INTRODUCTION

The Educational Research Workshop on Science and Computers in Primary Education was organised by the Scottish Education Department (SED) in co-operation with the Council of Europe's Council for Cultural Co-operation (CDCC) and the Scottish Council for Research in Education (SCRE). It was held at St. Andrew's College of Education (Craiglockhart), Edinburgh, Scotland, from 3-6 September 1984.

The aims of the workshop were:

1. to evaluate research with regard to science and primary education;

2. to draw attention to the consequences of research findings for educational policy (ie to contribute to the CDCC's primary education project);

3. to identify areas of future research;

4. to encourage European co-operation in this type of research.

The theme of the workshop was to discuss research into the teaching of science in primary education as part of environmental studies in the wider sense. Computers and technology were seen as applications of science. The workshop had eight commissioned papers presented in plenary session with discussion in three groups. The papers and the discussion focused on certain aspects of the theme.

1. The present situation

What evidence do evaluative surveys provide about the successes and failures of primary science? What evidence is there about the reasons for these outcomes? How can the evidence be assessed, to look at norms of performance, to look at the best practice and best results, to formulate targets that are both desirable and practical?

2. Analysis

Process aims and content aims are explained - sometimes one, sometimes the other, sometimes in opposition, sometimes in harmony. What is the correct relationship and correct balance of emphasis between these aims? What follows from this for the selection of the process objectives and the content objectives for primary pupils? How do both relate to the development of attitudes?

How can we distinguish and co-ordinate science aims, technology aims, and broader issues such as environmental awareness? More broadly, in the context of the broad aims of primary education, how do we assess the particular aims of primary science in relation to the curriculum as a whole?

In designing teaching we need to use a model of the learner and of the process of learning. How can research, on the preconceptions that pupils bring into school, on the development of reasoning skills and on concept development, help us to develop a model appropriate for design of teaching?

Teaching occurs through particular classroom practices and organisation conducted by the teacher. What does research tell us about existing practices, about their effectiveness and about the reasons why teachers adopt them?

3. Toward solutions

In staff development, what knowledge, what skills, what attitudes, do teachers need to acquire? Through what strategies can their professional development be encouraged? What has been learnt from attempts to encourage development by various and different means?

In curriculum development, can case studies of particular developments illuminate the problems of co-ordinating the various ideas and principles set out in Section 2 above? Is there experience which can guide attempts to formulate a comprehensive policy to develop teacher skills, curriculum and classroom practice in a co-ordinated way?

4. Microcomputers in primary school science

What can we achieve with computers? Can they provide ways to develop particular process skills, and skills of logical thought relevant to science? What can they do for children with special needs? What types of software are needed? What is the role of special programme of development in this area? In particular do broadcast TV course have a special part to play?

In addition to the eight commissioned papers, the BBC presented a paper and showed material developed by them for science education for 9-10 year olds and their work on the introduction of computers.

The Educational Research Workshop was chaired by Mr George Paton, Deputy Directore, Scottish Council for Educational Technology (SCET) and was attended by 60 delegates and observers representing 12 CDCC countries, UNESCO, the Hungarian Institute of Education and a number of teacher organisations. The Rapporteur General was Mr Frank Adams, Principal Curriculum Development Officer, Scottish Curriculum Development Service (SCDS), who presented a summary and conclusions of the workshop on the final day. Participants in the workshop visited a number of primary schools where they had the opportunity to observe children engaged in work in science and with computers.

In particular the Council of Europe would like to thank the Scottish Education Department (HMCI Jim H Thomson) and the Scottish Council for Research in Education (Dr. Bryan Dockrell and Mr John L Powell) for their excellent work in preparing and organising the workshop. The Council of Europe expresses its thanks also to the workshop Chairman (Mr George Paton), the Rapporteur General (Mr Frank Adams), the lecturers, group chairmen and group rapporteurs as well as to Sister Deirdre, Vice-Principal of St. Andrew's College of Education, who looked after the physical wellbeing of participants and the technical facilities.

Strasbourg 25 January 1985

Michael Vorbeck

Head of the Section for Educational
Research and Documentation
Council of Europe

SECTION 1: GENERAL REPORT,
COMMISSIONED PAPERS AND BBC REPORT

1.1 GENERAL REPORT

by

Frank Adams, Rapporteur General

1.1.1 INTRODUCTION

The Chairman, at the beginning of this week, reminded us that this week was to be a RESEARCH workshop rather than a workshop on curriculum development and it is important in reflecting on the workshop to keep that in mind. However, it is difficult, and perhaps undesirable, to make too clear a distinction between research and development as research must constantly inform and underpin curriculum development. Similarly, it is problematic at times to define curriculum for it can be interpreted, depending upon our background, as being simply a syllabus or list of content or it may have a wider interpretation to take in methodologies, organisation, assessment and all of the experiences planned and unplanned that a child will have in his years at school. The Committee on Primary Education (COPE) adopts a wide definition of curriculum taking, therefore, a view which relates to the individual child and which seeks to bring as many of the outcomes of his experience as possible into the conscious awareness of the teacher. Research, therefore, has much to contribute to our understanding of the child, of the experiences we believe are worthwhile for him and of the situations which will allow us as educators to provide the best possible conditions for that child to grow into a happy, healthy individual.

"... with a proper respect and concern for others as well as themselves, able to make rational choices, able to act as part of a group or with confident independence when that is appropriate." (Primary Education in the Eighties, COPE 1983)

That's all very well many teachers would say. It's easy to make these broad assertions but we are the ones who have to make it all happen. How is it to be done? Statements such as the one I have just made form the manifesto but within it there must be more specific guidance on how these aims for all of primary education are to be achieved and where the major contributions lie.

Science and the use of computers must be seen as contributing to the achievement of such an aim and this workshop has perhaps helped us to either see or begin to see afresh the important role that science and microcomputers play in a broad and balanced curriculum.

On the first day Professor Black (1) suggested that one of the difficulties that may have existed (or continues to exist) is the tendency to fail to look at an overall system and try to influence all of the elements within that system. Advances are made on some fronts while others are neglected. Perhaps this is inevitable - different people have different interests and it may be hard to agree on priorities when there are competing claims for finite - and perhaps diminishing - resources. Perhaps a priority is for us to agree on the system itself and what we do and do not understand within it. Clearly that is the aim of this workshop.

It seems to me that we have been operating this week on a system with at least the following components:

CHILD
- how does he learn?
- how do we know what he has learned?
- what criteria do we use to evaluate success?

CURRICULUM
- how does it relate to the "real world" of the child?
- what is the place of science?
- what should be taught?
- how should it be structured?
- how should it be taught?

TEACHER
- what skills and qualities are needed?
- how can they be developed?
- how should research help?

CONTEXT
- how is it to be defined?
- how is it to be organised?
- what are reasonable criteria for success?
- how can research help?

and I propose to make my remarks within the structure of this system without taking each element in turn. Some of the research presented this week has given indications of what we know and do not know about a number of these areas.

1.1.2 THE LEARNER

It is encouraging that there appears to have been no need or attempt to unearth the old issue of child-centredness v structure in the curriculum. The child has been firmly at the centre of the discussions that have taken place during this workshop. That may be so but some issues seem more

_____

(1) See list of commissioned papers under "CONTENTS".

difficult to resolve, eg how does he learn? What is the model of the learner that is at the centre of our concern? Important points have been made about the need for an active learner who is creating his own understandings of the world around him. Thus the child's explanations of the world are to be taken seriously but teachers need help that will allow them to judge when the "alternative framework", proposed by Professor Anderson, is perhaps likely to impede progress and when it is not. How is that to be judged? How can teachers distinguish between an "alternative framework" and a misunderstanding or misconception? It would seem to be good practice in either case to begin from where the learner is but are the routes to be followed from each the same? This workshop has identified the need for clarification of this issue and a research programme linking the implications of identifying pupils' difficulties as either "alternative frameworks" or misunderstanding and the subsequent action that teachers or curriculum developers might take seems to be needed. The criteria for judging success in the field of science also need clarification. It seems clear from the APU studies referred to by Professor Black that this is a complex area yet it is one in which it is tempting for some audiences to go from correlation to causation, eg class size issue. Professor Black suggested large-scale surveys were important but that smaller-scale research is not ruled out. What kind of research strategy is needed to link large-scale quantitative research with perhaps smaller-scale qualitative research so that we do not equate "quality with width"? Can research in assessment of performance help to clarify difficult areas such as process and help to lay the foundation for more extended development (Paper 1.2) or is there a danger that the process will become limited to that which is assessable? Can research say to the teacher what her expectations of the learner might be and whether we are asking too much or too little of children?

Implicit in all of our discussions about the learner has been a model of the teacher. Some delegates have been happy to accept a constructivist view of the learner but needed to add something more. Perhaps it was the teacher. The picture we have been building up of the learner might have been seen by some to imply a relatively passive role for the teacher - the teacher as restaurateur who presents an attractive buffet of possibilities but little more. Clearly there is more to it than that and much depends on sensitive intervention on the part of the teacher, particularly in terms of the crucial role that language and communication, pupil-pupil and teacher-pupil, play in the construction of understandings. The suggestion has been made that the teacher needs to adopt a more central role through her own understanding of science as she would in reading or in mathematics. Clearly to do this the teacher will require help, particularly if a lack of familiarity with science has been identified as one of the obstacles to development. What does the teacher need to know? It is perhaps in this area that most research needs to be carried out. If we are to build on pupil's alternative frameworks what are the activities that help the child to form concepts and progress from limited concepts to more sophisticated ones? How can we recognise changes in the child? These are important issues that relate to a wide spectrum of activities both in the primary school and at the transition from primary to secondary education. But who is to do this? The researcher - who may produce complex and unmanageable taxonomies or the teacher who may lack the background insights. The late Lawrence Stenhouse's concept of the teacher-as-researcher seems to me to be important in this issue. Through such a concept the teacher may be helped to develop an awareness of criteria that are meaningful to here within her own classroom situation.

1.1.3 CURRICULUM STRUCTURE

The network of issues about content, process and curriculum structure remains complex and a resistant to attempts at simplification. The issue of what should be taught and how is important whether the teacher is attempting to make provision within a national syllabus or within a school. Sinclair MacLeod suggested that a school policy for science should relate to philosophy, strategy and programme and so should any national syllabus. The question remains who is to decide what the philosophy, strategy and programme are to be and how? It seems clear that the debate is NOT content versus process but rather what do we mean by content and process? At the least I believe we can agree that content must exist as a vehicle for the development of a <u>scientific method</u> - which is widely applicable across the primary curriculum.

As Professor Black put it

"... the question at issue is whether the topics used for this purpose should be pre-specified" (Paper 1.2).

Wynne Harlen, quoted in a recent UNESCO publication "New Trends in Primary Science" sums it up as

"while children are investigating problems and developing scientific skills and attitudes what is the core of generalisations that they should at the same time acquire?".

The Primary Science Development Project in Scotland seems to suggest that teachers can agree on <u>broad areas of content</u>. Is that what we mean by a "core of generalisations"? Can a core be suggested and be relevant for all school contexts? Can we be sure of the generalisations that would be meaningful to children at different stages of the primary school and which could be built on in secondary education? Bruner's notion of a "spiral curriculum" is crucial in thinking about these matters.

<u>Context</u> is important to the teacher in terms of the school and its community - but also to the child. Can we balance pre-specified generalisations with room to respond to particular local/temporal/even individual demands? It seems clear that there should be a difference between ad hoc unplanned work and work which is responsive to the reactions of children. But is there? Would a core of content give teachers the confidence to react in a responsive way to questions which - if we have done a good job in process terms - cannot be entirely predicted.

What about process? Is process entirely about <u>skills</u>? I suppose it depends on how you define a skill. Is it a <u>psychomotor</u> process skill? If so there may appear to be no problem until you begin to try to work out how to mark progression. But what we call skills are not necessarily exclusively psychomotor. What we know about the world makes us better at applying a skill. What we mean by <u>know</u> is more controversial - I think that it is not simply <u>information</u>.

As Henri Poincaré put it

"Science is built of facts the way a house is built of
bricks; but an accumulation of facts is no more science
than a pile of bricks is a house".

Part of the process skills for the learner is knowing you've got them
or when to use them. That is being aware of your own thinking processes -
the area of psychology called meta cognition. How can we make children
aware of their skills? When can children begin to reflect constructively
on their own performance? Can all children do it in varying degrees?
What classroom activities will support its development. Research is
currently being carried out in the field of learning to learn by
Professor Nisbet and his colleagues at Aberdeen University and it may be
useful for more information on this to be made available within Europe
and in a way that can inform classroom practice.

Structure must however also include some thoughts about the place of
science in the primary curriculum. I have already suggested that context
is the important issue. Context for me implies purpose and an understanding
of purpose on the part of the child. Part of the issue is the source of
problems or topics for investigation. Whose reality is being operated on -
the teacher's or the child's? Meaningful learning is more likely to take
place when connections are made with past learning, with real problems than
when the ideas are inert. Is it any more meaningful to swing pieces of
plasticine on a length of string because that's what you've been told to
do than it is to write about transport through the ages or do a page of
long multiplication because that's what you've been told to do? I know
what's likely to be more fun. The curriculum development case studies
from Switzerland (Paper 1.6) and from Scotland (Paper 1.7) raised the issue
of whether science should be developed as part of a more or less
"integrated" curriculum or as a separate subject of study. The issue
doesn't appear to be simply about subjects or no subjects but more about
the contribution certain ways of thinking can make to our understanding
of the world. It is difficult to say what integration actually is. A
broad and balanced view of what constitutes experience of the world cannot
accept anything being "integrated away". Policies at both national and
school level which make clear the contribution of the various traditional
subjects to the development of an integrated view of the world can help
to avoid this.

It could be argued that the child in primary school brought up on a
diet of investigation and process will get to the stage when he/she
needs fairly specialised bits of information in order to understand a
particular phenomenon but that's not the same as storing up specialised/
subject information in case you'll ever need it. I believe teachers do
need practical help in this issue because the rhetoric of primary
education is about integration, interrelationships and seamless robes
but teachers are faced with problems of progression and continuity that
are increasingly complex unless research can help us to identify, for
example, certain process skills that go across the curriculum or a
manageable number of ideas about teaching and learning that fit a range
of curricular contexts, for example drafting and editing in writing across
the curriculum, so-called "discussion skills" etc.

1.1.4 CLASSROOM ORGANISATION AND MANAGEMENT

If we are to operate on all aspects of the system then it is clear that
concise help is needed to show teachers how to create a classroom/management
context which is reasonably simple but which can cope with active,
co-operative work on the part of all of the children some of the time.
We have been reminded of the importance of whole class work from time to
time by the work of Professor Galton among others. The important point
would appear to be that the teacher ought to be able to change her teaching
style depending upon the purpose of the activity. This must be part of the
increased awareness of possibilities that I suggested earlier ought to be
part of the characteristics of good teaching. What research might do is
to link purpose more clearly with mode of teaching and classroom management.

     Group One's report asked what are the conditions that are likely to
enhance learning? How can the task be matched to the pupil's level of
ability? This is a growing field of research and one which can be of
immediate relevance to the classroom, eg information on feedback from the
ORACLE (1) project underlines its importance in the teaching and learning
process. This is far from new but it is very important and immediately
suggests certain practical steps that can be taken in classrooms by
teachers.

     I commend to the workshop Professor Galton's paper (DECS/Rech (83) 25)
given at the Council of Europe Conference at Neusiedl (1983) because the
implications that it contains for research and development related to
classroom organisation and management throughout Europe are very important.

1.1.5 IN-SERVICE EDUCATION AND TRAINING (INSET)

Dr. Lauterbach has summed up the problem both in his metaphor of throwing
a rock into a deep well and seeing little effect (resource problem) and
through his research. If we begin from where the teachers are then it is
crucial to keep their perceived needs in mind as well as our perception of
priorities. The link between the need for research into classroom
organisation and management and the expressed needs of teachers for help
with classroom management is clear and should be amenable to more or less
instant help - not only through formal courses but in the informal ongoing
contact between teacher and teacher and teacher and promoted staff in
schools. Valuable in-school opportunities need to be exploited by the schools
themselves and they should receive the support they need to do this. Other
problems are less amenable - what can be done about differentiating
in-service to teacher needs just as we try to differentiate the curriculum
for pupil needs? Research such as that presented by Dr. Lauterbach can
confirm the truth we all know that the effects of INSET may be transient
for a range of reasons. What we now need is a vigorous exchange of ideas
and information about strategies to combat the factors that combine to
diminish INSET effects.

_____   _____

(1) Observational Research and Classroom Learning Evaluation, University
     of Leicester.

12

1.1.6 COMPUTERS

Up to now I have not mentioned computers. This is not an oversight nor is it a Luddite reaction to new technology. There have been many seminars, workshops and discussions on computers and primary education and a range of conclusions and recommendations exist about the kind of hardware, what software, what language and so on. What must be fundamental is that the · microcomputer is a resource for teaching and learning, albeit a very powerful one, just like any other resource for teaching and learning, albeit a very powerful one, just like any other resource available to the teacher. For the teacher the important feature must be the decisions that determine the selection and use of certain resources for certain purposes. The microcomputer is at the forefront of attention for many teachers at present. As M Robert so eloquently put it - when did government last specially fund a resource for use in schools? The microcomputer in many countries has been thrust into teachers' consciousness by government action and naturally there is a demand for software and for INSET. But it is important to be clear on why and to what end. The rapid introduction created a demand and it is probably easier to develop drill programmes than other kinds. But should a resource dictate the curriculum in this way? Clearly there have been and there continues to be great improvement but there is much that we still do not know and research must help us here - for example, can the computer - using appropriate software (logo/adventure games) stimulate a better quality of interaction among groups of children, because of its speed and power?

Should we be asking about the effects of having more than one computer in a school so that it is available on a long-term basis to all teachers? When and under what circumstances is the computer more than a frill? In other words should our research be more oriented to the curriculum, to teaching/learning and pedagogy than to software systems. The workshop is clear that the issue is not LOGO versus the rest but how the various strengths of the computer as a resource relate to the child as a learner. Researchers are already aware of the potential danger that the microcomputer can have in taking children away from the real physical world into an abstract model of the world and it may be salutary in a workshop on science to keep that in mind.

1.1.7 CONCLUSION

I began by emphasising the importance of research in this workshop. It is clear that research is important to teaching but we must be clear about our expectations of research. Sir William Pyle who was Permanent Under-Secretary at the DES from 1971-76 is often quoted as follows:

"I have to say of course that the great thing about educational research is that part of it is rubbish and another part (I will not be specific about the proportions) leads nowhere and is really indifferent; it is I am afraid exceptional to find a piece of research that hits the nail on the head and tells you pretty clearly what is wrong or what is happening or what should be done".

This of course will meet different reactions from different audiences but what it does make clear is that it is important not to raise false hopes in research either for the administrator/policy-maker or the classroom teacher. Research in education cannot always be an exact science. What is perhaps more important in ensuring the effectiveness of research is to make sure it gets known about and talked about. A recent journal article suggested that for research to be effective as a basis for curriculum policy it should:

have authority

have novelty

be more than common sense

suggest development

have coherence

have sympathy

ring true

be practical (which is not necessarily the same as simple)

- RESEARCH AS A BASIS FOR CURRICULUM POLICY
(ANDERSON, JOURNAL CURRICULUM STUDIES, 1982).

This may be an oversimplification but the underlying message is clear. Part of the researcher's task is to communicate the results of research but increasingly the researcher must think of ways of involving teachers in the formulation and implementation of research. Administrators and policy-makers must also be involved in planning research and must share with the researcher the task of making the results accessible and meaningful for those who will make use of them.

1.1.8 BIBLIOGRAPHY

Anderson, DCC, Research as a Basis for Curriculum Policy Making: a cautionary note, Journal of Curriculum Studies, Vol. 14, No. 1, 1982.

Consultative Committee on the Curriculum: Committee on Primary Education (COPE): Primary Education in the Eighties, Scottish Curriculum Development Service, Edinburgh Centre, 1983.

UNESCO 1984, New Trends in Primary Science.

Poincaré, H, La science et l'hypothèse, 1902.

In addition to limiting its range of topics to the plant and animal aspects of the environment, such work was further limited in skills to those of classification and observation. It also lacked any clear model of progression by which teachers could stimulate and evaluate children's development (Conran 1983).

The Oxford Project sought to help children to learn a first overall picture of the scientist's view of nature. This led it to base its work on a concept framework grouped under four themes: Energy, Structure, Life and Change (Redman et al 1968, 1969). Nuffield Junior Science started from a quite different view

"... the task in school is not one of teaching science to children, but rather of utilising the children's own scientific way of working as a potent educational tool" (Wastnedge 1967).

This latter philosophy, which was naturally combined with an emphasis on process skills, was to dominate subsequent developments.

Neither project attracted many users. The Nuffield approach was felt to be too open and too demanding for teachers, so it was followed by Science 5-13. This tried to support teachers' emphasis on process skills by using behavioural objectives, which were classified in a Piagetian framework of three levels, to guide the selection of opportunities for learning and to evaluate children's progress. The 25 books of this project were written for teachers to give guidance and examples, but they did not prescribe any schedule or hierarchy of content items to match the carefully structured set of 150 behavioural objectives (Ennever and Harlen, 1972).

Two further projects followed, one to help teachers to evaluate pupils' progress within the objectives framework of Science 5-13 (see Harlen 1977), another based on Science 5-13 but providing what the original project refused to provide - pupil's materials (Richards 1980).

This short history illustrates three main problem areas. The first is the conflict between content aims and process aims, the second is the struggle to develop a rationale for development of process skills, and the third is an oscillation, between providing materials for teachers and providing for both teachers and for pupils. Unfortunately, the history shows one other common problem. Surveys in 1978 showed Science 5-13 was being used in only 22 per cent of schools, and Nuffield Junior Science in only 7 per cent (Steadman et al 1978).

Moreover, this poor reception was part of a more general problem. In spite of the wealth of projects in the '60s and '70s, a systematic survey of primary schools by the government Inspectorate in 1978 presented a bleak picture. Only 10 per cent of schools were doing serious and effective work. Effort was usually superficial, and

"the work in observational and experimental science was less well matched to children's capabilities than work in any other area of the curriculum" (Department of Education and Science 1978).

1.2 SCIENCE IN PRIMARY EDUCATION

by

Prof. P J Black, London

1.2.1 SUMMARY

This paper starts by drawing some general lessons from a brief history of the development of primary science in England over the past twenty years. This leads to identification of seven main issues for subsequent discussion.

A review of children's attainments, based on national surveys in the United Kingdom, raises policy issues about the value of such surveys and also illustrates new evidence about process skills and about attitudes. This leads to a detailed discussion of the relationships between content aims and process aims in primary science. Whilst this should help to clarify aims, the curriculum structure then needs discussion by consideration of the nature of tasks set in the classroom. This naturally leads to an attempt to identify the distinctive role of technology and of its links to science in the primary curriculum.

The paper then raises the main questions about the pupil as learner which arise from its analysis of aims and of curriculum structure, but does not attempt to review this field. A discussion of evidence about classroom styles leads to further questions about methods required to implement new aims. After a brief consideration of the role of computer learning, the paper concludes with a review of its argument and the challenges this produces for professional development of teachers.

1.2.2 A HISTORY OF CHANGE

This section, like much of this paper, will draw mainly upon evidence and experience from the United Kingdom. The paper attempts to concentrate on fundamental and not on local issues. Whilst the author's reading of studies from overseas - some of which are quoted here - confirms personal experience that these issues are important in most countries, this paper cannot pretend to be a balanced international review.

In primary science, the United Kingdom's curriculum innovations started in the 1960s with two projects, called Oxford Primary Science and Nuffield Junior Science respectively. Prior to these, primary school science was mainly confined to nature study, of which a leading educator said

"Nature too seldom comes into the work and too often study is the last thing thought of".

Primary schools in England have been notable in the past 15 years for their development of child-centred and informal methods of education. If in spite of this, and in spite of the wealth of investment in projects, primary science could fail, this evidence at least carries the policy message that these two elements alone do not ensure success.

The problems are not unique to England. Martin (1983) reviews evidence of the low adoption rates of the many new process-based initiatives in the USA and Australia. The mismatch between central project aims and local school product can be equally serious in countries with centrally controlled curricula (Krasilchik 1983). Host (1983) gives a vivid description of the deterioration of primary science in French schools up to 1977, with a tedious and narrow concentration on observation and recording data, and with a schedule of content which led perceptive teachers to judge the work to be premature and to seek to abandon science altogether.

The above only illustrates one more general lesson. In educational development, it is not possible to produce change unless all aspects of the complex system are carefully considered. This paper will attempt to survey briefly the main aspects in order to stress this need for a comprehensive policy. This will be done by examining the following seven propositions in successive sections (numbered in brackets).

We need to start from carefuly study of children's present attainments (2).

We need to clarify the relative importance and interactions of process and content (3).

We need a comprehensive model of the curriculum in order to locate and interrelate work on science, on technology and on other interdisciplinary areas (4).

Essential questions about content learning and about process learning have to be answered within some model of the learner (5).

The future role of computers has to be planned by reference to a fundamental evaluation of the role of computer science in learning (6).

All of the above form the basis for a curriculum design, but such design can only be made effective if teachers can be helped to develop the new skills and new confidence (7).

1.2.3 CHILDREN'S ATTAINMENTS

Extensive surveys of performance in science have been carried out in England, Wales and Northern Ireland by annual testing. In each of the years 1980 to 1984 inclusive, samples of 12,000 children at age 11, which is the last year of primary schooling in most areas, have taken science tests. The results published so far (APU Assessment of Performance Unit, 1981, 1983, 1984) contain a wealth of data, including over 150 sample questions, with qualitative and quantitative data on the responses, together with overall scores and measures of associated variables. The only comparable national or international survey programmes (NAEP 1978, Comber and Keeves 1973) have not produced data which are as detailed or as comprehensive. The APU surveys are unique both in the attention given to a range of process skills and in the extent of practical tests. For example, in the 1980 survey about 3,500 children were given one of two kinds of practical tests in over 500 schools each of which was visited by an administrator trained to give the tests.

The surveys assessed performance in six main categories. Each set of questions was designed to test only one category and each set was given to only a fraction of the sample. The different sets were distributed amongst the sample schools to optimise the statistics of subsequent analysis. In addition to the six categories of performance scores, data on children's liking for science activities and school data, on policy for science teaching and on resources were also collected. The following paragraphs survey briefly the results in each of these areas.

In the first category, children's ability to use graphs, tables and charts was tested by paper and pencil exercises. Between half and two-thirds of children could read information from pie charts and bar charts for making qualitative comparisons, but reading quantitative information from line graphs or bar charts proved more difficult, and performance was much lower where children were asked to express in words the trends or patterns shown in graphs. About half could add data to a partially completed graph or chart.

In practical tests of the use of measuring instruments (the second category) most could read the scales of simple instruments correctly, but could not interpolate between scale divisions. The third category also used practical testing to assess skill in making and interpreting observations. Children were given both real objects to handle, and photographs and moving film. Performance was better with photographs than with real objects. Most children could observe broad similarities and differences between objects and classify them on the basis of their observations. However, they were better at recording differences between objects than similarities. Where children were asked to make observations to classify or group or predict, and then to explain the reasons for their results, they always performed better in producing the task outcome than in explaining reasons. Questions requiring observation of fine details of objects also produced low scores.

In the paper and pencil tests of the fourth category, children were presented with information and asked to define patterns, make predictions or draw conclusions. Here again, children could more easily select or state an outcome than they could explain how they used information to arrive at it. In some sets of questions, all the information required was given in the questions. Where these concerned everyday situations, children were weak at basing conclusions strictly on the data provided: they all too easily went beyond the evidence in the way that many adults to in daily life. Other sets of questions required the same logical operations, but needed also some application of science concepts for interpretation of the data. For these, success rates fell as the concept "burden" increased.

Further written tests, in the fifth category, required children to plan, in whole or in part, investigations in a systematic way, to solve problems or test hypotheses. For example, where children were told that a snail refused to move across a surrounding ring of salty water and asked to propose a plan to find out whether it was the salt or the water that repelled it, about half could produce an acceptable approach. However, most failed to add details of controls or interpretation required to make the test fair. This was a typical result - children could foresee a general strategy and the first steps for tackling a problem, but essential components of execution, including any of the detailed actions required to put vague aims into effect in terms of explicit and quantitative measurements, were beyond the majority. Similarly, only a few could discuss how the observations or measures would be used to establish the result. It also appeared that some would think that an "everyday" problem does not require careful measurement because it is not "scientific".

The sixth category also set practical problems, as in the fifth, but in a practical context where children were asked to select from given equipmdnt to carry out a modest investigation. For example, pupils were given three different balls and three pieces of floor material and asked to determine whether the balls bounced equally well on all three. A large majority found an appropriate way to apply similar tests to the three. However, few correctly controlled the important variables or repeated observations or measurements as a routine check. Nevertheless, performance of any task with equipment did produce a more competent attempt than appeared likely when identical tasks were set as a paper and pencil exercise in the fifth category.

Children's attitudes to science can be explored under two aspects. One is their attitudes within science. Thus, tester observation and questions, asked within the category six questions described above, established that less than 5% appeared bored, uninterested, or scared, but that almost half were uncritical in that they did not respond to hints about possible improvements when invited to be critical in a closing discussion. For the second aspect, tests of attitudes to science showed a high level of liking for practical activities particularly amongst boys. The scores fell for girls when physical science activities were considered, for all when measurement appeared to be important, and for boys when writing and recording were stressed. Association of "liking" scores with performance showed low but significant correlations (about 0.20) with some, not all, cateogory scores. It has been established elsewhere that liking for science declines in the early years of secondary schooling (Ormerod and Duckworth 1975) and Martin (1983) reviews studies which show that the same decline has been reported in some primary research although, as above, it seems to occur more with the physical sciences than with other areas.

Data collected about schools policy and resources were analysed with the performance data. Although significant correlations were established, further careful and complex analysis is needed if useful policy conclusions are to be drawn. It is clear that any measure of social deprivation or of home background gives the largest score variations. Scores also show a clear progression from inner city (lowest) to the wealthy outer suburban (highest) areas, which may also be due to the home background factor. However, scores are also higher where class sizes are over 25 than when there are fewer than 25 children in a class. This is an unwelcome result to teachers. It may arise because small classes associate with other factors which give lower scores (small rural schools, special treatment for low ability children); however, although the complex multivariate analysis required to explore any such effect is still in progress, the crude result is enough to show that class size on its own is not a very important determinant of performance.

Data on school policies showed that 85% of schools included science
activities in their curriculum, but only about half of these included them
as specific activities rather than as an aspect of broader topics. Overall,
schools spent about 5% of their teaching time, and about 5% of their
resources for books and materials, on science. Schools were also asked to
place in rank order lists of possible goals and emphases for their science
work. The greater emphasis was given to making observations, recording
them and drawing conclusions. Goals concerned with identifying variables,
designing experiments and critical examination of experimental methods all
received low priority.

These last results are in accord with the performance results. General
skills, which are widely applicable across the curriculum, are well developed.
The more specific science skills are poorly developed. This is not because
children lack enthusiasm or initial competence in those types of activity
which could provide opportunity to develop the skills needed.

Survey results of this type could serve policy-making in several
different ways. It was originally intended that the national surveys would
provide data on trends over time. It is too early to comment on this aspect
but the range of the survey aims gives rise to one problem. Highly reliable
data can only be obtained with homogeneous measures, which could constrict
the range of skills assessed and so reduce the value for curriculum and
teaching.

The data could also indicate future priorities if they showed clear
associations between performance and resources or policies. This may be
possible, but greate care is needed before correlations can be interpreted
as evidence of causes.

Finally the data can serve policy by giving a detailed map of the
strengths and weaknesses in pupils' work. The above account shows how the
surveys are doing this. In addition to detailed trends which suggest
teaching needs, or problems needing in-depth research, the sample questions
are in themselves valuable. Teachers are finding them valuable because they
give concrete expression to process aims which many supported in the abstract
but were hitherto unable to express in concrete practice.

1.2.4 PROCESS VERSUS CONTENT?

The survey in Section 1.2.2 recounts a history of tension between process
aims and content aims. Process skills must be exercised on some content,
so the question at issue is whether the topics used for this purpose should
be pre-specified, because they are important in their own right, or left to
the free choice of pupils or teacher because the topics are merely vehicles
to motivate work for the process skills.

Nobody can deny that such skills as the power to make generalisations
on the basis of observations, or the ability to argue whether or not a given
hypothesis is consistent with the data, must form an essential component of
science education even if learning of content is also important. Unless
children understand how concepts derive from and make sense of data, they
cannot have an authentic grasp of these concepts: they cannot see the links
in the derivation except by effective use of process skills.

Thus it is possible to accept that young children need some scientific knowledge and yet to give priority to process skills because without such skills that knowledge cannot be acquired.

Some also argue that the process skills might as well be exercised on content which has its own value for children. One such argument is that some science content can meet young children's immediate needs, eg in bodily hygiene, in care for the environment, in respecting all forms of life: such aims are of particular importance where compulsory education in science may end at or shortly after the primary stage. A different argument is that some content is needed for laying a basis on which the more abstract concepts of science will be built in the future. It is also pointed out that carefully chosen content can provide good opportunities for developing process skills where a random choice may not.

These arguments are explored by Kerr and Engel (1980), Harlen (1978) within a United Kingdom context and by Host (1983) in describing the basis for development in France derived from the work of the Institut National des Recherches Pedagogiques.

The conclusion that specified content ought to be learnt meets two main objections. One is that children should study topics which are meaningful to them and imposition of an external schedule will lead to uninspired work remote from their interests. Both Host and Harlen reject this argument because they envisage that common content objectives should only be specified in very broad terms, eg

-   living things depend on each other for survival and all animals depend ultimately on plants for their food,

-   air contains water vapour, some of which condenses out in various conditions to give rain, dew, mist, snow, hail, ice or water.

These can be pursued in a variety of particular topics, themes or projects, which the teacher may deploy according to local and individual interests.

A second objection comes in two forms. One is that the level of abstraction of a topic, must be matched to the development of the child. This comes in its strongest form from a Piagetian: to meet it, it is necessary to be precise about terminology and to analyse content in a spectrum from knowledge of specifics at one end to grasp of deep abstract concepts at the other. The work of Shayer and Adey (1981) is a good example of such analysis. A second form of this objection would be that work must first explore the common theories that children already hold about the natural world. These two points of view are considered briefly in Section 1.2.6.

All of the arguments point to a need for a carefully structured framework of content within which a teacher may have some freedom of manoeuvre to match to children's local and personal interests. The most recent policy statement of HM Inspectorate in England and Wales (DES 1983) emphasises such a policy, taking an exemplary set on content aims and setting out a year-by-year sequence for them.

For process skills, the problems appear to be different. Whilst many different lists and definitions of process skills have been set out, there is a substantial degree of agreement between them. However, there does not exist the amount of detailed research on the possible levels or stages of progression within process skills such as we do have for content. Thus, the HMI Inspectorate policy statement quoted above makes clear that process skills are important and gives a list of them. However, whilst for content there is a full analysis of progression and structure, the discussions of processes lacks these detailed features. One interesting feature of the APU work is that it seems to be the first comprehensive attempt to set out a detailed structure for the process skills and the results at age 11 may form a starting point for further work on the development of such skills.

The distinction arising in these APU results, between general process skills, developed in many areas of primary school work, and specific skills peculiar to science, may be very important here. The scientific ones may best be developed on tasks which need the rigour and careful control of scientific methodology. A study of condensation, where a child often believes that the moisture on the outside of a cold drink has leaked from inside, may be one of a set of studies leading eventually to the theory of water vapour in the air. That example shows both the need to explore and challenge everyday conceptions, and the need to design tests of hypotheses and to make generalisations. One reason for studying science in primary work is that its content, suitably chosen, provides an excellent vehicle for the consolidation and extension of children's process skills. Thus process skills need to be exercised on science content if they are to be developed as fully as possible.

Thus processes and content learning must develop in close interaction. In the work of scientists, there is an intimate symbiosis: without skills the scientist is helpless, but without its unique and peculiar structure of abstract concepts science is no more than organised common sense.

However, process skills are of no value unless children are willing and able to use them when faced with a problem. The same can be said of knowledge, whether of specifics or of abstractions. These points have two implications. The first follows if it is accepted that children will be willing to use methods and ideas of science if they have already enjoyed learning them and already experienced success in using them. It is also relevant here to note that some skills, such as care before jumping to conclusions, are as much as matter of attitude as of intellect. So the relevance of the development and monitoring of attitudes ought to be obvious.

The second implication is that content and skills must be based on realistic tasks which make sense to and are rewarding to children. This is not the same as saying, as some do, that children's own problems must initiate such tasks. It does say that analysis into content and skill elements is dangerous if we lose sight of the human need to experience the reality of tackling problems using both.

1.2.5 TASKS AND TECHNOLOGY

None of the arguments about content or process is meant to imply that
either is to be taught by didactic methods. The focus of the work ought
to be problems or tasks for solution or exploration in which children
observe, make generalisations, propose hypotheses or solutions, and then
test out their ideas. The curriculum designer ought to select or propose
task activities which will both interest children and provide occasions
to develop useful process skills and the knowledge basis out of which
generalisations and concepts can be formed. Thus a child's curriculum
in science might be a sequence of tasks which, viewed superficially,
might seem to provide no more than a varied and attractive menu, but within
and between which a systematic development of process and content skills
can proceed.

Whether or not the teacher is the designer of such a curriculum, he or
she has the additional duty of seizing the opportunities as they arise,
to encourage, reinforce and extend children's knowledge and process skills.
One of the conclusions of the surveys described in Section 1.2.3 was that
such opportunities were not being used. It may also be part of such a
strategy to make the knowledge and process activities explicit by
encouraging children to reflect on what they achieve and the way in which
they achieve it. Indeed, it may be argued that unless a child's grasp of
knowledge or of process skills is self-conscious, he or she cannot be said
to fully possess them and may be unlikely to use them in other contexts.

Viewed in this way, the tasks are the vehicles for scientific
development. This argument is relevant to technology, because technology
is generally regarded as encompassing a particular type of task. Consider
the following statement from the 1978 HM Inspectorate survey:

> The study of mechanical artefacts supported by constructional
> activities is an aspect of work in science which is seldom
> explored ...

This statement may be a statement about science but is not a statement
about technology. Technology is concerned with solving problems, meeting
needs. In technology, the task, making the artefact or other form of
solution, is the end, the resources are the means. The knowledge and skills
of science may be some of the resources, but other skills, such as those of
design, of craft or of evaluation of solutions, may also be needed. Thus
technology work has profoundly different values and aims from science. It
also is synthetic in that it brings together and uses a wider range of skills
across the whole curriculum than science tasks usually do.

These points are illustrated in the account by Evans (1980) of
successful technology work with 8-12 year olds, in which he criticises
those who fail to see the intrinsic value of constructive problem solving
and regard it only as applied science. The point can be made more general,
for in the primary curriculum many valuable tasks can cut across the
various discipline or resource areas. A task may be a means to promote or
to use science skills and knowledge but may have its own virtue as technology,
or as an exercise in communication or expression, or in many other ways.
In such a broader view, projects in which children learn about science

from secondary sources should not be ruled out. Study of the environment
is a rich source of suitable tasks and should be seen in a similar light
to technology - a field in which the problems and needs have primacy and
a variety of resources is required.

1.2.6 PUPILS AND THEIR LEARNING

It is not the concern of this paper to review this field or to discuss
the various empirical and theoretical perspectives that inform it. It is
relevant here only to draw together certain questions about children's
learning which arise from the arguments of Sections 1.2.2 to 1.2.5.

In the concept area, what theory or model can guide the appropriate
progression, from specifics to abstractions at various ages? If work
should start with children's own explanations, do these have sufficient
consistency across a group to form a basis? Sociologists have long ago
pointed out that life-world knowledge is both robust, because socially
derived and supported, and profoundly different from scientific knowledge,
being episodic, fragmentary and inconsistent as between one area of
experience and another (see Solomon 1982). How is such knowledge to be
challenged, extended or contradicted within science teaching? What process
skills are needed for the learning to be effective?

Similar questions are rarely asked about process skills, but they have
naturally arisen in Section 1.2.4. How do they develop, and do children
have their own everyday process skills which teaching has to extend or
challenge? Apart from questions about structure and progression, how is
transfer of skills to ensure readiness to use across different contexts,
to be achieved? And, as asked in 1.2.5 above, do children need to reflect
on the skills and content they have learned, to make them objective and
explicit to themselves, if they are to fully possess them?

It may help in selecting the right questions here, and in judging
answers to them, to regard content and process as similar rather than
profoundly different. After all, in an artificial intelligence programme
to perform scientific problem solving, one can imagine that both process
skills and content knowledge would be represented as procedures helping
to transform data from the input state to the desired solution state.

1.2.7 CLASSROOM PRACTICES AND PROCEDURES

There is a long tradition of research in which classroom intereactions
have been recorded and analysed. Amongst the most important landmarks are
the books by Bellack (1966), Simon and Boyer (1968) and Flanders (1970)
in the USA. There are various styles for such research, ranging from
extremes of the quantitative, which categorises and counts discrete
events, to the qualitative, which aims to write a subjective participant
account to capture the mood and significance underlying the events
observed.

Such work is extensively used in teacher training, to promote awareness
and an analytic process. It has rarely informed policy. However one major
research in England, known as the ORACLE Project (Galton, Simon and Kroll
1980) has, through a major quantitative survey of primary classroom
procedures, produced results of undoubted significance for future policy.

Before this research, it was widely believed that primary classrooms in England had been transformed. Physically this was clearly true: the straight rows of desks, facing the teacher and the blackboard, had given way to sets of small tables around which children sat in groups. The children appeared to be working in these groups, with the teacher acting to initiate and guide their own active learning.

The ORACLE Project's careful observations over a large sample of such classrooms showed surprising features. Children sat in groups but they rarely worked together: they worked individually and talking to one another was only used as a distraction from work. The majority of teachers rarely taught the class as a whole and hardly ever worked with groups as such. Written materials specified tasks for individual work, and pupils only spoke to teachers about work on an individual basis. In a class of 30 this meant that any one pupil could expect to speak with a teacher about learning for between 5 and 10 minutes per day. In fact, some pupils continually sought attention, others worked steadily and asked to be seen only with completed work, whilst others again worked intermittently and avoided contact. Because of the short time of contact with any one pupil, teachers interactions were mainly of a superficial sort - to check work, point out errors, and specify the next tasks. Any discussion to explore reasons for a child's product, or to extend the child's powers, would take time, and lead to a long queue of others waiting attention. Most teachers resolved this dilemma by curtailing individual discussions to a minimum.

A few teachers spent about 20% of their time on whole class teaching, and it was only in classes taught this way that pupil-teacher interactions were concerned with higher level skills of critical judgement or reflection. Not surprisingly, in pre- and post-tests, of all the classes concerned, only these particular classes showed significant gains on those higher skills which need critical discussion.

These results surveyed primary classes over all areas and did not separately analyse particular areas such as science. However, it seems clear that if children are to learn by guided work on practical activities involving critical discussion of their efforts, this can only be compatible with the logistics of time and class size if a class can work in small groups which come together from time to time to assemble, compare and reflect upon their outcomes. To conduct such work requires special skills. The ORACLE finding that there is an almost complete absence of work of this type, in any subject areas, is a serious problem.

1.2.8 COMPUTERS

In terms of the above analysis the possible use of computers can be approached in two ways. A suite of computer programmes could be made to provide a model world, within which children could try out and develop the process skills of scientific investigation. For use in this way, it would be essential that some work with real world objects should accompany the simulated work.

However, computing and computer science are a new and powerful language in society, a new way to develop dialogue and advance thought. Learning to use computer science in all parts of the curriculum should therefore be as central a theme as learning to use one's native language in all areas of

the curriculum. Seen in this light, the role of computers has to be
discovered; one source of ideas would be to examine carefully the part
that they are coming to play in the work of scientists and technologists
and then to look for parallel activities suited to young children.

Thus, working with computers within science and technology tasks
becomes something to be experienced and learnt about, a new resource or
perhaps a new type of task, not merely a means to an end. For this reason,
computers in learning present problems and prospects different in kind, not
merely in degree, from, say, programmed learning.

1.2.9 STRATEGIES FOR CHANGE

The argument above has sketched out the main strands for development. One
is to develop a strategy for defining the content of primary science. A
second is to set out a parallel policy for process skills. A third is to
establish a clear curriculum model in which content and process can
interact within selected tasks, activities which can serve not only science,
but, with different emphasis, technology and other areas of concern. All
of these three have to be designed in the light of a single consistent model
of the child as learner.

The fourth quite different need is to develop models, and experience,
of the methods of classroom organisation and teacher pupil interaction
required to promote and guide pupils active and interactive work. A fifth
is to clarify the role of computers within the curriculum model.

For all of these, it is in principle possible to promote change by
using surveys fundamental research, and development work in order to form
a central policy which is then to be disseminated to all teachers. However,
it is possible, for these various strands, to argue that a central product,
manufactured in order to be disseminated, is of no value. This argument
asserts that teachers must be involved in working out their own solutions in
order for any real change to occur. Such argument can hardly be applied to
every one of the strands discussed above. Whether or not it is true of any of
them, it is certainly true that the changes needed may involve such radical
redefinitions of classroom role, together with a new perspective on the
nature of school science, that any plan to impose change quickly is bound to
fail.

Any discussion of the problems and prospects for the professional
development of teachers is outside the scope of this paper. The problems
of setting out an ideal strategy have been the main concern here. However
if changes cannot be designed so that teachers can adopt them with hope of
success no development will occur. This need may well dictator that the
ideal aims may have to be approached slowly and along a carefully chosen
route.

1.2.10 BIBLIOGRAPHY

Assessment of Performance Unit. Science in Schools. Age 11, Report No. 1
    (1980 survey). Her Majesty's Stationery Office, London 1981.

Assessment of Performance Unit. Science in Schools. Age 11. Report No. 2
    (1981 survey). Department of Education and Science, London 1983.

Assessment of Performance Unit. Science in Schools. Age 11. Report No. 3 (1982 survey). Department of Education and Science, London 1984.

Bellack, A A et al. The Language of the Classroom. Teacher College Press: New York 1966.

Comber, L C and Keeves, J P, Science Education in Nineteen Countries: An Empirical Study. Wiley, New York 1973.

Conran, J. Primary Science 1950-82: A Personal View, in Richards and Holford (q.v.), pp 17-27.

Department of Education and Science. Primary Education in England: A Survey by HM Inspectors of Schools. Her Majesty's Stationery Office, London 1978.

Department of Education and Science. Science in Primary Schools. A discussion paper produced by HMI Science Committee. DES London 1983.

Ennever, L and Harlen, W. With Objectives in Mind. Macdonald Educational, London 1972.

Evans, P. Science: Pure or Applied? Education 3-13, Vol. 8 (1), pp 16-23, 1980. Reprinted in Richards and Holford (q.v.), pp 187-199.

Flanders, N. Analysing Teacher Behaviour. Addison Wesley, New York 1970.

Galton, M J, Simon, B and Kroll, P. Inside the Primary Classroom. Routledge and Kegan Paul, London 1980.

Galton, M J and Simon, B. Progress and Performance in the Primary Classroom. Routledge and Kegan Paul, London 1980.

Harlen, W et al. Match and Mismatch. Oliver and Boyd. London 1977.

Harlen, W. Does Content Matter in Primary Science? School Science Review. Vol. 59, pp 614-625, 1978. Reprinted in Richards and Holford (q.v.), pp 54-69.

Harlen, W (ed). New Trends in Primary School Science Education. Volume I. UNESCO, Paris 1983.

Host, V. Science in Primary Schools in France, pp 30-37, in Harlen - New Trends (q.v.).

Kerr, J and Engel, E. Can Science be Taught in Primary Schools? Education 3-13, Vol. 8 (1), pp 4-8, 1980. Reprinted in Richards and Holford (q.v.), pp 45-52.

Krasilchik, M. The Teaching of Science in Brazilian Primary Schools, pp 24-29, in Harlen - New Trends (q.v.).

Martin, M D. Recent Trends in the Nature of Curriculum Programmes and Materials, pp 55-67, in Harlen - New Trends (q.v.).

National Assessment of Education Progress: Three National Assessments of Science: Changes in Achievement 1969-77, NAEP Report No. 08-S-00, NAEP Education Testing Services, Princeton 1978.

Ormerod, M B and Duckworth, D. Pupils' Attitudes to Science: A Review of Research. NFER Windsor, United Kingdom 1975.

Redman, S et al. Young Children and Science: The Oxford Primary Science Project. Trends in Education 12, pp 17-25, 1968 (reprinted in Richards and Holford (q.v.) pp 131-138).

Redman S, Brereton, A and Boyers, P. An Approach to Primary Science, Macmillan Educational, London 1969.

Richards, C and Holford D. The Teaching of Primary Science: Policy and Practice. Falmer Press, Lewes, England 1983.

Richards, R et al. Learning Through Science: Formulating a School Policy. Macdonald Educational, London 1980.

Shayer, M and Adey, P. Towards a Science of Science Teaching. Heinemann, London 1981.

Simon, A and Boyer, G E. Mirrors for Behaviour. Philadelphia, Pa.: Research for Better Schools, 1968.

Solomon, J. Learning about Energy: How Pupils Think in Two Domains. European Journal of Science Education, Vol. 5 (1), pp 49-59, 1983.

Steadman, S D et al. An Enquiry into the Impact and Take-Up-of-Schools Council Funded Activities, Schools Council Publications, London 1978.

Wastnedge, R et al. Teachers' Guide I Nuffield Junior Science. Collins, London 1967.

1.3 A FRAMEWORK FOR DISCUSSING APPROACHES
AND METHODS IN SCIENCE EDUCATION

by

Prof. Björn Andersson, Sweden

1.3.1 SUMMARY

This paper addresses itself to the question: How should the pupil be
stimulated to construct scientific concepts and reasoning patterns that are
new to them?

To answer the question, a constructivist model of learning, based on
the work of Piaget, is used as a guide-line. The model states that the
individual tries to understand something new with the help of existing
thought structures. We need, therefore, to be informed of the pupil's
initial state. The model does not, however, tell us what specific
conceptions the pupils have of electricity, heat, light, matter etc. We
must find that out by focusing research activities on this problem.

The model offers guidance on what measures might be taken in order to
help the pupil to change from his initial state to a desired state. It
does not, however, predict how the pupil will function in a content-specific
teaching situation. This must be discovered by special research efforts.

Research in recent years has demonstrated, for the age range 12-18
that the pupils initial state, ie his reasoning prior to teaching, is
markedly different from the content of the teaching programme, and that
only to a minor extent it develops to the desired state as a result of
teaching. The majority of the pupils remain quite unaffected by the school
courses in respect of their understanding of scientific concepts and key
ideas.

Research into the initial state of the students has also opened up a
new world for the teacher. A lot of important new knowledge about students
"alternative frameworks" has been generated. We are not in a better position
to guide the students. However, the primary school is a relatively neglected
area. Therefore, some suggestions are put forward regarding research
projects concerning primary school science (7-12 years of age), including
finding out about the initial state of the learner and describing processes
leading to a desired state.

1.3.2 PROBLEM AND SYNOPSIS

Anyone who wishes to research into approaches and methods in science
education has to delimit and define the field in order to formulate questions
that are researchable. A given question should deal with a central aspect

of science education and lead to important new knowledge. This paper attempts to show that the question: *"How should the pupils be stimulated to construct scientific concepts and reasoning patterns that are new to them?"* meets these requirements, provided that it is answered with the aid of what is termed a constructivist model of learning.

1.3.3 CONCEPTUAL CHANGE - THE MAIN GOAL OF SCIENCE EDUCATION

Science education is a primary school (7-12 years of age) has many functions. It has to stimulate critical thinking, the ability to solve problems, social and linguistic development, etc. These functions are both necessary and essential, but not solely confined to the science subjects. Neither can these subjects, on the basis of research results, claim to be superior to others in developing the pupils in these respects. From this it follows that the unique and most central task of science education is to help the pupils to learn scientific concepts, theories and ways of reasoning. It is a question of bringing about lasting conceptual changes in individual pupils so that they become "scientifically literate" (Karplus 1964).

1.3.4 THEORETICAL BASIS - A CONSTRUCTIVIST MODEL OF LEARNING

To investigate how "scientific literacy" might be developed a theory or a model of learning is required as a guide-line. The model used by the author originates essentially from Piaget (see, for example, Flavell 1963 and Furth 1969) and is an example of a constructivist view of learning. The word constructivism expresses the idea that the individual himself constructs or creates ideas and ways of reasoning in response to impulses and stimulation from the world around him. The process of thinking itself is also an active construction.

Piaget assumes that man is endowed with a strong desire and will to learn. This is an essential link in a biologically determined endeavour to understand and exercise control over one's environment. But the individual's curiosity lands him in situations that he does not understand. His mental equilibrium is disturbed, he is not completely adjusted or *adapted* to his environment. But, according to Piaget, intelligence is a biological system, which like others of this kind strives to organise its parts into a whole, in increasingly better equilibrium with its surroundings. That is why disequilibrium is an impetus to learning and development. The individual strives to restore his equilibrium by *self-regulation*, that is, by his own reasoning and creativity.

Accommodation does not mean that only existing structures are used. It may also take place, for instance, through syntheses of structures, generalisation and differentiations. Consequently, the individual constructs many different structures during his life-time, and these become more and more integrated and flexible when it is a question of maintaining equilibrium with one's surroundings, that is, of understanding and predicting events. The individual increases his ability to cope in new and unknown situations. Piaget speaks of intelligence as an organ for non-specific adaptation. He also observes what most people have experienced, namely, that it is stimulating to begin to be able to use new ways of reasoning. Thought structures during their period of development are compared to hungry animals searching for food in order to grow.

1.3.5 SOME CONSEQUENCES OF THE CONSTRUCTIVIST MODEL OF LEARNING

The model just presented helps us to structure research to obtain an answer to the question: "How should we stimulate the pupils to construct scientific concepts and reasoning patterns that are new to them?"

The model states that the individual tries to understand something new with the help of existing thought structures. If follows, then, that it is desirable to be acquainted with the ones that exist in the area of education concerned. We need to be informed of the *pupil's initial state*. But, although Piaget and others have described the development of reasoning in such a comprehensive manner, the model does not tell us, for instance, what conceptions the pupils have of electricity, heat, light, matter, etc, before they begin science lessons. This is because Piaget and others have been interested in the development of reasoning in general. Our interest, on the other hand, lies in a specific subject area. We must therefore, to a large extent, find out about the pupils' initial position by focusing research activities on this problem.

From the initial state we want the pupils to change to a *desired state*, that is, to construct the knowing that is included in the school science courses. It is therefore necessary to clarify what characteristics school science. The findings affect, among other things, what aspects of the pupil's intitial state are studied.

1.3.6 SOME CHARACTERISTIC FEATURES OF SCHOOL SCEINCE

Consider an experiment that can conveivably be included in a science programme for the upper elementary school:

Diagram 1

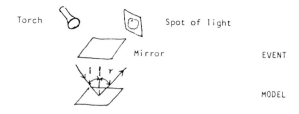

A torch is shone onto a mirror. A spot of light is intercepted on a screen. The pupil perhaps reads in a text-book that this is because the torch emits light, which is reflected in the mirror. The angle of incidence is equal to the angle of reflection. To understand all this the pupil is required to co-ordinate many varieties of concepts, including:

scientific concepts and   – light exists and propagates
key ideas: rectilinearly in space

reasoning patterns: – serial ordering of angles,
                                    eg the bigger the angle of
                                    incidence, the bigger the
                                    angle of reflection

spatial concepts:	- line, angle, plane, perpendicular
temporal concepts:	- first the ray comes in, then it goes out
cause-effect:	- the ray bounces on the mirror
concepts of science:	- in science you do not learn absolute truths, but set up a model, which is then tested

We can conceive that science at all levels concerns how systems change in *space-time*. Change is seen as evidence of *interaction* (cause-effect). Change is described and explained by creating and using *reasoning patterns* and *scientific concepts* and *key ideas*.

1.3.7 QUESTIONS ABOUT THE PUPIL'S INITIAL STATE

With a description of the characteristic features of school science as a starting point, we can now formulate a number of special questions about the pupils initial state, for example:

scientific concepts and key ideas:	How do the pupils predict and explain phenomena to do with electricity, heat, light, matter, etc?
reasoning patterns:	How do the pupils solve problems that require the reasoning patterns classification, serial ordering, proportionality, control of variables, reasoning with models etc?
space and time	What are pupils conceptions of position, motion and perspective? In what way do they comprehend 3D-drawings, cross-sections, etc?
subject and learning	What conceptions have the pupils of the purpose of the science subjects? What are their conceptions of knowledge, learning etc?

These are questions of a fairly simple type, that can be answered by interviewing the pupil, using eg a problem as a starting-point. This means that the pupil first of all predicts the outcome of an experiment and then explains how he/she reasoned.

More difficult questions concern, for instance, how various types of concept are integrated, co-ordinated, systematised and differentiated.

B

1.3.8 QUESTIONS ON LEARNING

As one's understanding of the pupils initial state develops, one can start posing questions about learning. What happens to the pupils' concepts of electricity (light, heat, and so on) when they are stimulated by a certain education programme? Is it possible to describe the construction process in a pupil in detail?

Similar questions may be posed about reasoning patterns, space, time, and so on.

1.3.9 THE PRESENT POSITION REGARDING RESEARCH - A SHORT ORIENTATION

During the past six to seven years many studies have been made with regard to how pupils of various ages explain and predict physical and chemical phenomena. One major result is that it has been established that their reasoning prior to teaching is markedly different from the content of the teaching programme and that only to a minor extent does this reasoning develop as a result of teaching. The majority of the pupils (about 70-80%) remain quite unaffected by the school courses in respect of the understanding of scientific concepts and key ideas.

The pupils' reasoning has been designated in various ways according to the investigators points of departure. The teacher in charge of instruction who thinks he has done a good job is inclined to call the pupils' strange answers "misconceptions". Recently, for instance, a well-attended seminar entitled "Misconceptions in Science and Mathematics" (1983) was held at Cornell University. The science education researcher who thinks he understands the pupils' way of reasoning uses the designations "alternative frameworks" (Driver, 1983) and "children's science" (Osborne, Bell and Gilbert, 1983). By this one wishes to show that one respects the pupils' conceptions, which are the result of their thinking. Like the researcher, the pupils are trying to understand the world around them. Their ideas should be considered as alternatives to established ones. (One problem with the designation "children's science" is that many adults also think in the same way as the children). In the author's research group, the phrases "everyday physical conceptions" and "everyday chemical conceptions" are sometimes used in order to emphasise that these are constructed to form an understanding of experiences of light, heat, electricity, etc, in daily life. The pupils' attempts at understanding the words and expression of adults reinforce these conceptions.

Research into alternative frameworks (1) has opened up a new world to the teacher and reveals a dramatic gulf between pupils' conceptions and course requirements.

---

(1) See for example Gilbert & Watts (1983), Driver & Erickson (1983), Tiberghien (1984), McDermott (1984), Andersson (1984).

33

For example:

i. The D C circuit

If you give a round battery, an electric light bulb and a piece of copper
wire to "pupils", aged seven to seventy, they often connect them like this
to get the bulb to light up:

Diagram 2

    After a great deal of thought they try other variants, such as:

Diagram 3

    Sometimes they say that a plus current and a minus current go to the
bulb. This is usually drawn in cross-section as follows:

Diagram 4

    It is evident that the pupils use a source-consumer model. The
electricity or current exists at a source from which it is led over to the
consumer.

Diagram 5

    Everyday experience provides ample support to this model. An
electrical apparatus is supplied with one flex to a wall socket, which is
enough to start it. (The pupils think of the flex as containing one wire
only).

Diagram 6

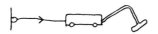

In our daily life we also talk of electricity as a consumable commodity. "Don't waste electricity", "Work out how much electricity is used", "How expensive electricity is" are some common expressions.

In Sweden we present the pupils in Form 7 (aged 13) with a closed circuit model. In the course, it is taken for granted that this model is easy, which is why it is not presented as a problem to be solved. Instead, series and parallel connections are rapidly gone into, and this is followed by theoretical concepts, such as current, voltage and resistance. No consideration is given to the fact that the pupils initial state is a source-consumer model. The result is that most pupils lose the thread of what they are supposed to learn from the start. Studies show that about 80% of the pupils use a source-consumer model to solve simple problems in electricity, not only in Form 7, but also in Forms 8 and 9 (aged 14 and 15). Thus, the model is not appreciably affected by the lessons on electricity (Andersson and Kärrqvist 1979).

Work on studying teaching with the aim of getting the pupils to exchange their "alternative frameworks" for school science is progressing to a certain extent (see Driver and Erickson 1983, for a review). One of the strategies recommended is based on the idea of making the pupil aware of his alternative way of reasoning, eg by showing that a prediction is not borne out by the results of the experiment. After this, the teacher introduces the scientific way of reasoning, in the hope that the pupil experiences this as better and more productive. It is too soon to draw any general conclusions from the attempts to get the pupil to move away from his alternative way of reasoning to the reasoning of school science (2).

1.3.10 REASONING PATTERNS

The previous section concerned pupils' conceptions in the various areas of physics and chemistry. In other words, we treated the aspect of the *content* of scientific reasoning. We now go over to the aspect of <u>form</u>. This aspect refers to the fact that we use various forms of reasoning or *reasoning patterns*, which may be applied to a variety of contents. One such reasoning pattern is *proportionality*, which occurs in various connections, for instance, the definition of density, Ohm's Law, Boyle's Law and chemical calculations.

Another reasoning pattern is *control of variables*. To be able to draw a conclusion from an experiment, all factors except the one to be investigated are kept constant. This reasoning pattern is used not only in physics, chemistry and biology, but also in various behavioural sciences.

A third example of a reasoning pattern is *hypothetico-deductive* reasoning. This means that one makes assumptions about how a system works and then deduces consequences, which are then tested experimentally. If the predictions made are borne out by the results of the experiment, a given assumption gains in credibility.

Other important reasoning patterns are *classification* and *serial ordering*.

_____

(2) See also Children Learning in Science, University of Leeds.

We know quite a lot about how pupils use various reasoning patterns as one of Piaget's chief interests has been to study how they are developed and integrated.

With regard to control of variables, it may be mentioned that children find it difficult to cope with more than one variable at a time. They easily confuse two variables, and do not understand that it is impossible to draw any definite conclusion if two variables are changed simultaneously.

The large number of books that Piaget has written on the forms of scientific reasoning has led to extensive follow-up research and further development of his ideas. The interest among researchers in science education may be explained by the fact that the reasoning patterns in question occupy a central position in scientific thinking (3).

Attempts to develop reasoning patterns by means of teaching programmes have generally been positive. For instance, Lawson and Wollman (1976) have demonstrated that four lessons have led to a considerable improvement in the ability of 13 year-olds to understand and perform control experiments. Kurtz and Karplus (1974) have reached positive results regarding proportionality. The length of the teaching programme was 12 hours and 13 year-olds were involved here, too.

It is noteworthy that the point of departure for these studies is the fact that a given reasoning pattern is often found in an intuitive, but correct, form, which provides a good starting-point for teaching. The logic of control experiments is matched by, for instance, an intuitive feeling for a fair comparison. The pupils know that if two 100-metre sprinters are to compete, then one does not put ski-boots on one and spikes on the other. As far as alternative frameworkers are concerned, on the other hand, a conception must sometimes be *replaced* by another.

The positive results of different training programmes for reasoning patterns constitute a criticism of Piaget's structuralistic ideas. Piaget believes that reasoning at a certain stage is governed by a general structure. Without the thought structure for formal operations, for instance, it is impossible to cope with problems to do with proportionality, control experiments, etc. It takes years to develop the structure in question. But the short training programmes are successful. This indicates that we are dealing with independent reasoning patterns, and not, as Piaget has claimed, something that has a general and universal thought structure as a necessary prerequisite.

Criticism of this kind regarding Piaget's structuralism has contributed to the fact that interest in researching into reasoning patterns has waned in favour of content-oriented conceptions. It would be unfortunate, however, if all the work on the form of reasoning were pushed aside, as it has led to very valuable knowledge about pupils of different ages. The field must, however, be freed from Piaget's structuralism. An attempt in this direction is the use of the term

---

(3)   Important work has been done by Professor Robert Karplus' group at Lawrence Hall of Science, Berkely. See, for instance, Karplus (1979), Karplus, Lawson, Wollman et al (1977); Lawson, Karplus and Adi (1978).

reasoning pattern instead of "formal operational scheme" and similar
expressions from Piaget's system. It is perhaps possible to integrate
the two research fields "content" and "reasoning pattern". A connecting
link may be the hypothetico-deductive reasoning that is an important aid
in testing, and possible discarding, conceptions of content. In general,
it is possible to regard reasoning patterns as tools with which to work on
the content.

1.3.11 SPACE, TIME, SUBJECT AND LEARNING

Very little research that has a direct bearing on science has been undertaken in the areas mentioned in this heading. An exception is a study by
Nussbaum and Novak (1976) concerning pupils understanding of the earth as
a heavenly body (ages 7-15 years). The study clearly demonstrates the
difficulty that the pupils have in co-ordinating their own view of the
earth with an imaginary view from a point out in space.

1.3.12 CONSEQUENCES FOR THE ELEMENTARY SCHOOL (7-12 YEARS) - SOME ESSENTIAL RESEARCH TASKS

Research into the scientific reasoning of school children, especially "the
alternative framework movement", has led to such a large body of new
knowing that one is justified in speaking of a major revolution. One can
wonder why all these discoveries were not made earlier, for instance, by
the thousands of teachers who have given lessons in physics, chemistry
and biology for many years. It is probable that this may be explained by
the fact that researchers have deliberately used a constructivist model
of learning. If you use this kind of model, it becomes, for example, both
necessary and meaningful to enquire into the initial conceptual state of
the pupils.

A considerable number of signs indicate that teaching is governed by
another model, which may be designated *empiricist*. According to this,
what is termed the transmission of knowledge does not present any
particular difficulties. The sources of knowledge are experiments, books,
film-strips and the teacher. Knowledge is transmitted from these sources
to the individual, who may be described as a relatively passive receiver.
This view of learning results in, among other things, the orientation
courses so typical of lower secondary school (upper level of the
comprehensive school, 13-15) and which expose the pupils to very abstract
material in a short time. The pupils are assumed to acquire this knowledge
if they only keep their eyes and ears open. The teacher spouts out
information at a rapid rate and pupils go through "cook-book" laboratory
sessions in order to absorb new knowledge rapidly and effectively. The
constructivists point out that this type of teaching lies far above their
initial conceptual position.

All this has a strong bearing on teaching at the primary stages
(7-12). A primary prerequisite for a dynamic science education programme
at these stages is that the teachers apply a constructivistic model of
learning. This model leads to paying attention to the pupils' initial
state, after which the teacher tries to stimulate the pupils to construct
concepts that are new to them. This requires a great deal of time for
discussion and for solving problems.

A constructivist model provides the teacher with an inquiring and creative attitude to his own teaching. Instead of copying established teaching patterns, the teacher seeks for new ways in a continuous struggle to achieve something better.

One important task for research is to find out what model of learning elementary school teachers use. It is probable that empiricist conceptions are common. A potential project would include interviews with teachers and video-taping of lesson preparations and lessons, and interview with teachers in connection with these video-recordings.

If one found that empirisist models are common, the *question would arise how one should stimulate the teacher to move from empiricism to constructivism.* This is not an easy task. The language is full of expressions that communicate empiricism conceptions (4). We all harbour an old and tenacious empiricist within us, which turns up and distorts a constructivist message. Thus, for instance, many people believe that Piaget is an advocate of "discovery teaching", in the sense that the pupil is to investigate and discover for himself so as to obtain the set knowledge of school courses direct from experiments instead of from books. This kind of empiricist Piaget has scarcely existed. Constructivist experience indicates that there is no guarantee whatsoever that individual exploring leads to the knowing that the school course prescribes.

An empiricist view of Piaget results in working groups being given the task of weeding out concepts from the course syllabus, with reference to Piaget's research. This kind of work has been done and may in itself be positive. It is, however, of limited value as a measure of reform unless one, at the same time, clearly sets out the fundamental constructivist approach, which is a prerequisite for dynamic and vital teaching and learning.

In order to run good science courses at elementary school it is not enough to move from an empiricist to a constructivist model of learning. It is also necessary to have a somewhat more detailed knowledge of how one should apply the latter model to the given teaching material - that is, science.

As already mentioned, the model states that the individual tries to understand something new with the aid of existing concepts and ideas. But it does not tell you what these are within a given area, for instance, electricity, heat and matter. It is, therefore, *a matter of urgency to carry out research into the scientific reasoning of pupils at the elementary school.* This level has, for instance, not been affected to any marked extent by "the alternative framework movement". The reader is referred to the section "Questions about the initial state of the pupils" for a more detailed structuring of the problem area.

We need to know how far the pupils can move from a given initial position. New educational programmes need to be produced with the aim of making a detailed study of the pupils' learning with regard to key ideas, reasoning patterns, spatial concepts, etc. The main purpose is to give the

---

(4) See, for example, Reddy, 1979.

teachers insight into the nature of scientific learning so that they are
better able to guide and stimulate their pupils. It is *not* a question of
prescribing procedures that lead to well-defined goals.

Finally, it should be pointed out that the research on alternative
frameworks carried out up till now provides a basis for the hypothesis
that elementary school teachers have, to a considerable extent, not
mastered the school science course. They have alternative ways of
reasoning, similar to those of the pupils (compare, for instance, the
example about electricity, see 1.3.9.) What is termed "children's science"
may therefore also be "teachers' science". Many informal observations
from pre-service and in-service courses support this hypothesis. A
systematic survey may, however, need to be done. Under no circumstances
should the problem be denied. It is a challenge to indicate how the
elementary school teachers should be stimulated to construct, on their
own, the scientific conceptions that are needed to help the pupils to
take the first step on the way from "children's science" to "school
science".

1.3.13 BIBLIOGRAPHY

Andersson, B (1984): Chemical Reactions. Elevperspektiv. No. 12. The EKNA-group, Dept of Educational Research, University of Göteborg, Box 1010. S-431 26 Mölndal, Sweden.

Andersson, B & Kärrqvist, C (1979). Elektriska kretsar. Elevperspektiv No. 2. The EKNA-group (as above).

Andersson B & Kärrqvist, C (1983): How Swedish pupils, aged 12-15 years, understand light and its properties. European Journal of Science Education, Vol 5, pp. 387-4-2.

Archenhold, W F; Driver, R H; Orton, A & Wood-Robertson, C (Eds) (1980): Cognitive development research in science and mathematics. Leeds: Centre for Studies in Science Education, University of Leeds.

Childrens Learning in Science Project. Centre for Studies in Science and Mathematics Education. The University of Leeds, Leeds L S 2 9 JT.

Misconceptions in Science and Mathematics. Proceedings of an international seminar June 20-22, 1983. Write to J D Novak, Dept of Education, College of Agriculture and Life Sciences, Cornell University, Itacha, New York 14853, USA.

Driver, R (1983): The pupil as scientist? Milton Keynes: Open University

Driver, R & Erickson, G (1983): Theories-in-action: Some theoretical and empirical issues in the study of students' conceptual framework in science. Studies in Science Education, Vol 10, pp. 37-60.

Flavell, Y H (1963): The developmental psychology of Jean Piaget. Princeton, N Y: Van Nostrand.

Furth, H G (1969): Piaget and knowledge. Englewood Cliffs, N Y: Prentice-Hall.

Gilbert, J K & Watts, D M (1983): Concepts, misconceptions and alternative conceptions: changing perspectives in science education. Studies in Science Education, Vol 10, pp. 61-98.

Guesne, E (1978): Lumière et vision des objects: Un example de représentations des phénomenes physique pre-existant à l'enseignement. Proceedings of GIRP, edited by G Delacôte. London: Taylor and Francis.

Jung, W; Pfundt, H; v Rhôneck, C (Eds) (1982): Problems concerning students' representation of physics and chemistry knowledge. Ludwigsburg: Pädagogisch Hochschule.

Karplus, R (1964): The Science Curriculum Improvement Study. Journal of Research in Science Teaching, Vol 2, p. 293.

Karplus, R (1979): Continuous functions: Students' viewpoints. European Journal of Science Education, Vol 1, No. 4, pp. 397-415.

40

Karplus, R; Lawson, A E; Wollman, A E et al (1977): Science teaching and
the development of reasoning. Lawrence Hall of Science, University
of California, Berkeley, California 947 20. (It is a workshop
material in five parts, namely Physics, Chemistry, Biology, Earth
Science and General Science).

Kurtz, B & Karplus, R (1974): Intellectual development beyond elementary
school VII: Teaching for proportional reasoning. School Science and
Mathematics, Vol 79, pp. 387-398.

Lawson, A E; Karplus, R & Adi, H (1978): The acquisition of propositional
logic and formal operational schemata during adolescence. Journal
of Research in Science Teaching, Vol 15, pp 465-478.

Lawson, A E & Wollman, W T (1976): Encouraging the transition from concrete
to formal cognitive functioning: an experiment. Journal of Research
in Science Teaching. Vol 13, pp. 413-430.

McDermott, L (1974): Critical review of research in the domain of
mechanics. In Research on physics education: proceedings of the
first international workshop. Editions du Centre National de la
Recherche Scientifique, 15 quai Anatole-France, F-75700 Paris.

Misconceptions in science and mathematics: Proceedings of the International
Seminar at Cornell University, 1983. Write to J D Novak, Dept of
Education, College of Agriculture and Life Sciences, Cornell University,
Itacha, New York 14853.

Nussbaum, J & Novak, J (1976): An assessment of children's concepts of
the Earth utilising structured interviews. Science Education, Vol 60,
pp. 535-550.

Osborne, R Y; Bell, B F & Gilbert, Y K (1983): Science teaching and
children's views of the world. European Journal in Science Education
Vol 5, pp. 1-14.

Reddy, M Y (1979): The conduit metaphor - a case of frame conflict in our
language about language. In ortony, A: Metaphor and thought.
Cambridge University Press.

Research on physics education: proceedings of the first international
workshop. See McDermott, L (1984).

Sjøberg, S (1981): Jean Piagets teorier: Bade vitenskapsteori og
utviklingspsykologi. In Kongressrapport, Den 11: e nordiska
kongressen för lärare i matematik, fysik och kemi. Can be obtained
from LMFK, Södra kretsen, Lärarhögskolan i Malmö, Box 23501, S-200 45
Malmö.

Stead, B & Osborne, R (1979): Exploring science students' concepts of light.
A paper presented at the first national conference of the New Zealand
Association for Researfh in Education, Victoria University of
Wellington, 7-10 October, 1979.

Tiberghien, A (1984): Critical review on the research aimed at
elucidating students' understanding of temperature and heat (10-16
years of age), electric circuits (8-20) and light (10-16). In
Research on physics education: proceedings of the first international
workshop. Editions du Centre National de la Recherche Scientifique,
15, quai Antole-France, F-75700 Paris.

1.4 STAFF DEVELOPMENT WITH REGARD TO SCIENCE
EDUCATION IN PRIMARY SCHOOLS

by

Dr. Roland Lauterbach,
Federal Republic of Germany

1.4.1 SUMMARY

This paper focusses on the practising teacher of science , technology and
nature study at the primary school level. It intends to draw conclusions
from research and development relevant for the improvement of teaching this
subject area and to suggest measures for staff development, commonly
labelled teacher in-service training or teacher in-service education.

1.   Attention is given to those qualifications of primary school teachers
which directly affect teaching science, technology and nature study,
concentrating on those expected to become part of the professional profile
of teachers.

2.   Research and development data concerning activities, models, concepts
and patterns relevant for teacher in-service training in primary science
are presented and are discussed in relation to their effectiveness.

3.   Consequences for possible policy decisions on in-service training are
suggested relating research and development to the proposed qualification
profile of primary science teachers.

1.4.2 PROFESSIONAL PROFILE

1.4.2.1 *An experience of professional jeopardy*

     "I have always been fascinated by the problems involved in theorising
about and researching into education. Thus I was taken aback by my reaction
to these activities when I returned to the classroom. Once working again as
a teacher I lost all desire to keep up-to-date with the literature. This
was not because my mind went soggy or because I became too involved with
the minutiae of day-to-day problems. It was simply that the world of the
academic journals seemed completely irrelevant to classroom life. Inherent
in the nature of social science and educational research is a propensity to
generalise and develop second order abstractions from the concreteness of
particular examples. In addition, such activities are conducted in an
ambience of intellectual detachment and scepticism. But as a teacher I had
to act in particular and concrete situations and, moreover, be committed to
and believe in what I was doing."

(McNamara 1976, 155)

1.4.2.2 *Terminology and concept*

McNamara's autobiography reflection poses a fundamental problem for
INSET (1): Is the true professionality of teachers substantially different
from or even imcompatible with the concept of "teacher" proposed by
educational theory and research? Moreover, is there a third or even fourth
and fifth professionality concept for existing INSET, for administration
and for the public? In his critical analysis of the professionalisation
concept HOYLE characterises *professionality* as "the attitudes towards
professional practice among the members of an occupation and the degree of
knowledge and skill which they bring to it" (Hoyle 1980, 44). The
professional profile describes the qualifications teachers need to practise
their profession satisfactorily. Satisfaction seems primarily defined in
terms of client (pupil) satisfaction. But this is only one side of it. Of
equal importance, though not articulated in the professional (self-) concept,
is the teacher's satisfaction.

At least two views of the concept have to be distinguished: The
professional reality of the practising teacher (how she or he *is*) and the
desired, expected or proposed practice (how she or he *ought to be*). Reality
and proposition differe considerably, and this is not necessarily a question
of quality on profile terms.

Jackson (1968, 116 ff) reports the views on teaching held by a group
of American elementary school teachers identified as good practitioners:
Their approach to teaching was intuitive; their concepts of educational
theory were interpreted to fit their own common-sense notions of pupil
development; they did not seem to be interested in evaluating their work in
an objective manner; educational objectives had little relevance for them;
their satisfaction came from the immediacy of events; they valued their
autonomy and their personal relationships to pupils; for their pedagogical
moves and evaluation, they relied on what seemed to be marginal ("fleeting
and sometimes cryptic") signs from pupils.

Teacher training and corresponding research literature propose quite
contrary professional qualifications: theoretically sound concepts, rational
methodology, objective evaluation, systematic planning and observation,
behavioural objectives, compliance with syllabi. And indeed, most evaluation reports accompanying new curricula as well as research reports
illustrating new methods of teacher training (Voss 1983, Joyce and Showers
1980, Good 1980) give evidence that teachers improve their teaching when
they receive formal training, be it in questioning, classroom management,
or in other dimensions considered important for better teaching.

---

(1) INSET is used throughout as an abbreviation for in-service education
and training.

Yet the effects do not nearly keep up with the expectations (2). Therefore, it may not be surprising that criticism on theory and research-based teacher training has gained momentum. Empirical research, so far, has not resolved the perennial question why successful teachers do not necessarily conform to formal qualification criteria and vica versa. But then, some successful teachers do.

Consequently, the relationship between teaching practice and research, between teaching reality and research-based proposition needs re-orientation.

Perhaps we need to take a step backward and reconsider if our own professionality as image designers of the teaching profession is enhancing the teachers' professional practice, or if it is ensuring our own professional existence. I am not clear on that. Therefore, I will review evidence that the recognition of the teachers' professional competence in research and training can revitalise the teaching profession, research and training leading to results that may generate the needed perspectives for improvement.

1.4.2.3 *Profile demands for primary science teachers*

In an exploration of teachers' planning concerns Peterson, Marx and Clark (1978) identified (through a "think-aloud" technique) the following order of importance: subject matter, instructional processes and students, materials of instruction, and objectives.

Before turning to the subject matter aspect which concerns us here most, we should take note of professional prerequisite qualities which seem more important for successful teaching.

1.4.2.3.1 *General qualifications*

When students achievement is taken as the success criterion for teaching three results stand out.

1. Brophy and Evertson (1976) found that the only belief that consistently separated high and low effective teachers (external judgement) was the extent to which teachers believed that they had the power to achieve the desired effects, ie could teach effectively (3).

2. Process-product studies, in general, relate positively student achievement to teachers' *managerial abilities*. The importance of this qualification complex seems to be the most consistent result in different studies (Good 1980, Anderson, Evertson and Brophy 1979). This is especially notable for primary education (Stallings and Hentzell 1978).

---

(2) The latest review is by Yager and Penick 1983, who reanalysed the results of three national evaluation studies on science education efforts in the US during the sixties and seventies.

(3) Supportive studies on *personal efficacy* exist (eg McDonald and Elias 1976), but most of them are concerned with self-fulfilling prophecies, mainly on the low expectations teachers have of students.

A recent study on interests and expectations German teachers have for INSET topics in educational science supports the results indirectly. Eigler and Nenninger (1982 , 1983) found that "class management" courses had the highest preference of a single topic area followed by those on "motivation" and "evaluation". Most important, though, was an interest pattern analysis showing that combinations of topics centering on "classroom-management" are considered most valuable for enhancing competence and performance in instructional practice.

3. Good (1980) also emphasises *active teaching* as a fairly consistent indicator on student achievement. Its conceptual orientation values that the teacher sets and articulates the learning goals, actively assesses student progress towards those goals, and frequently makes presentations to the class that illustrate how to do the assigned work (4). The supportive American studies are specified for certain conditions and expectations of school learning with the results varying considerably depending on subject (convincing in mathematics, not science), age of pupils (younger children more than older ones), the teacher's role definition (eg role perception in tune with behaviour, Doyle and Ponder 1976), and the expectations children have of school learning. Additionally the school environment can have considerable modifying effects as some school climate studies indicate (Anderson 1982).

For INSET we may at this point conclude:

a. *Self-confidence* has to be built up and maintained in teachers that what they teach is worthwhile and how they teach will be effective.

b. *Classroom management* competencies (with supportive and specifying topics) need to receive high priority, especially the sensitive perception and anticipation capabilities for person, social interaction, and classroom organisation.

c. *Tuned teaching* fitting the role concept of a teacher, the expectations of the children, and the teaching context of both has to be attained, or context, expectations of children and role concepts have to change.

These three dimensions seem an appropriate supplement from research to extend McNamara's experience and Jackson's finding at the beginning of this chapter.

1.4.2.3.2 *Qualification requirements for primary science*

The Commission of Science Education of the American Association for the Advancement of Science (AAAS) identified in their report of the Teacher Education Project (1970) 31 competencies needed by primary science teacher, classifying them into five categories: scientific knolwedge, processes of science, attitude toward science, scientific inquiry, and continuous learning. There has been little modification of this list, except for a stronger emphasis on solicitating behavioural expressions: the cognitive potential to act is not sufficient for the actualisation of that potential.

---

(4) Similarly the concept of direct instruction - Powell 1978.

A teacher's point of view on qualification requirements hardly had time to develop. While reviewing teacher in-service efforts Moore and Blankenship (1978) identified varying need patterns of teachers depending on school, age of pupils, subject matter, previous training, personal background, interest (hobby) etc.

Science teachers are a quite specific group in this respect. For them subject matter, experimentation and didactics (usually understood as modes of transmitting subject knowledge, methods and experiences) range first in priority. A nation-wide study on characteristics of science teacher in-service training, which the IPN conducted in the Federal Republic of Germany in 1980 (Block et al 1981), substantiated the high appreciation for these areas by lower and upper secondary science teachers and their trainers.

For primary school teachers, required also to teach science in addition to all other aspects of the curriculum, the situation is different. In priority ratings of subject matter, science rates low (Stake and Easley 1978). And there are some additional impeding characteristics of primary school teachers in relation to science education.

1. In many countries primary school teachers have little or no training in the sciences during their pre-service phase. There is not enought time to deal with science, nature study or technology systematically in addition to all the other subject areas. And if Jaus' (1978) study on teaching environmental science, indicating that teachers usually do not teach subjects or topics they have not been trained in, can be generalised, all hope must rest on INSET.

2. Most primary school teachers are women. In the industrialised countries their share of teaching positions is between 70-90%. Girls' and women's interest in the sciences and in technology is far lower than the boys' (Kelly 1981). Only for some biological topics this is not the case. These interest patterns are not confined to school subjects and topics. They are even more pronounced when the out-of-school activities are surveyed (Weltner et al 1979). These observations seem to be consistent for adults, including school teachers (for an overview and broad discussion of the topic Kelly 1981, Lehrke, Hoffmann and Gardner 1984). The strongest point in this case is made by the preliminary results of a long-term effect study for physics education. Fifty-two per cent of the variance explaning the lower results of women is given just by the fact that a person was a woman (Häusler et al 1984).

3. With dropping birth rates and reduction of teaching positions in many industrial countries fewer young people enter the profession. Pre-service or even secondary school science experience and know-how through an up-dated science education, therefore, has less and less chance to enter the primary schools by means of young teachers. Status studies indicate that young teachers receive recognition from colleagues because of their up-dated qualifications in subject matter areas. Especially in the sciences, older teachers are willing to learn from the younger ones.

For some countries the situation is not that discouraging. Because of syllabus requirements and considerable efforts in teacher training, science, technology and nature study has been established. Correspondingly, more or less successful attempts have been made to train primary teachers in selected scientific contents, methods, attitudes and behaviours. Yet, a number of problems remain. A few of them will be touched upon briefly here:

1.4.2.3.2.1 *Knowledge*

There is already sufficient evidence that science concepts are of little help for pupils when they are asked to solve everyday problems (eg Vicentini-Mossori 1980, Duit et al 1981, Osborne et al 1983). Moreover, the notions children have of a science concept are often of greater functional adequacy for them than school science concepts. Presently, there still is too little awareness or consideration of this in science teaching and INSET.

Maybe some of the problems associated with alleged difficulties of science could be handled right from the start, instead of ignoring them or postponing their treatment. Vicentini-Mossori (1980) is in agreement with our own observations that the school science of teachers often has little to do with science or at least with scientific concepts and methods. Viennot (1979) and Saltiel (1980) found out that even university physics majors and student teachers in France, Belgium and Great Britain revert to pre-scientific, eg Aristotelian, views when dealing with real or applied problems in elementary mechanics.

And a last point: the body of knowledge in the sciences seems quite homogeneous, its methodology well structured. INSET deals with it on these grounds. Epistemology and sociology of knowledge have questioned this perception considerably. To put it positively: Science is a living human endeavour containing ingenuity as well as misconceptions, order as well as confusion. Yet, school science and INSET tend to ignore these facts.

If science teaching is to make sense, teachers have to understand and accept the children's notions and ideas as functionally adequate though less powerful; they have to be knowledgable of the science content they want to achieve and of its quality; and they have to be aware of their own functional conceptionalisation, because they themselves will demonstrate it when they talk and act in the classroom.

1.4.2.3.2.2 *Method*

For method questions teachers find themselves confronted with problems similar to the ones they have with children's notions and scientific knowledge. On the one hand, the children's ways of investigating are not those of science as part of the terminology (eg observations, description, classification) suggests and some science educators idealise; on the other hand, the top scientists depend on their ingenuity and, often, "extra" rational problem-solving capability for their special area. As with knowledge, there is the teacher's own problem-solving capability for science problems. Without substantial training it is probably no more specialised than that of any other non-expert. Jean Piaget's developmental psychology of step by step growth for solving "simple" problems relevant for mathematical and scientific understanding, together with Thomas S Kuhn's paradigm acquisition process the young student has to go through, should make science educators cautious in this matter.

Wright (1979) reports that students of elementary science method courses solve less than 40% of paper-and-pencil tasks dealing with multiple variables, up to 75% when interacting with hands-on problems. For unsuccessful problem-solvers he identified (through questioning) a holistic approach without sorting out relevant details. Reif (1983) reports that expert problem-solvers in physics first deal with problems qualitatively before applying calculating strategies. They have a hunch about the solution, they feel sure how to solve the problem, before they actually go into the details of procedure. Students ("non-experts") often try to proceed systematically right from the start - and they often fail. Consequently, training emphasis will have to be on both holistic problem perception and identification of relevant variables.

For the time being, we have to accept that a good way to improve problem-solving abilities in the sciences is to solve problems in the sciences. But many of the problems we pose in school science are pre-solved. And what often is called problem-solving or inquiry is just finding the method or solution the curriculum or the teacher is expecting. Divergent answers are not easily accepted, because they divert from the pre-conceived path of the curricular outline, leaving many teachers at loss. The pupils learn to look for cues of acceptance rather than for "their" correct solution.

1.4.2.3.2.3 *Attitudes and interests*

The world-wide educational, political, and economic goal of improving science and technology know-how has been underlayed with the intention to develop a positive attitude towards science and technology in children as early as possible. It is interesting to note that there never has been any indication that children of primary age do not have such a positive attitude. On the contrary, attitude and interest studies show that children generally have a positive feeling towards nature, technology and science regardless of gender, school science experience or social environment (Ormerod 1981, Kelly 1984, Lehrke et al 1984). Differences develop with age, be it gender specific preferences (technology for boys, nature for girls) or interest as well as disinterest in specific school subjects.

The early diffuse positive indication can still be increased. Bredderman's (1983) meta-analysis of the effects of the US elementary science programmes (ESS, SAPA, and SCIS) show positive attitude effects. But he cautions that they may be lost when the pupils are later enrolled in traditional science classes.

The teachers' task may well be to help children differentiate their attitudes and interests in science, nature and technology, thus preventing indifference and aversion. But we do not know to what extent primary teacher attitudes impart likes and dislikes (low relationships reported from meta-analysis by Druva and Anderson 1983, Shrighley 1983) onto the children.

One might speculate on the hypothesis that as long as there has been little science in primary grades there have been no effects; with an increasing number of science topics attitudes of teachers will mediate to children (5).

For teacher attitudes towards science a correlation with gender was already mentioned. We also know that these attitudes cannot be completely concealed by a person and that children are aware (often subconsciously) of the teacher's attitudes (Smith 1979).

Furthermore, the primary teacher's attitudes towards science influence his or her teaching style and efforts to teach it.

Nevertheless, the consequences cannot be to teach teachers positive attitudes towards science, but to offer chances for developing them. To know and to be able to think or act is categorically different from valuing. Human rights, morality, self-determination in a democracy, and the uncertainty of the best judgement in historically undecided questions delimit any indoctrinating measures. The teacher's own experience, knowledge and judgement will have to decide on this question.

While research will have to clarify justification for objectives on the "attitudes to science", as well as those on "scientific attitudes" (because they too are questionable on substantial grounds: Schibeci 1983), INSET has to confine itself to offering experiences with science, nature and technology, to clarifying issues and problems connected with them, and to supporting awareness of self, of self-expression, and of its effects on children.

1.4.2.3.3.4 *Behaviour*

Behavioural expressions (gesture, posture, facial expression) of a person strongly affect the participants of an interaction. For science education Jungwirth (1971) showed that students complied with the inferred non-verbally expressed expectations of teachers and not with the verbal statements. This, probably, explains why teachers who are interested and practice inquiry into science are more effective in achievement categories. Quite often though the attitude concept is used to explain the tendency of an individual's behaviours. Wicker's (1969) review found only low consistency between attitude and behaviour. Ajzen and Fishbein (1980) suggest and show that intention of behaviour may be a more indicative influencing factor.

Lehmann and Langeheine (1984) in their study on environmental conscious-ness confirmed that there is more to activating behaviour than having the potential to behave. The knowledge of negative behavioural effects (eg littering) as well as of corrective behaviours (no littering, recycling), the cognitive and behavioural competence to act, and a highly positive attitude towards the correct behaviours were not enough to solicit these

---

(5) A comparative long-term study on interests at the IPN (Lehrke and Hoffmann) may give some answers.

behaviours. Similar results are know from public health studies on smoking, dieting, or physical training. Here we meet a phenomenon that seems constantly ignored in education: knowledge, ability, and favourable attitudes are not enough to make people act.

1.4.2.3.3.5 Some consequences

For the specific requirements in primary science teaching, we may conclude that at least the following grounding efforts are needed:

a. New topics as well as up-dated *knowledge* about nature, technology and 'the sciences will have to be dealt with permanently. Moreover, the conceptual understanding of school science needs constant attention. It has to be related to the children's notions, the everyday functionality, the scientific meaning, and the tacher's interpretation.

b. The same holds true for the method aspect of science. The sciences, technology and nature study have a rich arsenal of *processes* and procedures to handle information, objects and organisms, to gain insights and to solve problems. As no single method should dominate at the expense of another, an open methodology is needed. The criterion for method selection is the method's adequacy for fulfilling the task or solving the problem at hand.

c. The installment of scientific *attitudes* and *interests* in teachers is not a matter of in-service efforts. But attitude and interest development is. Attitude and interest formation and change is an individual as well as a collective process. It needs to be understood and experienced in order that teachers become able to assess and deal with its effects in and for science teaching.

d. *Behavioural expressions* seem to be the overt educational core qualities. Primary science teachers need to be trained in behavioural skills, such as dealing with organisms, environment, natural and technological objects, scientific apparatus and information. Of greater concern are the holistic effects of behaviour, requiring concistency with the intentions of teaching, and the conditions for putting the behavioural potentials into action.

1.4.2.4 INSET and profile considerations

In the light of desirable profile characteristics, INSET has to recognise that it is an open-ended task in need of an alert, differentiated and flexible support system capable of responding to the viable need patterns of its teachers.

A tentative assumption on professionality gives rise to optimism. Primary school teachers, in general, seem well qualified in the basics of teaching, ie they are confident as primary school teachers, they manage their classes, and they have adopted or developed modes of teaching fitting their and their children's expectations. Furthermore, they have contributed to conditions of teaching in a manner which is often excellent as far as material and ideational environment is concerned. These are the grounds of professionality to rely on for self-directed development.

51

The requirements for teaching science, technology and nature study are
cautiously indicated above. They are of concern to teachers (6), because
they generate insecurity even in their traditional competence domain: New,
strange or even disliked subject matter can upset self-confidence in
knowing what and how to teach. Experimentation, environmental (out-door)
studies, or technical constructions require a change of classroom management; instructional habits relying on directive teaching common in reading,
writing and mathematics are questioned by exploratory or inquiry learning.
For INSET this means finding a course of action which relies on and values
the teachers' know-how, while at the same time offering options for change.

This seems necessary, because teaching strategy or patterns of
strategies may be the most important identifiable factor for change as far
as teachers' influence on achievement is concerned (7).

1.4.3 ACTIVITIES, MODELS, AND PATTERNS IN INSET

1.4.3.1 Results and their relative value

Research on primary science INSET poses some difficulties. Nevertheless, in
combination with pre-service studies and relevant INSET in related areas,
some guidelines for action can be derived.

1.4.3.1.1 Individual effects on teachers: eg attitudes

The typical research reports are ambivalent. They tend to be optimistic;
but small populations and marginal effects, as far as practical consequences
are concerned, suggest their cautious interpretation.

All in all, research on attitudes indicates that changes tend to occur
in a positive direction through favourable experiences, manipulative
measures, and reflective experiences. Contrary to Morrisey's (1981) and
Voss' (1983) recommendations for continuing research on inducing positive
attitudes (eg long-term effect studies), I would defend the thesis that in
order to raise professional qualifications the teachers' knowledge,
experience and consciousness of attitude development and manipulation for
children and self have to be the future research tasks.

The scope of most of the rather specific studies (not only for the
attitude aspect, illustrated here) is limited for the following reasons:

–   Most of the reported studies present positive results, if they were
    intended. Be it in knowledge gains, increase in problem-solving
    ability, science process acquisition, attitude changes or behavioural
    modification.

---

(6) It should be noted that older teachers will have different concerns
     from younger ones already trained in primary science.

(7) Mean effect size of .34 for new science teaching techniques in the
     meta-analysis reported by Wise and Okey (1983).

-   Control groups also tend to improve.

-   Even where changes are statistically significant, they are relatively small compared to starting conditions.

-   Programme effects are measured on short-term basis (pre-post-test).

-   The participation of practising teachers in research is extremely low and it is on a voluntary basis.

-   This may explain that the starting conditions (knowledge, readiness, attitudes) are already pro-science oriented as the comparisons with control groups clearly indicate.

-   Information gathering often relies on questionnaires and interviews asking teachers to describe effects, while classroom and behavioural observation over time is the exception.

Results like these are helpful, but limited in their power for instigating new approaches of INSET or, more so, for policy decisions. Needed are data of an intermediate level of models and methods for drawing policy consequences.

1.4.3.1.2 *System effects*

The report and analysis of more than 50 INSET activities and models (Bolam 1977, Bünder et al 1978) clearly documented that a lot of development work exists most of which appears sensible and successful in its own right. But less than 10% of the models reported tangible results of measured improvement against external or even the self-set criteria. Of these only a few are interesting for primary science education.

The Swedish DELTA-Project used the seven study days teachers had during the year for compulsory participation in a centrally organised primary math INSET programme. Materials were read at home; study days were used for clarification of materials and discussion among teachers; activities of new math were applied in own classrooms. Result: 45,000 participants, materials for teachers, new math in the syllabus. The audit office evaluated: quality - "good", quantity - "excellent" (Bünder et al 1978, 59). Similar organisation results were achieved for the introduction of English into Swedish primary school (60), while a project to improve co-operation and partnership among students has been judged "doubtful" (58).

These results raised the question whether a new subject or topic just needs to be installed by order, law or syllabus and in-serviced aggressively in order to be effective. If it is a matter of no choice, teacher may comply. A similar procedure was used in most states of the Federal Republic of Germany with the implementation of New Math around 1970. It was a failure. The introduction of science into primary schools at about the same time has to be viewed in a more differentiated way, varying between delayed acceptance of science requirements on face value, its reinterpretation in light of traditional "Heimatkunde" (Vernacular Studies), and its reorganisation in new conceptual models for a new subject "Sachunterricht" (Study of things) (country report by Frey and Lauterbach 1984). Depending on the intentions (state-wide briefing or teacher development) different INSET models were applied. Except for very specific information on some curriculum projects, no quantitative data about effects on teachers' professional qualifications are available: because of the syllabus demands, teachers teach the required topics - at least according to textbook contents.

Present-day American practice can be an illustrative example to help reflect the problem at hand, especially as INSET is voluntary (as in most countries, when teacher qualification is intended and not just programme or syllabus implementation). For the United States three national studies on curriculum effectiveness were conducted: they included curriculum effects on teachers, like the National Science Foundation's "Case Studies in Education" (Stake and Easley 1978, Volume XIII, Chapter 16). The effects are neither encouraging nor discouraging.

Teachers taught science, but more or less like any other subject, believing their socialisation task to be paramount. And the evaluators sum up: "Scientists and other intelligentsia have little effect; parents and other teachers have much". (16 : 23).

In their meta-analysis of the three national studies Yager and Penick (1983) mention as one major accomplishment between 1956-76 the "massive efforts to affect teacher in-service programmes" (466). But among the unsolved problems are those that concern us. The effects on the classrooms remained low: textbook teaching, predominance of lecture, limitation to certain science knowledge and processes, discipline orientation, rare or no experimentation, low priority of science.

Encouragement for continued efforts in research and development is given by Bredderman (1983). He has just published a meta-analysis of 57 controlled studies on the effectiveness of the three major activity-based US elementary science programmes (ESS, SAPA, and SCIS) in over 900 classrooms. He identified improvement in science process tests, affective outcomes, and in science content. His summary: "The overall effects of the activity-based programmes on all outcomes areas combined were clearly positive, although not dramatically so." (1983, 504). Because the available data was obtained from studies made in conjunction with teacher training efforts (pre- as well as in-service), the readiness of teachers to act programme-conform may have contributed considerably to the positive results.

To find the reasons for the discrepancy between effects in the classroom and those in experimental or INSET settings is in itself a research task that is still at the beginning. Lombard (1982) has reported on work done in the USA but a comparable large scale evaluation for science education is not available in Europe. But for INSET in general initiatives have already started. For example in 1981 the Joint Federation-Länder Committee for Educational Planning and Research Promotion (BLK) in the Federal Republic of Germany published a report of INSET experiments with rich information on various approaches. The valued criteria were the number of teachers involved, courses offered, materials produced (Arlt et al 1981).

The quality of effects has to be inferred from the descriptive case data. In 1980 the IPN organised a symposium on evaluation of INSET; in 1981 a joint workshop with German-speaking and Scandinavian countries was concerned with the topic (Teschner et al 1983); beginning in 1983 a subgroup of ATEE (Association for Teacher Education in Europe) started a project on INSET evaluation studies in which members of different European countries participate. The main thrust of this work is directed at finding out how to use evaluation for INSET. Some of the work to rely on, methodologically and anticipatory, comprises the mentioned US studies or the promising Swedish studies on school management and team training (Henricson 1983).

In the meantime we have to rely on the existing wealth of case descriptions about INSET experiments and models. The main difficulty with judging the effects are their historical, cultural, political and geographical singularity.

Three generalisations can be made regardless of content, subject area or locality:

1. The participating persons, teachers as well as trainers, researchers and administrators improve in their professional qualification.

2. The created experimental settings produce new knowledge, procedures, materials and (micro-) environments.

3. The context determines what an experiment or model is worth, be it for the participating teachers and trainers or for the educational system as a whole.

1.4.3.2 *The case of curriculum-oriented INSET* (8)

Shortly after the introduction of science into primary education at the end of the sixties the need for appropriate INSET was recognised. Its predominating paradigm to start with was a directive description of teacher (as well as pupil) behaviours, rationalised and approved by research and evaluation. Matters are changing and today it is more important that the original efforts generated, step by step, new knowledge for INSET, and resolved a number of its problems, practically as well as theoretically. A brief historical review can expose which of the gains are worth keeping for curriculum development has nòt been ineffective in its own right.

During the experimental phases of curriculum development, teachers were counselled by members of the curriculum teams, they participated in planning and feedback sessions, some were engaged in the development. Though some of these teachers had to cope with individual difficulties, on the whole they improved in nearly all professional aspects as did the curriculum researchers in theirs.

Awareness for INSET arose because the new curricula were not readily picked up by teachers after they were published. And even when a curriculum was bought, it often remained in the cupboard. The curriculum teams responded, eg by:

---

(8) The following historical outline of curriculum-oriented INSET for primary sciences intends an idealised generalisation of the author's experiences in curriculum adaptation and development, research and INSET in the Federal Republic of Germany. The listed activities and their discussion are verified (eg Lauterbach 1979).

a. publishing articles on theoretical aspects and about practical
   experiences;

b. sending newsletters;

c. presenting lectures, films and demonstrations.

As no marked effects were registered, the curriculum teams turned to
systematic planning of INSET activities. They utilised the existing INSET
structures, often with financial and material support from publishing
companies, or even set up new ones. Teachers were invited to participate
in activity-oriented seminars and courses. The time schedule varied from
a series of afternoon sessions or a blocked weekend, week or fortnight to
combinations thereof.

A qualitative change was the involvement of teachers in the curriculum.
Short lectures, films, demonstrations, reading and discussion sessions
remained part of the programme. But additionally teachers:

d. gained direct experience in handling animals and plants, in setting up
   experiments or in solving problems, as required in the curriculum;

e. simulated classroom activities from the curriculum in the role of
   students;

f. micro-taught colleagues and invited groups of children in curriculum
   activities;

g. acted in protected (positively perceived) environments and received
   feedback on their own activities; uncertainties were immediately
   clarified;

h. interacted intensively with other teachers and with trainers.

Process and product evaluation generally indicated positive effects of
INSET immediately after the courses. These effects were lost, sometimes
they turned negative after a few weeks, stabilising themselves at a low
positive level after a period of two to three months. The use of the new
curriculum elements was highly inconsistent. Teachers selected mostly
activities in which they had been trained or which fitted their previous
experience.

To compensate the fade-out effects INSET was modified:

i. time was alloted during courses to adapt activities to the teachers'
   own classroom conditions;

j. teachers were asked to try out adaptations in their own classrooms;

k. variable and extended time schedules were introduced: eg after an
   initiation phase of a week, the teachers met at regular intervals for
   one afternoon (weekly) or at weekends (monthly);

l. after the courses, trainers visited the teachers and teachers kept up
   communication with their trainers by letter or tape on curriculum and
   classroom problems.

These measures had a stabilising effect. Though in the course of time a tapering out of interest or "normalisation" was noted:

- less contacts between INSET institution or trainers and teachers;

- returning to teaching requiring less preparation and effort (textbook);

- developing new interest areas.

A reorientation of perspective occurred for curriculum development and INSET. The needs of specific groups of teachers and the specific environments of teaching became more important than the contents. The qualitative difference from previous INSET was marked by the intention of need-oriented assessment and utlisation of curriculum offers for the teachers.

For INSET this meant eg:

m.   assessing and selecting curriculum offers by teachers (utilisation of curriculum analysis schemes);

n.   rewriting activities for a specific teacher, classroom and school;

o.   small-scale evaluation.

The qualitative change is, among other things, a result of the critical distance teachers - and subsequently teacher trainers - had developed towards theory-based curricula. Their applicability on face value had been questioned. The specifity of different school environments, teachers' individual prerequisites and interests, and pupils' spontaneous ingenuity could not be discovered. The starting positions seemed reversed. Theoretically structured and research-based curricula were, at best, used as a quarry for personal building intentions. INSET responded with a set of measures to permit and foster curriculum construction by teachers, eg:

p.   establishment of small working groups of teachers over longer periods of time (up to a year or two);

q.   school-based curriculum development.

The results were ambivalent. While some teams and schools were unable to cope with workloads and standards to produce original products, others did. Disregard of scientific standards was compensated by functioning products, reinstating confidence in one's own teaching capability. INSET answered by setting up a new infrastructure, eg by:

r.   providing a counselling and support system for teacher working groups;

s.   setting up a communication, printing, documentation and dissimination service for new topics and "grey" (teacher-made) materials;

t.   establishing procedures for participation in decision-making for INSET programmes (topic areas, priorities).

This last phase of INSET appears in singular examples already transgressed. It may be characterised by mutual appreciation of a threesome partnership between researchers and subject experts, teacher trainers, and

teachers. Each of these groups acting self-confident in their competence
areas, openly posing questions and asking for assistance, where needs are
identified, and recognising the chances and limitations of contributions the
others are able to make.

The idealistic summary should not conceal the remaining original
problems:

a. For most of the primary school teachers as individuals in a specific
    school the question of what to teach in primary science and how to do
    it is not answered confidently by the teachers themselves.

b. For INSET the generalisation and installation of model experiments has
    about the same status.

1.4.3.3 *Patterns for INSET*

Although diversity and ingenuity in model development and realisation are
needed further on, some guiding principles for future INSET are desirable.
Theoretical instrumentation of practical experiences is necessary in order
to form policy decisions.

From the activities and models to involve and qualify teachers in
primary science teaching and from historical reconstruction of curriculum-
oriented INSET, two general patterns of INSET can be inferred, overlapping,
enhancing as well as impeding each other. The first one is concerned with
developmental stages, the second with topography of control.

1.4.3.3.1 *Stages of development*

Fullan's (1983) overview of curriculum implementation and evaluation in the
USA and Canada classifies the projects into programmed and adaptive-
evolutionary approaches. The first projects of the programmed approach
(teachers were to comply as closely as possible with described behaviour)
began in the sixties, while those of the adaptive-evolutionary approach
(intending modification through teachers for their environment) started in
the mid-seventies. In a comparison of these approaches Fullan as well as
Berman (1980) conclude that both are necessary regardless of a number of
disadvantages; their effectiveness depended on the specific situation.

This type of classification can be applied to the curriculum development in the German-speaking countries as well (Lütgert and Stephan (1983)),
pin-pointing the contrary conceptualisations of the teacher as instrument
(programmed) or the teacher as individual (adaptive-evolutionary). Other
classifications are described by Holford and Sutton (1980). The historical
reconstruction in part 1.4.3.2 has shown that we are dealing with successive
stages of historical problem-solving in our societies in which the previous
stage is necessary in order to generate the next. When we start to operate
on this next stage in one context, we may well remain in the previous one
in another. The identified pattern is instructive and suggestive: project
teams and individuals seem to pass through it with every new experience.

Hall, Wallace and Dossett (1973) developed a model on *stages of concern* (9) through which one is supposed to pass during an adoption process. While testing this model in an adaption study of ISCS, James and Hall (1981) concluded three phases: adoption, implementation and redirection. The evidence they gathered from teachers, using ISCS from 0 to 5 years, retains appreciation for their model, but clearly lends more support to a generative, adaptive and open-ended developmental approach.

In an independent evaluation of the implementation follow-up study to the primary science curriculum project "Children and their natural environment" it was investigated how written curriculum materials were transformed into action by teachers. Here, too, three phases were identified: (1) copying attempts, (2) flexible adaption to the teachers' own aims, and (3) reflection of the teachers' own interaction behaviour and attempts of its modification (Mühlhausen 1983). In their own study, the curriculum authors describe a similar sequence (Haller et al 1983). They propose Piaget's accommodation-assimilation paradigm to explain the teachers' interaction with the curriculum, proposing four influencing variables on the side of the teachers: reflexiveness, role understanding, planning behaviour, and level of pretentiousness. This proposition is compatible with other implementation reports (Welch 1979, Lütgert and Stephan 1983). It paves the way to extend the perspective for INSET beyond previous attempts.

To comply with the developmental view and to release teachers from the defensive and receptive role which the concept of "concern" implies, six *stages of intention* during an adoption are proposed.

Awareness — Teacher (workgroups, staff of a school) perceives an offer/ requirement as possibly relevant, eg reads title of INSET course in "Science processes for primary schoolchildren".

Subjectivation — Teacher (...) subjects her-/himself to offer in order to get to "know", to experience what is relevant ("contents"), eg participates in course on science processes, reads about it, watches a film on experiments with candles.

Adoption — Teacher (...) adopts contents as her/his own, redefining it in her/his own terms, eg propagates the need for science processes, experimentation as "systematically trying out an idea (hypothesis)".

Application — Teacher (...) applies contents in her/his own settings on the basis of perceived "fit", eg lets children try out how long a candle burns in different size jars.

Construction — Teacher (...) uses content to construct "new" systems of operation, eg arranges for three different experiments at the same time, comparing the results later on.

---

(9) Stages of concern: awareness, informational, personal, management, consequence, collaboration, refocusing.

Development   Teacher (...) generates new contents from old, eg has
               children speculate on what keeps a candle burning, think
               out results, ask new questions.

This pattern proposes that teachers (individually as well as in a group
within a specific in-service set-up) will have to pass through these stages
for every adoption. External conditions facilitate stage transition, in
case they fit the state of readiness; they impede it if they do not.
"Intention" should signal that adoption is not just an internalisation of
external requirements but a conscious process of reflection intending action
by the person and by the group.

Classifying INSET approaches according to stage compatibility can serve
as take-off point for future research and development. Pre-post test
research in INSET, for instance, barely transgresses subjectivation (stage 2)
with an announced option for adoption (3), while most of curriculum-specific
INSET with a continuous support system reach application (4). Construction
(5) has been promising in some school settings, while development (6)
appears maybe only as a description of some researchers' or trainers'
perception of their experience.

1.4.3.3.2 *Topography of control*

Immediate effects of many INSET efforts are most probably diminished by the
change of social cont l conditions when teachers return into their school
setting. Easley's (1982) recommendation for more naturalistic studies to
uncover social interaction mechanism affecting implementation or Shrighley's
(1977) search for extrinsic professional reinforcement would fit into this
pattern. According to the sociology of social control (eg Bernstein 1971,
1974) there are different modes of control an individual is subjected to:
eg self, knowledge, language, other people, institutions, material
environment. This concept is supported by social psychology in those
aspects dealing with interactive behaviour (eg Watzlawik et al 1974, 1981).
A person perceives, conceptualises and acts differently according to the
perceived expectations of the partner(s) and the interpretation of the
context in which the action takes place. Awareness of these control
conditions for a special situation is usually low.

For clarifying the questions at hand a rudimentary pattern of percep-
tional control is proposed.

1. The *material environment* exerts social control. Place, time, organisation, facilities, arrangements, or equipment are some of the environmental
factors influencing a teacher's actions qualitatively as well as quantitatively. Lang (1982) reported that the arrangement of tables and chairs in
a school science laboratory support or impede communicative behaviour of
children; with a conscientious interpreation of open-school effects in
teachers Weinstein (1979) also points out that the material environment is
an influencing factor on communication and type of activity: certain
activities will be done differently, less often or they will not be
initiated at all.

The material con rols are generally quite effective, because the
authorities inducing the controls are de-subjected. To the teacher (and
trainer) their manifestations appear as more or less objective "conditions":

Space-time for preparing and teaching of activities, presence or absence of equipment and technical apparatus or of laboratory and nature trail. Ainley (1981) showed that the existence or lack of facilities in a teacher's own school as compared to the INSET setting does affect teachers' actions, though not all teachers in the same way (Stake and Easley 1978 or the list of impeding factors mentioned in Lombard 1982).

2. *Knowledge* can exert social control, if it is presented and perceived as authoritative (Bernstein 1974). This is done in primary science curriculum and INSET by claiming identification with science in aims, contents and rationale:

-   a solid body of scientific facts, concepts, laws, and principles;

-   a perfected complex of scientific methods;

-   an ideologically grounded set of scientific values; and

-   a paradigm constituted by a network of scientific behaviours.

But INSET also proclaims authority in knowling how to teach, be it in its weak forms of the written and spoken word or in its strong forms like drill and practice courses. This knowledge appears objectively secured and guaranteed by research and evaluation, nearly as solid, perfected, valued and paradigmatic as science itself.

As soon as primary teachers return into their daily routine of many subjects, the importance of authority of science drops below that of reading, writing and mathematics (eg Yager and Penick, 1983).

And the authority of better science teaching, ie through inquiry, shows its vulnerability, when teachers are not able to deal with more lively children, divergent ideas, or inventive experimenters in their classroom.

3. The most powerful controls seem to be exerted by the *social context*. This includes the partners of interaction, the interaction itself, the normative rules for maintaining authority, the institutional frame. The most convincing results, despite some methodological difficulties, are gathered in Anderson's (1982) summary of school climate studies showing considerable effects on pupil achievement. More specific on teacher behaviours is Campbell (1977) in his study on teacher flexibility. He found to his surprise that the group taught is mainly responsible for differing teacher behaviours. Leithwood and Montgomery (1982) investigated that the role perceptions of principals affect teachers, as do supervisors (Stronk 1977). It is the perception of self, other, etc that determines the types of effectivity of control).

During INSET the social recognition of doing science is high for the teacher. The trainers are personalised authorities due to their status, aided by the socially high-ranking image of the scientist. The other participants act as social enforcers of training efforts. After returning to the school setting, social reinforcement for teaching science declines quickly. Teachers, principals, or parents consider other areas more important (Shrigley 1977). With the lack of extrinsic professional reinforcement the teachers' motivation to continue with a possibly troublesome implementation tends to fade out. Sheldon (1978) could show that the participation of administrators in a three-week awareness conference for science was more effective for change (at least for one year) than just the teachers' participation.

1.4.3.4 *Summary of results*

1. Research studies on professional re-qualification of practising teachers are manifold but limited to small populations. They indicate that, in principle, intended improvement can be achieved through INSET. But the measured qualification effects tend to be lower and of less duration than expected or hoped for.

2. For macroscopic effects of innovations and INSET activities quantitative effects can be registered as well, but the available data is either non-conclusive on qualitative improvement or not encouraging.

3. Model developments tend to report optimistically. But their singular, highly favourable and protected experimental setting permits not assertation, if the experiences can be generalised or duplicated and what their long-time effects may be.

4. On the basis of research and development data two patterns in adoption processes are identified. One refers to the development of intentions for adoption on the side of the teachers, the other relates to the conditions of control enhancing or impeding implementation.

1.4.4 POLICY CONSIDERATIONS

Because policy conditions for INSET vary with the political, cultural and economic context, differing between countries and even within a country, the expectations for valid suggestions fitting all contexts would be inappropriate. I shall confine myself to draw conclusions from the presented research data, thereby inferring a developmental context for INSET.

1.4.4.1 *Possible policy consequences*

1. To insure continued improvement of primary science education teachers have to adopt science teaching in their professional profile as being not less important than any other professional task. (Similar expectations are postulated for teacher trainers, school and political administrators.) Professionality includes permanent involvement with a readiness to improve by critically applying new knowledge and techniques as well as by participating in development.

To make this possible a permanent INSET service system would be required that fosters co-operation and communication on equal terms between different groups of professionals in education.

2. - To instigate the adoption of primary science teaching INSET has to arrange attractive and effective opportunities for contacting, experiencing, reflecting, practising and developing science teaching, taking care to respond with its offers to the teachers' level of readiness for further involvement (stages of intention).

This would require an alert and adaptable INSET service with successive elaboration of its organisation to satisfy the demands (needs) of teachers.

3.   In order to help teachers decide, if new and possibly irritating experiences should be risked (eg science for reluctant teachers, try out inquiry teaching), sufficient and manifold information and, especially, direct experiences have to be offered that connect to the teachers' general qualifications: support self-confidence, clarify classroom management, tune teaching strategy to teacher.

This would require an INSET system in close contact with research and development to identify and utilise the most appropriate models and in-service training strategies.

4.   In order to stabilise the intentional stage teachers have reached, eg application of a questioning technique in the teachers' own classroom, the previous experiences and knowledge need actualisation, modification and steady encouragement to continue efforts.

This would require a specific and individualised INSET support system that allows and stimulates teachers to make use of it regularly and easily.

5.   In order to facilitate adoption the discrepancies between control conditions of in-service settings and school settings have to be reduced.

This would require that INSET complies with the specific conditions of the participants' schools, or that schools are changed to fit the INSET context, or that INSET and schools co-operate closely in a non-directive manner.

6.   The most striking conclusion to be drawn from research and development data is that INSET should establish a network of experimental and developmental settings.

The comparison of the US national studies on science education in schools with the meta-analysis of curriculum effect studies or, for that matter, with research reports on INSET activities and models, clearly favour the latter in terms of desirable results. Similar inferences can be made, when case descriptions of INSET models are projected against the daily school routines. Therefore, it can be expected that experimental and developmental settings will at least achieve the following:

1.   all participants improve their qualifications: teachers as well as teacher trainers, researchers, and administrators;

2.   the environments of these settings profit from them directly: the teachers' schools, the organising in-service units, the associated research institutions, and the responsible administration;

3.   society as a whole and the people comprising it obtain new knowledge, products and processes for future use.

A possible presentiment of this approach may be the modelling of school-based INSET. But there, the general fate of models cannot be precluded: They lose their effectiveness, when they become the established norm.

1.4.4.2 *School-based INSET*

In their 1983 volume on "Issues in the In-service Training of Teachers", the Association for Teacher Education in Europe (ATEE) (Chadwick 1983) lists school-based INSET as one of the key issues. To resolve or even discuss it adequately requires knowledge about decision-making processes and power relationships in the educational system for which it is considered. For the context to inferred above I would argue as follows:

In Chapter Two of this paper enough evidence has been presented to suggest serious consideration of school-based INSET for primary science, though not without caution. "School-based" when fully realised means localising INSET in a school or at least at an inter-school level.

Some expected advantages are:

1. From the professionality point of view:

   - Teachers can draw on their concrete professional knowledge and competency concerning their school, classes and children.

   - Ambitious or theoretical change demands for science teaching will need joint efforts with trainers to affect the changes on the level of the possible.

2. From the effectivity point of view:

   - By using the available knowledge and experience of effective INSET, its results should at least be replicated.

   - The effects of training are identifiable in the true setting, ie the setting where they are needed.

3. From the developmental point of view:

   - The intentional status of the individual teacher as well as of the group can be jointly identified and responded to.

   - The risk threshold for stage transition is lowered for the individual teacher without lowering the quality of the group results.

4. From the control point of view:

   - Material environment condition can be taken into account; if necessary and possible, they will be changed.

   - Consideration and, consequently, change of the social context is part of school-based INSET.

   - Devaluation of science knowledge and INSET experience by teachers will be slight, while over-valuing of science knowledge will diminish

This positive picture may be somewhat surprising. But the outlined retrospective of curriculum oriented INSET suggests that school-based INSET is a necessary historical consequence and our present reflections are signs of societal consciousness.

c

64

1.4.5 BIBLIOGRAPHY

AAAS Commission on Science Education: Preservice science education of
elementary school teachers. AAAS Miscellaneous Publication 70 - 5,
1970, 6.

Ainley, J: The importance of Facilities in Science Education,
In: Ejse 3 (1981) 2, 127 - 138.

Anderson, C S: The Search for School Climate: A Review of the Research.
In: Rev. of Educational Research, 52 (1982), 3, 368.

Anderson, L; Evertson, C; Brophy, J: An experimental study of effective
teaching in first grade reading groups. In: Elementary School
Journal 1979, 8. 193 - 223.

Arlt, W; Döbrich, P; Lippert, G: Modellversuche zur Lehrerfort- und
weiterbildung. Bund-Länder-Kommission für Bildungsplanung und
Forschungsförderung. Stuttgart: Klett, 1981.

Ajzen, J; Fishbein, M: Understanding attitudes and predicting social
behaviour. Englewood Cliffs, NJ: Prentice-Hall, 1980.

Bajora, W H: An Analysis of Attitudinal Differences Between Teachers
Involved in Science: A Process Approach. Diss. Abstracts International,
42 (1981) 2, 520 - A.

Berman, P: Thinking About Implementation Design: Matching Strategies to
Situations. In: Mann, D/Ingram, H (eds): Why Policies Succeed or
Fail. Berkely, Calif.: Sage Publications, 1980.

Bernstein, B: Klassifikation und Vermittlungsrahmen im schulischen
Lernprozess. In: Zeitschrift für Pädagogik 17 (1971) 2, 257 - 287.

Bernstein, B: Class Codes and Control Volume I: Theoretical Studies towards
a Sociology of Language. London: Routledge & Kegan, 1974.

Bethel, L J; Ellis, J D; Barufaldi, J P: The Effects of NSF Institute on
Inservice Education. In: Science Education 66 (1982) 4, 643 - 651.

Bloch, J A; Bünder, W; Frey, K; Rost, J: Charakteristiken der Lehrerfortbildung im naturwissenschaftlichen Bereich in der Bundesrepublik
Deutschland. IPN-Arbeitsberichte 46. Kiel: IPN, 1981.

Bolam, R: Innovation in the In-Service Education and Training of Teachers,
Towards a Conceptual Framework: OECD/CERI TE 77. 06; 1977.

Bredderman, T: Effects of Activity-based Elementary Science on Student
Outcomes: A Quantitative Synthesis. In: Review of Educational Research,
53 (1983) 4, 499 - 518.

Brophy, J; Evertson, C: Learning from teaching: A developmental perspective.
Boston, 1976.

Bünder, W; Nentwig, P: Modelle zur Lehrerfortbildung aus neun OECD-Mitgliedsländern. IPN-Arbeitsberichte 34. Kiel: IPN, 1978.

Champbell, J R: Science Teacher Flexibility. In: Journ. of Res. in Sc. Teaching 14 (1977) 6, 525 - 532.

Chadwick, G (Ed): Issues in the Inservice Training of Teachers. Bruxelles: ATEE, 1983.

Doyle, W; Ponder, M: The practicality ethic in teacher decision making. Paper read at the Milwaukee Curriculum Theory Conference Milwaukee, Wisconsin, November 1976.

Druva, C A; Anderson, R D: Science Teacher Characteristics by Teacher Behaviour and by Student Outcome: A Meta-Analysis of Research. In: Journ. of Res. in Sc. Teaching 20 (1983) 5, 467 - 479.

Duit, R; Jung, W; Pfundt, H: Alltagsvorstellungen und naturwissenschaftlicher Unterricht. Köln: Aulis Verlag Deubner, 1981.

Easley, J R; JA: Naturalistic Case Studies Exploring Social-Cognitive Mechanisms, and some Methodological Issues in Research Problems of Teachers. In: Journ. of Res. in Sc. Teaching 19 (1982) 3, 191 - 203.

Eigler, G; Nenninger, P: Erfassung von Lehrerfortbildungsinteressen als Beitrag zu einer Lehrerfortbildungskonzeption. In: Unterrichtswissenschaft (1982) 4, 378 - 399.

Eigler, G; Nenninger, P: Möglichkeiten und Grenzen einer Interessenorientierten Lehrerfortbildung. In: Unterrichtswissenschaft (1983) 3, 227 - 243.

Frey, K; Lauterbach, R: Primary Science Education in the Federal Republic of Germany. Educational Research Workshop on Science in Primary Education. Edinburgh/Scotland 3. - 6. September 1984. Kiel: IPN, 1984, polycop.

Fullan , M: Implementation und Evaluation von Curricula: USA und Kanada. In: Hameyer, U; Frey, K; Haft, H: Handbuch der Curriculumforschung. Weinheim, Basel: Beltz, 1983.

Good, T L: Research on teaching. In: Hall, G E; Hord, S M; Brown, G (Eds): Exploring Issues in Teacher Education: Questions for Future Research; Research and development center for teacher education. Austin, 1980.

Good, T; Grouws, D: Teaching Effects: A process-product study in fourth grade mathematics classrooms. Journal of Teacher Education, 1977, 28.

Green, M R: The Predictors of Science Teaching Performance in Elementary School Teachers. Paper presented at the annual meeting of the National Association for Research in Science Teaching, 1981.

Häussler, P; Hoffmann, L; Rost, J: Zum Stand der physikalischen Bildung Erwachsener. Kiel: IPN, 1984 (in preparation).

66

Hall, G E; Wallace, B; Dossett, B: A Developmental Conceptualisation of the
Adoption Process within Educational Institutions. UTR - D, 1973.

Henricson, S-E: In-Service-Teacher-Training and its Evaluation in Sweden.
In: Teschner et al 1983, 167 - 177.

Holford, D; Sutton, C: Science Teacher Education: The Art of the Possible
In: McFadden, C P (ed): World Trends in Science Education. Halifax,
Nova Scotia, Canada: Atlantic Institute of Education, 1980.

Hoyle, E: Professionalisation and deprofessionalisation in education. In:
Hoyle, E; Megarry, V: World Yearbook of Education, 1980, NY 1980.

Jackson, P: Life in classrooms, New York, 1968.

James, R K; Hall, G: A study of the concerns of science teachers regarding
on implementation of ISCS. In: Journ. of Res. in Sc. Teaching 18
(1981) 6, 479 - 487.

Jaus, H H: The Effect of Environmental Education Instruction on Teachers'
Attitudes toward Teaching Environmental Education. In: Science
Education, 62 (1978) 1, 79.

Joyce, B: The ecology of professional development. In: Hoyle, E; Megarry, J:
World Yearbook of Education 1980, New York, 1980, 19.

Joyce, B; Showers, B: Training ourselves: the message of research. In:
Educational Leadership 37 (1980) 4.

Joyce B; Showers, B: Improving inservice training: the message of research.
In: Educational Leadership (1980) 2, 379 - 385.

Jungwirth, E: The pupil, the teacher and the teacher's image. In: J. Biol.
Educ. 5 (1971) 4, 165 - 171.

Koballa Jr, T R: The Effect of Integrative Complexity on the Systematic
Design of a Persuasive Communication for Changing Attitudes of
Preservice. In: The Pennsylvania State University, 1981. Dissertation
Abstracts International 42 (6): 2598 - A, December 1981.

Koballa, Jr, T R; Shrigley, R: Credibility and Persuasion: A Sociopsycholo-
gical Approach to Changing the Attitudes toward Energy Conservation of
Pre-Service Elementary School Science Teachers. In: Journ. of Res. in
Sc. Teaching 20 (1983) 7, 683 - 696.

Keiny, S; Jungwirth, E: Changing Science Teachers' Role Perception and
Teaching Behaviour, by Means of an Experimental Course in Human
Relations. In: Science Education 66 (1982) 5, 789 - 797.

Kelly, A: The missing half - Girls and science education. Oxford, 1981.

Kelly, A: The Development of Girls' and Boys' Attitudes to Science:
A Longitudinal Study. In: Lehrke et al, 1984.

Kelly, A: Sex differences in science achievement: some results and hypotheses.
In: Kelly, A (Ed) 1981, 24 - 41.

Lang, M: Planungshilfen zum Kommunikativen Lerner. Weinheim und Basel: Beltz, 1982.

Lauterbach, R: Unterrichtsplanung als didaktische Entscheidungssituation: Eine Untersuchung zur Interessenvertretung der Schüler im naturwissenschaftlich-technisch orientierten Lehren des Primarbereichs. Fachbereich Erziehungswissenschaften, Universität Hamburg, 1979.

Lehmann, L; Langerheine, R: Umweltsozialisation (Environmental Socialisation) Internal Paper. Kiel: IPN, 1983.

Lehrke, M; Hoffmann, L: Interessen am naturwissenschaftlich-technischen Unterricht: Untersuchungen und Erklärungen (in Vorbereitung).

Lehrke, M; Hoffmann, L; Gardner, P L: Interests in Science Technology Education. Proceeding of the 12th IPN-Symposion, 1984 (in preparation).

Leithword, K A; Montgomery, D J: The Role of Elementary School Principal in Program Improvement. In: Review of Educational Research 52, (1982), 309 - 339.

Lombard, A S: Effects of Reasoning Workshop on the Teaching Strategies of Secondary Science Teachers. In: Science Education 66 (1982) 4, 653 - 644.

Lynch, J; Plunkett, H D: Teacher Education and Cultural Change. London: George Allan & Unwin Ltd, 1973.

Martin, R E: The Influence of Communicator Credibility on Pre-service Elementary-Teachers' Attitudes Toward Science and Science Teaching. In: The University of Toledo, 1981. Dissertation Abstracts International, 42 (6): 2622-A, December 1981.

McDonald, F; Elias, P: The effects of teacher performance on pupil learning. Beginning teacher evaluation study: Phase II, final report; Vol. I, Princeton, N.J.: Educational Testing Service, 1976.

McNamara, D: On returning to the chalk face: theory not into practice. In: British Journal of Teacher Education 2 (1976) 2, 147 - 160.

Moore, K E; Blankenship, J W: Relationships between science teacher needs and slected teacher variables. In: Journ. of Res. in Sc. Teaching 15 (1978) 6, 513.

Morrisey, J T: An Analysis of Studies on Changing the Attitude of Elementary Student Teachers Toward Science and Science Teaching. In: Science Education 65 (1981) 2, 157 - 177.

Olson, J K: Science Teacher Participation in Curriculum Development: The Teacher's Point of View. In: Journ. of Res. in Sc. Teaching 16 (1979) 5, 391 - 400.

Ormerod, M B: Factors differentially affecting the science subject preferences, Choices and attitudes of girls and boys. In: Kelly, A (Ed): The missing half. Manchester: University Press 1981, 100 - 122.

68

Osborne, R J; Bell, B E; Gilbert, J K: Science Teaching and Children's View of the World. In: EJSE 5 (1983) 1, 1 - 14.

O'Sullivan, P S et al: A Model for the Effect of an In-service Program of Junior High School Student Science Achievement. In: Journ. of Res. in Sc. Teaching 18 (1981) 3, 119 - 207.

Peterson, R W; Carlson, G R: A Summary of research in science education, 1977. In: Science Education 63 (1979), 429 - 550.

Peterson, P L; Marx, C W; Clark, R M: Teacher planning, teacher behaviour, and student achievement. In: American Educational Research Journal 15 (1978) 3, 417 - 432.

Powell, M: Educational implications of current research on teaching. In: The Educational Forum, 1978, 43.

Reif, F: Wie kann man Problemlösen lernen? - Ein wissenschaftlich begründeter Ansatz. In: Der Physikunterricht, 17 (1983) 1, 51 - 66.

Rosenshine, B: Content, time and direct instruction. In: Peterson, P; Waldberg (Eds): Research on teaching: Concept, findings and implications. Berkeley: McCutchan Publ. Corp., 1981.

Sallam, S M A: The Effects of Inquiry Instruction in a Geoscience Course upon pre-service Elementary Teachers' Attitudes Toward Teaching Science and the Acquisition of Integrated Science Process Skills. Diss. Abstracts International 42 (1981) 4, 1575 - A.

Saltiel, E: Kinematic concepts and natural reasoning: study of comprehension of Galilean frames by science students. In: EJSE, 3 (1981) 1, 110.

Saltiel, E: Spontaneous ways of reasoning in elementary kinematics. In: European Journal of Physics 1 (1980) 1, 73 - 80.

Schibeci, R A: Selecting Appropriate Attitudinal Objectives for School Science. In: Science Education, 67 (1983) 5, 595 - 604.

Schwedes, H: Die Rolle der Affektivität im Physikunterricht. In: Westermanns Pädagogische Beiträge (1973) 11, 606 - 609.

Sheldon, D S: Long-Term Impact of Curriculum Awareness Conferences on School Administrators and Key Teachers. In: Science Education 62 (1978) 4, 517 - 521.

Sheldon, D; Halverson, D: Effects of a Televised Science In-Service Program on Attitudes of Elementary Teachers. In: Journ. of Res. in Sc. Teaching 18 (1981) 3, 249 - 254.

Shrighley, R L: The Function of Professional Reinforcement in Supporting a more Positive Attitude of Elementary Teachers toward Science. In: Journ. of Res. in Sc. Teaching 14 (1977) 4, 317 - 322.

Shrighley, R L: The Attitude Concept and Science Teaching. In: Science Education, 67 (1983) 4, 425 - 442.

Shrighley, R L et al: ISEE-ITV and Professional Reinforcement: Teacher's Model for Implementing Curriculum Change at the District Level. In: Science Education 63 (1979) 1, 3 - 8.

Smith, H A: Nonverbal Communication in Teaching. In: Review of Educational Research 49 (1979) 4, 631 - 672.

Spooner, W E: Kindergarten Students' Attitude Toward Science and Achievement. In: Science Diss. Abstracts International 42 (1981) 5, 2057 - A.

Stake, R E; Easley, J A: Case Studies in Science Education. Booklet XIII. Urbana-Champaign, Illinois, CJRCE & CCC, University of Illinois, 1978.

Stallings, J; Hentzel, S: Effective teaching and learning in urban schools. Paper presented at the National Conference on Urban Education, St. Louis, Missouri, July 1978.

Stronk, D R: The Comparative Effects of Institutes for Changing the Philosophy of Teaching Elementary School Science among Teachers and Administrators. In: Journ. of Res. in Sc. Teaching 14 (1977) 4, 323 - 328.

Stronk, D R; Koller, G R: Evaluating the Effectiveness of an In-Service Science Program Through the Use of Materials. In: Journ. of Res. in Sc. Teaching 18 (1981) 5, 403 - 408.

Szabo, M; Welliver, P: Technology and Psychology: Broadcast ITV and Inquiry-oriented verbal behaviours of elementary science teachers students. In: Journ. of Res. in Sc. Teaching 15 (1978) 6, 441 - 454.

Teschner, W P; Harbo, T; Gran, B; Haft, A (eds): In-Service-Teacher-Training Models, Methods and Criteria of its Evaluation. Lisse: Swets & Zeitlinger, 1983.

Vicentini-Mossori, M: Common-sense knowledge and scientific knowledge. In: McFadden (Ed): World Trends in Science Education. Halifax: Atlantic Institute of Education, 1980, 276 - 281.

Viennot, L: Spontaneous Reasoning in Elementary Dynamics. In: EJSE 1 (1979) 2, 205 - 221.

Voss, B E: A Summary of Research in Science Education - 1981. In: Science Education 67 (1983), 285 - 419.

Watzlawick, P (Hrsg.): Die erfundene Wirklichkeit. München, Zürich: Piper, 1981.

Watzlawick, P; Beavin, S H; Jackson, D D: Menschliche Kommunikation - Formen, Störungen und Paradoxien. Bern, Stuttgart, Wien: Huber, 1974.

Weinstein, C S: The Physical Environment of the School: A Review of Research. In: Review of Educational Research 49 (1979) 4, 577 - 610.

Welch, W: Twenty Years of Science Curriculum Development. In: Berliner, D
(Ed): Review of Research in Education. Washington DC, 1979, 282 - 306.

Weltner, K u.a.: Das Interesse von Jungen und Mädchen an Physik und Technik.
In: NiU - P/C, 27 (1979), 183 - 189.

Wicker, A: Attitudes vs. actions: The relationship of verbal and overt
behavioural responses to attitude objects. In: Journ. Soc. Issues 25
(1969), 41 - 78.

Wise, K C; Okey, J R: Meta-Analysis of the Effects of Various Science
Teaching Strategies on Achievement. In: Journ. of Res. in Sc. Teaching
20 (1983) 5, 419 - 435.

Wright, E L: Effect of Intensive Instruction in Cue Attendence of solving
Formal Operational Tasks. In: Science Education 63 (1979) 3, 318 - 393.

Yager, R E; Penick, J G: Analysis of the current problems with school science
in the USA. In: EJSE 5 (1983) 4, 463 - 469.

1.5 LEARNING PROCESSES (AND OBSTACLES THERETO)
     OF SCIENCE PUPILS AGED 6-14

                        by

        Prof. André Giordan, Switzerland

1.5.1 SUMMARY

Pupils' own conceptions have so far been systematically ignored by
traditional science teaching. We propose a change in approach based on the
hypothesis that the most important of these conceptions constitute an
essential stage in the transmission of operational scientific knowledge
and must consequently be treated as such.

     This paper poses the problem of their educational significance. The
appendices outline a methodology for describing and classifying them and,
to illustrate this, detail a study carried out on the learning of the concept
of fertilisation.

1.5.2 PRELIMINARY REMARKS ON SCIENCE TEACHING

Diagram 1: Conceptions of the life of the foetus

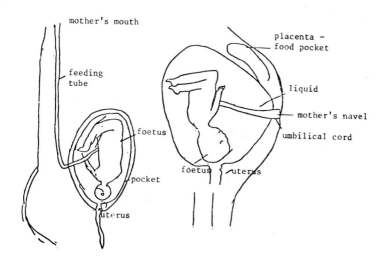

72

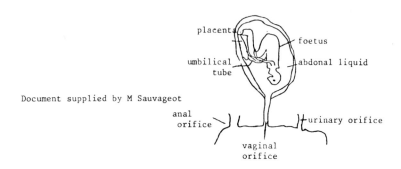

placenta

foetus

umbilical
tube

abdonal liquid

Document supplied by M Sauvageot

anal
orifice

urinary orifice

vaginal
orifice

Despite efforts to update it, science teaching is still hampered by serious shortcomings, some of which I exposed as early as 1976 (1). Since then, research in Europe and the United States has revealed that most of the scientific knowledge taught at school is forgotten in a few years or even a few weeks ... if it is ever really acquired. It can hardly be called operational and is difficult to transfer to other levels of education. University teachers often complain that the fault lies with secondary school, while secondary school teachers unanimously blame primary school. This knowledge does not help us to assimilate information, especially the flow of information produced by the media. It is also difficult to apply in daily life or working life when it comes to decision-making (2).

I do not propose to discuss these questions in detail here, but to illustrate them with a survey carried out on changes in humans at various levels of education.

In particular, I asked children aged 10 to 12, three weeks after a course taught by a qualified teacher using traditional methods, what happened to a piece of bread and a glass of water once they had been absorbed.

An analysis of the results showed that these pupils, who had managed to memorise the knowledge transmitted, nevertheless had difficulties with several points (as shown by the diagrams below):

(1) A Giordan: "Rien de sert de courir, il faut partir à point" (thesis, Université Paris V, Paris VII, 1976), also incorporated into "Une pédagogie pour les sciences expérimentales" (Centurion, Paris 1978). The book also demonstrates the importance of enabling pupils to acquire a scientific approach and investigative methods prior to scientific knowledge. A Giordan (under his own responsibility) PUF - Paris 1978.

(2) J F Kapterer - B Dubois: Echec à la Science - NER - Paris 1981.

- overriding importance of the stomach, as the focal point of
  digestion, by comparison with the other organs;

- non-existent or insufficient relationships between tracts
  and glands;

- existence of two separate systems for liquids and solids;

- inability to understand intestinal absorption;

- inability to understand the function of digestion, etc ...

Diagram 2: Various conceptions of the digestive tract (10 years)

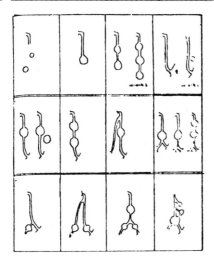

These difficulties are understandable in young pupils. However, I
submitted the same project to pupils aged 14 and 17, three weeks after
further lessons on the subject. I also circulated the questionnaire to
adults (teachers undergoing training) to complete the sample.

This time I was surprised to see the same difficulties recur
systematically even after well-planned courses - at least according to
traditional criteria. This naturally raised questions about the usefulness
of school syllabuses at the various levels.

74

Diagram 3: Persistence of conceptions of the digestive tract and digestion

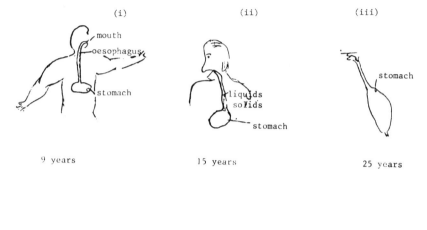

(i)   (ii)   (iii)

9 years   15 years   25 years

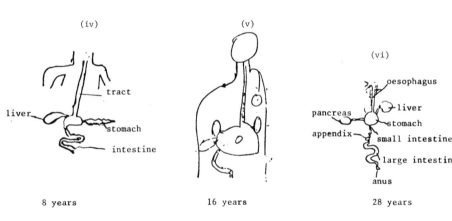

(iv)   (v)

(vi)

8 years   16 years   28 years

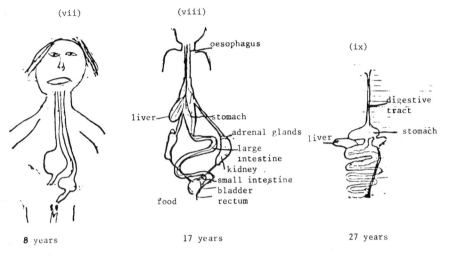

(vii)

(viii) oesophagus

(ix)

liver — stomach

adrenal glands

large intestine

kidney

small intestine

bladder

rectum

food

liver — digestive tract

stomach

8 years

17 years

27 years

1.5.3 THE CRISIS IN SCIENCE TEACHING

Much is said, for many reasons, about the crisis in the teaching of
mathematics or the mother tongue, yet the crisis in science teaching is no
less serious, and comes at a time when the world is being radically altered
by science. Two million scientific papers are read every year in all sorts
of fields and six million scientists meet annually to review varied subjects.
The spin-off from their work helps to shape daily life in the usual areas
of transport, communications, data-processing and medicine, but also in more
unexpected areas such as food or sexuality.

Yet the community has great difficulty in assimilating the scientific
knowledge taught at school or disseminated by the media. Even the scientific
approach and method have made very little headway in our societies: the types
of argument used in daily life or political affairs are a case in point.
Paradoxically, there has in fact been an upsurge in the number of clairvoyants,
fortune-tellers, healers of all kinds and official or unofficial sects,
together with an increase in the space devoted to horoscopes in the press and
in sales of books on a wide variety of religious beliefs. There are thus
10,000 clairvoyants in the Paris area and 50,000 healers in France (according
to Ministry of the Interior estimates for 1982), accounting for an annual
budget of 4.4 million francs in 1981 (according to Ministry of the Budget
estimates). As a final example, 12 million French people believe in flying
saucers and "martians" (survey by Dubois-Kapferer).

I do not propose to discuss the root causes of these problems:
preparation of successive reforms by officials who are usually cut off
from both research and classroom realities, outdated epistemological ideas,
lack of wide-ranging discussion of the place and function of scientific
knowledge in European society, limited timetables and resources on the
spot, lax teacher training etc. I intend to concentrate on a single
parameter which has rarely been mentioned, but nevertheless acts as a
restraining factor: science teaching forgets whom it is aimed at - pupils.

Pupils are currently both "present" in the educational process and
"absent" from it. More specifically, classroom ituations reveal a
substantial gap between the teacher, who plans lessons with his/her adult
logic, as a specialist in a given field, and the pupils, who try to
understand this language with the help of their own prior conceptions.

Traditionally, teachers preparing or giving lessons bother very little,
if at all, about the pupils' reference frameworks and conceptions. They
base their teaching on the usual syllabuses or on current set books. At
best, they read up the state of scientific knowledge on the question or
the version conveyed by popular books.

Yet my work has shown - and it is now confirmed - that pupils faced
with a scientific problem or a phenomenon stemming from their environment
always have their own method of tackling and explaining it. That is how
pupils - if they are motivated - try to understand the things a teacher
asks them to do or tells them.

If the teacher fails to take account of this, it is hardly surprising
that the knowledge he/she wishes to pass on should not replace the
children's preconceived ideas.

To clarify this point, here is an example drawn from one of my own
classes.

A group of five pupils were studying the breathing of aquatic animals
in a tank in the classroom. They had already studied the breathing of
goldfish. An analysis of their summaries, copied from the previous year's
science notebooks, showed that they had observed water movements and gills.
In fact they had made microscopic reproductions of them. In brief, the
notebook said: "How does the goldfish breathe? Water containing dissolved
oxygen enters through the mouth and leaves through the gill covers after
passing through the gills. The oxygen then passes into the blood. The
alternate opening and closing of the mouth and gill covers enables the
water to circulate".

In the course of their investigation I asked them, "How does the
goldfish breathe?" A pupil replied, "It absorbs oxygen dissolved in water
through its gills".

I then asked them to explain the point more fully. The group went into
a huddle and answered, "We're going to dissect a fish to see where the
lungs are".

To get over my surprise and try to understand how two types of explanation (gills and lungs) could exist side by side, I suggested that they draw me an explanatory diagram.

Diagram 4

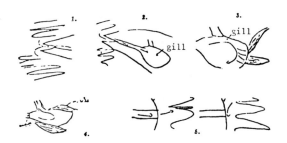

1. Water enters through the mouth.

2. It passes into the gills.

3. The oxygen contained in the water passes through the walls of the gills into the small neighbouring veins.

4. The muscles of the gills move and the water is ejected into a respiratory tract leading to the gill covers.

5. The gill covers act as valves. The respiratory tracts which lead the water into the gills and eject it are also equipped with valves. They are located at the point where the respiratory tracts merge with the gills.

78

Diagram 5

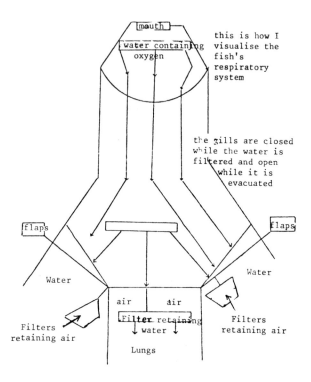

this is how I
visualise the
fish's
respiratory
system

the gills are closed
while the water is
filtered and open
while it is
evacuated

As they were unable to agree, I was offered two explanatory diagrams:

- Diagram 4: the gills fulfil the same function as lungs; they fill with water and empty out by means of valves adapted to the system;

- Diagram 5: air can only operate in a gaseous state; the gills act as filters retaining the air in gaseous form.

These two diagrams provide a very significant illustration of the gap between what the teacher teaches and what the pupils understand (1).

(1) A Giordan (under his own scientific responsibility): L'élève et/ou les connaissances scientifiques. P Lang, Berne - Frankfurt.

Since then I have encountered many examples of the same kind, all extremely revealing of the distance between the teacher who transmits knowledge according to his/her own logic and the pupils who interpret the teacher's words, or the activities suggested, according to their own reference system. On each occasion the examples also showed that the knowledge memorised at school co-existed with a stubborn prior knowledge which, at best, allowed itself to be slightly distorted in order to gain a firmer hold.

Hence the idea behind my later work: science teaching cannot ignore or even get rid of pupils' conceptions; it must understand, recognise and acknowledge them so as to interact with them.

1.5.4 IMPORTANCE OF PUPILS' LEARNING PROCESSES

This educational hypothesis thus attempts to promote a different approach based on the idea that pupils build up their own knowledge, usually in a manner conflicting with previously or recently acquired ideas.

This hypothesis, which I have attempted to corroborate by a series of experiments (1), runs counter to the current attitude of quasi-indifference to pupils' reference frameworks, arising from teachers' assumptions that their lessons will spontaneously replace any prior or individual conceptions or that pupils' minds are virgin territory.

Many teachers think, as Cramaussel writes, that pupils' thinking is like a network of fine, tangled threads which anyone trying to untangle is liable to break at any moment. Once this principle is established, it is pointless and tedious to dwell on pupils' thoughts, since they amount to mere "sayings" clearly at odds with reality and since the logic of adult thought naturally takes the place of this incoherent mess. Consequently, anything pupils say simply deserves to be dismissed as the expression of a dreary verbalism, fit for no more than a collection of platitudes, since in any case pupils are but "tireless worriers" who content themselves with the random replies they receive.

Ignorance of children's own conceptions is therefore deep-rooted and remains entrenched as long as the aim is to pin the reasoning and reference frameworks of a teacher bent on "getting through the syllabus" on to pupils' thinking, without bothering about what they really learn; in other words, as long as the sole concern is to see what pupils memorised for the previous week's test, rather than what they have really acquired by way of learning tools.

Yet, as my analytical work has shown, it is not so easy to acquire operational knowledge or, in fact, to change one's explanatory basis. Bachelard (1938) noted and emphasised the difficulties involved in changing models, which he explained by the fact that scientific explanations lack glamour by comparison with pupils' own ideas and that the need is first and foremost for changes in the level of culture.

---

(1) I wish to point out at this stage that the hypothesis does not entail allowing pupils to do whatever they like, as did non-directive teaching methods. The teacher and teaching situations dismissed by such methods are of paramount importance.

My work has focused on the difficulty of challenging conceptions worked out over a long period of time, usually in close association with daily practice, and accordingly on the importance of what Rumelhard (1980, 1981) calls the "already there": as I see it, knowledge does not fill a vacuum, but gradually replaces "spontaneous" (1) conceptions expressing the pupil's established vision of the surrounding world. Although they are fairly vague and difficult to express, and do not derive from rigorous analysis, these conceptions reflect a certain way of perceiving reality. This makes it difficult for pupils themselves to challenge them, even if the internal contradictions are immediately apparent to the analytical eye of an adult and specialist.

This led to further studies, some attempting to understand why certain conceptions remain entrenched in learners' minds, despite systematic learning, even where this is effective (Astolfi 1980, 1983), others defining and classifying them (Rumelhard 1980, Giordan et al 1983, Weil Barais 1984), and still others viewing these obstacles as part of various learning processes (Zimmerman et al 1982, Elbin 1983, Raichwag 1983, Ducros 1983, Bazan 1984).

Since then research of this kind has been in full swing (2).

1.5.5 INITIAL REVIEW OF EXISTING WORK AND PROSPECTS FOR RESEARCH

An initial review (3) can be attempted at this stage in order to outline the importance of these ideas in educational terms.

This work appears to have drawn attention to the role of pupils and the stages they pass through in building up their own knowledge. We now understand more clearly why some conceptions remain entrenched for a long time, avoiding confrontation with reality, and why they deflect the teacher's statements or explanations, resisting all efforts to break or shift them. Disregarding them in fact results in pupils having two parallel explanatory systems in their minds, neither with any hold over the other. One is used in school situations determined by the teacher, while the other invariably reappears when the situation is less school-oriented.

However, all this research needs carrying further in order to cover a wide range of subjects and gain a better understanding of the mechanisms involved. For practical reasons, it could be split up according to two complementary groups of questions. The first group of projects could be based on the following broad question: How do learners appropriate and construct their scientific knowledge?

---

(1) These "spontaneous" conceptions are coherent in children's and adolescents' eyes and are in no sense a game.

(2) A Giordan and J L Martinand: Actes des Journées internationales sur l'éducation scientifique. Paris, Nos. 1 to 6 (1979 to 1984).

(3) This work was first done on an ad hoc or practical basis, then shifted to conceptual areas: nutrition, growth, development, respiratory systems, reproduction and heredity in biology, electricity, magnetism, energy in physics.

It may seem an obvious question, but as I have just shown, it is always forgotten in practice, which explains the many gaps between what the teacher teaches and what the pupils understand.

It must be admitted that so far only psychologists have looked into it. But fundamental psychology has primarily sought to devise an overall classification of stages in operational development of logical structures minimising or disregarding learning mechanisms and processes and the content they relate to (1) - information which is essential to science education.

The above factors and the inadequacy of most psychological research of this kind - which rarely deals with the conditions governing the passage from one level to another - should lead us to pose the problem in fresh terms and tackle new areas of thematic content.

1.5.6 A TEACHING APPROACH GEARED TO PUPILS' CONCEPTIONS

A second series of studies could centre on another question: How can learners be helped to build up scientific knowledge with the support of their own learning processes (questions, reasoning, arguments, reference frameworks)?

This work on conceptions generates a fresh outlook: henceforth, the teacher/pupil relationship changes and pupils, ie learners, take their rightful place in it.

The research thus provides the basis for devising different types of educational practice. Models (in the scientific sense) of educational interaction remain to be developed, but it is unfortunately too early to embark on that stage yet.

As things stand, a highly pragmatic approach is essential, so I would urge, in terms of classroom practice, that pupils' conceptions and the obstacles they reflect be regarded as indicators enabling teachers to view teaching in a rather similar light, if I may say so, to medicine. Just as a doctor examining a patient looks into the symptoms, not so much to treat them as to assess the situation and propose a course of treatment on the basis of the data collected, teachers could use these obstacles to assist them in their diagnosis (2).

---

(1) Pupils are not only children as studied by genetic psychology. They are faced with an educational programme framed by the education system and they have a number of teaching aids at their disposal, the most important being the teacher. To this must be added, briefly, the idea that the appropriation and dissemination of knowledge are too complex a subject to be understood with the aid of a single methodological approach.

(2) Research on teacher training shows that teachers find it easier to choose their teaching methods when they gain a clear grasp of the difficulties facing them.

At the same time, a further series of research projects is needed on this point to develop theories of "change" in connection with formal and informal learning situations, focusing in particular on types of situation and intervention which offer a positive response to the learning obstacles observed.

A trend is emerging and should perhaps be boosted further. A more rational approach to problems has never come naturally. Historically, it even amounted to a conquest. Research of this kind also needs to prove itself and reach a wider audience. Hence the importance of reflecting right now on the strategies to follow and reaching some sort of explicit consensus, so as to confer a proper status on this type of research and develop, alongside (and in conjunction with) educational science and fundamental science, what might be called "science for education", or more specifically in this case, "science for the dissemination or appropriation of science".

Martinand (1983) proposes to define this pragmatically by analogy with "engineering science", the aim being not to produce educational recipes, but to develop a range of diversified tools for the use of practitioners and also decision-makers, to ensure that the correct decisions are taken at the various educational levels (1).

1.5.7 BIBLIOGRAPHY

Astolfi, J P. Les procédures d'apprentissage en sciences. Compte rendu des Journées d'études. INRP, Paris 1981.

Astolfi, J P. A propos des représentations. Intervention au Séminaire de Génève. INRP, Paris 1983.

Bachelard. La Formation de l'esprit scientifique. Vrin, Paris 1938.

Bazan, M. Le concept de respiration. Thèse 3ème cycle. Université de Paris VII, Paris 1984.

Bilbao, P. Evaluation de l'information sexuelle faite à l'école française. Thèse 3ème cycle. Université de Paris VII, Paris 1981.

Chastrette, M. Quel est le niveau des bacheliers en chimie? Actualité chimique. 1978.

Ducros, A. La circulation du sang. Mémoire. Université de Paris VII, Paris 1984.

Elbin, J. La fécondation des plantes. Mèmoire. Université de Paris VII, Paris 1983.

Garcia Barquero, P et al. Conoscimientos de biologia al terminar e curso de orientación universitaria. Madrid 1984.

---

(1) J L Martinand: Présentation des 5èmes journées sur l'éducation scientifique. Actes JES 5ème - Paris 1983.

83

Giordan, A. Présentation des 2èmes Journées sur l'éducation scientifique. Actes JES 2. Paris 1980.

Lestournelle, L. La grande misère de la formation scientifique. Cahier pédagogique, 1976.

Martinand, J L. Les obstacles épistémologiques. Séminaire de DEA. Université de Paris VII, Paris 1981.

Martinand, J L. Présentation des 5èmes Journées sur l'éducation scientifique. Actes JES 5ème. Paris 1983.

McCloskey, M. L'intuition en physique. Pour la Science (transl). Paris 1983.

Raichwag, D. L'information sexuelle. Mémoire. Université de Paris VII, Paris 1983.

Rumelhard, G. Thèse de 3ème cycle (unpublished). Université de Paris VII, Paris 1980.

Viennot, L. Le raisonnement spontané endynamique élémentaire. Hermann, Paris 1979.

Vuilleumier, B. Obstacle à propos de chaleur. Acte JES 5. Paris 1984.

Weil Barais, A. In Astolfi, J P et al. Experimenteur (Chapter 2), Privat, Toulouse 1984.

Zimmerman, M L et al. Obstacle à propos de chaleur. Acte JES 5. Paris 1984.

1.6 THE NATURAL SCIENTIFIC ASPECTS OF "MAN AND ENVIRONMENT"
IN THE CURRICULUM OF PRIMARY SCHOOLS
1ST TO 6TH SCHOOL YEAR
(DEVELOPMENT 1574-1584)

by

Armin Beeler, Switzerland

1.6.1 INTRODUCTION AND SURVEY

The curriculum "Man and Environment" (M + E) combines several subjects such
as local history and topography, general history, geography, biology,
physics, sociology and economy. In the German speaking part of Switzerland
this subject combination is called "Sach-Unterricht". In general this
subject is taught five hours per week.

The canton of Lucerne covers an area with about 300,000 inhabitants.
That means, some 1,200 teachers are confronted with this curriculum. Due
to the fact that the Commission of Education of the canton of Lucerne
introduced new teaching material for the subject "history" they were forced
to reorganise the teaching of "Man and Environment" as well as the other
subjects linked up with "history" such as local history and topography,
geography and biology. I was asked to take over this task.

In order to implement this reform, a commission of teachers working
voluntarily and, from 1978 onwards, a fully employed scientific commissioner
were appointed. This full-time post was occasionally separated into two
half-day posts.

This case study mainly treats the natural scientific aspects within the
curriculum. It will begin with a presentation of central theses as
determined in the report "Basic ideas for a reform of local history and
topography teaching as well as the teaching of factual subjects as geography,
history and biology at the primary school" which began our work in 1974.
I will then pursue the development of these theses until 1984 by describing
the methods of evaluation, the scientific and the political influences, the
forms of testing and evaluation up to the stage of 1984 by which we can
deduce the actual problem situation.

Just a word about the scientific aspect of the curriculum and its
development and testing methods:

- Results of scientific research are mainly referred to in the basic
  report of 1976 and the outline of the 1st curriculum of 1978. Among
  others we took the following books into consideration: Studies in
  Cognitive Growth by Jerome Bruner, Cognitive Psychology by Jean Piaget,
  Basic form of teaching by Hans Aebli, Genetic learning by
  Martin Wagenschein, Fundamental meaning of elementary perception by
  Hugo Kükelhaus. These basic ideas have been accepted up to now
  without any restriction.

- The 1st commission (1976-78) made up by secondary teachers as
representatives of all the subjects concerned, was in charge of
the scientific adjustment of the contents of the curriculum.

- The methods of developing and testing the curriculum do not entirely
correspond to the intrinsic scientific claim of the curriculum
research. For this our manpower and financial resources were too
meagre.

In short we could summarise the evolution of our curriculum from 1974
to 1984 as follows:

Basic report prepared by a commission of experts in each subject of our curriculum and of teachers and educational experts.	1976

Presentation for public consultation The basic report of 1976 is made available to the public interested in school problems such as teachers, political parties, newspapers and school officials of neighbouring cantons. The feedback is evaluated.	1977

Hearings with teachers concerned 417 teachers of the 3rd and 4th classes of the primary school received talks on the basic report and were asked to give a written comment on it, which was evaluated.	1977

1st curriculum outline was prepared by a second commission consisting of primary teachers and educational experts over a period of several weeks.	1979

Second presentation The outline of the curriculum was shown to all representatives of school authorities for further comments.	1979

2nd curriculum outline In the light of the above comments the second outline of the curriculum was completed with the assistance of the educational authorities.	1980

Curriculum testing with evaluation 95 teachers in all parts of our canton were engaged in the testing and evaluation procedure leading to the provisional curriculum of 1982	1980-82

Provisional curriculum From 1982 onwards 100 teachers in groups of 12 were introduced to this provisional curriculum per year. This introduction course consisted of approximately eight meetings over the period of one year.	1982-84

The idea was to introduce all teachers in such group courses to a teacher's work on the basis of this provisional curriculum. During this procedure up to 1988, the provisional curriculum is open to any criticism or suggestion for improvements. From 1988 onwards it is expected that the revised curriculum could be declared as compulsory for all teachers of our canton.

1.6.2 THE DEVELOPMENT OF THE THESES 1974-84

1.6.2.1 *Basic curriculum theses*

Thesis 1: On conceiving a curriculum we have to take into consideration the age of the children as well as the children's scope of preparedness to act, that means, we have to refer to basic phenomena as human beings, creatures, things, processes, and should not insist on the demand for an entirely systematical concept of the presentation of facts.

This thesis of the basic report has always been supported by all authorities and teachers concerned. The main intention was to move beyond the original subjects of geography, history, biology and to create a concept which took the basic phenomena of living into consideration. On the basis of former teaching concepts from Germany and Austria, we conceived a frame of basic requirements of man, similar to that occasionally referred to in geography. "Man must live in society, must work, supply himself, educate himself, relax and move within society"(1).

---

(1) Partzsch, Dictionary of space scruting and space order. O J/H Bobek, geography, 1948.

Before the 1st curriculum model was developed an analysis of all available German educational publications about practical teaching was made. All the themes that had to do with those basic requirements of living were collected by the commission and ordered by the grade of importance for the life of the child. Coherent phenomena were co-ordinated to thematic circles which had to replace the former subjects. The following was the structure of the 1st curriculum outline:

- work x	- healthy-ill man x
- building-living x	- clothing x
- shopping-money	- Lucerne-Switzerland x
- food x	- media
- spare time	- plants-creatures-living space xx
- history-concept of time	- school-family-human being in society
- state and society	- transport x
- our earth x	- weather-water xx

This classification is based on phenomal principles as shown above. The aspects of natural science, ie the biological, physical, technical aspects refer to many themes and are marked with one or two asterisks. The ones marked with two asterisks seem to be above all natural-scientific. But it is important to show the teachers during the introductory courses that physical phenomena, as for instance measurement of temperature, always have a subjective aspect as they induce perceptions and feelings which have to do with the theme.

In the course of the development of the phenomenal teaching concept some problems arose from the thematic classification:

- By this new classification many new themes were introduced into the teaching programme of the primary school. In many comments on this new thematic concept we were confronted with a fear of too much material producing an unacceptable pressure on the teachers as well as on the pupils. We took this criticism very seriously but in no case did we want to exclude these new themes as they seemed indispensable to us for educating pupils to become young people with the capacity to act. Therefore we had to establish the compulsory curriculum basically from the beginning (see Thesis 3). That meant we had to renounce the compulsory presentation of certain subjects and stick to a generally formulated teaching aim.

- Referring to the 1st curriculum outline (1979) we received the criticism that the natural-scientific aspects were definitely dominated by socio-cultural themes. But in spite of such critical feedback we decided to consider the theme "plant-creatures-living space" as compulsory and suggested that this theme was used twice a year at a minimum.

- In opposition to the basic report of 1976 we did not take chemical aspects into consideration any longer.

-   In the course of the curriculum testing the theme circle "water-weather", which had to deal with the physical problems of water, proved to be too narrow to cover all the interesting physical phenomena, as far as the children were concerned. In the provisional curriculum of 1982 this theme circle was then called "laws of nature".

(Further information on natural-scientific aspects is contained in paragraph 1.6.2.2 (Theses about natural-scientific aspects).)

Thesis 2: Education for self-reliance: the process aims (learning of working-learning-thinking-methods, introduction of the moral qualities of responsibility towards man and environment) are as important as the content aims.

This thesis caused a visible change in the teachers' approach to teaching. A list of process aims had already been introduced in the original basic report. The presentation in 1977 of the basic report produced the following information:

-   School authorities and politicians emphatically supported the introduction of process aims into the new teaching scheme. These aims were looked upon as the decisive mark of the whole reform.

-   Of 417 consulted teachers only 18 expressed some doubts about that point: they asked for further information and instruction about how these aims could be reached.

From this discrepancy between the authorities who supported the process aims and the teachers who proved to be disinterested and methodologically inexperienced on the other side, one of the most important taks of our reform work arose: to win the teachers' support for this aim and to offer them methodological help.

Within the curriculum testing period (1980-82) we informed the participating teachers about the methods which would put the process aims into practice. At the same time we collected examples of practical experience. The evaluation and the testing showed that a publication concerning the methodology appropriate to the process aims was in high demand. I met this demand by publishing the book "Selbst ist der Schüler" (pupils and self-reliance), Klett and Balmer, Zug 1982. This publication is now part of the reform work.

Process aims must also be considered as essential for natural-scientific teaching.

The following statements of aims are looked upon as specially important in the provisional curriculum of 1982:

i. Basic working methods for immediate information collection:

    - observing and collecting observation results;

    - collecting and ordering.

Comment: If the child has direct contact with nature the development of the ability to observe will become the central focus
of teaching. We have to consider here the need to develop the
differentiation of the child's perception. The undisturbed,
intensive process of observing shows positive effects on the mental
health of the child (1) but the overstimulation in every day
conditions, mainly by the media, spoils the child's ability to
observe. As we concentrate exclusively on directly observable
phenomena in the realm of natural science a continuing observation
training must take place. Blackboard biology and physics should
therefore be discouraged.

ii. Basic ways of thinking:

- experimenting - predicting - concluding - comparing - transferring -
creative thinking.

Comment: As well as observation training it seems to us that the
training of a number of ways of thinking could be very important
for work in the realm of natural science. Once again the main
emphasis does not lie on knowledge about nature but on the training
of the thinking process based on natural phenomena. The above-
mentioned ways of thinking are neither chosen nor ordered by
systematical points of view. They are the result of experience with
pupils: it should not surprise us that the most common ways of
thinking are not necessarily easily followed by children.

iii. Fundamental attitude of responsibility towards the environment

Comment: Above all we take the term "environment" to mean biosphere.
Today scientific education at the primary school has to be coupled
with an ethical concept of responsibility. By an appropriate choice
of themes and by the inclusion of methods of social learning
(conversation, role-play, project-teaching) this aim could be
achieved.

Education to self-reliance (Thesis 2) has been developed as the
essential part of the reform. It is accepted by all sides but some
difficulties are encountered when trying to put it into practice as it
demands a radical change of thinking. Not only the "what", but the
"how" becomes important in teaching and as process-oriented methodology
is very seldom provided for during the teachers' training course, the
teachers do not have a model to follow. As well as the difficulty of
training in these ways of working and thinking, such methods make demands
on time. Therefore we had to try as much as possible to reduce the
material pressure. This could be achieved by cutting out all the
compulsory subject-teaching in the teaching programme.

In short this means, the working principles in natural science should
be reduced to the development of corresponding working-, thinking- and
attitude-patterns.

---

(1) Kükelhaus, op cit.

> Thesis 3: An open curriculum is most suitable to cover the requirements of the phenomenal approach (Thesis 1) and the education for self-reliance (Thesis 2).

In the basic report of 1976 we described this "open curriculum" as follows: "It contains binding suggestions as general aims, basic teaching exercises, teaching aids, testing material, which do not restrict the freedom of teaching but on the contrary support the development of creative power as far as distinct aims, phenomena and methods are concerned".

In 1984 we conceived an open curriculum in the traditional sense (aims, contents) but not an open curriculum in the scientific sense (aims, contents, teaching aids, exercises, testing material). What has led to this change?

i.   The financial and manpower resources were not sufficient to provide the conditions for the development of a system of education and teaching aids which are needed for the complete curriculum.

ii. Above all, the teachers involved in the construction process in 1977 and the evaluation in 1981-82 opposed the testing of the material and process aims. As it was not possible for us to develop valuable tests, we preferred to leave it. The educational authorities would have appreciated such tests, but we convinced them that the tests could be replaced by following instructions:

       "The teacher has to keep a diary which should contain a daily record of the themes dealt with and the material and process aims pursued. This diary has to be shown to any school officials (inspectors) and must be placed at the disposal of teachers taking over the class".

     The teachers involved not only accepted keeping such a record but even asked for it. Today this diary is looked upon as an integrated part of the teacher's work.

iii. A real curriculum should contain corresponding teaching aids. As the production of own teaching aids was beyond our power we decided to select from the supply of teaching aids produced in the German-speaking areas for a teacher's library. This method did not prove to be ideal because the market of teaching aids in such a large area changes quickly. Any lists of teaching aids had to be renewed each year and therefore could not be considered in the publication of a curriculum. So it is up to the school to decide what teaching aids should be selected. With the exception of a history book no other books are accepted for the pupils. If the children have to deal with phenomena, a book is an obstacle. This thesis is now accepted by the teachers and it proved to guarantee a lively realistic form of teaching.

iv. The decisive experience of the testing period 1980-82 enabled us to pursue the thesis of the open curriculum with even more accuracy. The 2nd curriculum outline of 1980 had the following structure: (1) General aims with phenomenal description and pedagogic explanation; (2) Suggestion about the distribution of themes over six years; (3) Precise methodical suggestions to each theme. This third part is no longer referred to in the provisional curriculum of 1982. The teachers involved argued that such methodical hints were no longer of any interest after an intensive discussion of these curriculum themes. This allowed the curriculum to be reduced from 200 to 100 pages.

1.6.2.2 *Theses of the natural scientific aspect of the curriculum*

We have already considered natural-scientific problems in Theses 1 and 2. In the following theses we have to look at the natural scientific problems as far as special subjects are concerned.

Thesis 4: Physics (particle model): The idea that substance and energy are made from particles is looked upon as a basic principle for teaching physics in the primary schools.

This thesis was introduced in the basic report of 1976. Today, in 1984, it is forgotten and is not referred to for explaining physical phenomena. What has happened? Our physicist and chemist of the first commission (1976-78) accepted this particle model theory as suitable for teaching purposes at the primary school. It was tested in American teaching courses and was introduced to modern German curricula (for instance in Bavaria in 1972). After the public consultation in 1977 there was still no opposition. It seems now that this thesis was only accepted by the natural scientists and that the other people involved in the first commission did not express their own opinions, because the non-scientists actually could not understand what the problem was about. Indeed it was the second commission, made up of primary teachers, which pointed out that this thesis was in opposition to the phenomenal approach to curriculum teaching projects. In physics the particle model theory needs systematic presentation of the teaching material and cannot be based on a study of environmental phenomena.

Therefore the particle model was given up during the modification of the 1st curriculum outline of 1979. Nobody, not even the physicists, opposed that change. As the phenomenal approach grew in influence the physical themes of the curriculum were presented in a thematic way (for instance in such a sequence: work, building, living, feeding, cooking, health, clothing, transport, weather).

The change towards the phenomenal approach in teaching physics had some other consequences as well as far as the equipment was concerned. In the basic report of 1976 equipment such as test tubes, bunsen burners etc was required and precisely described. Nowadays it is hardly mentioned. We prefer that children observe phenomena as they appear in everyday life and in nature. Boiling water in a pot and not in an Erlenmeyer test tube.

But a problem still remains as far as the work between teachers and pupils is concerned. It is very difficult to explain everyday physical problems to children because this must happen in a simplified form which still guarantees absolute correctness. The teachers must have at their disposal knowledge about physics and an appropriate training to be able to master the problems which arise. This cannot be guaranteed in our canton for the moment. We have the impression that we are on the right track, but it is still the beginning. The general opposition to technical-physical thinking caused by our environment and civilisation problems makes it very difficult to motivate our teachers for such purposes.

Thesis 5: <u>Biology: the direct approach to biological phenomena</u> is the basic principle of teaching biology at the primary school.

This thesis is a simplified version of Thesis 1. But it has decisive consequences for the development of the curriculum. The commission tried in their 1st outline of 1979 to establish a list of all possible bio-themes that children might experience at first hand. This list has always been brought up-to-date and has today the following structure:

We classify our environment in the following themes: meadows/fields/ hedges - forest - water - village/town. Each theme is divided into three parts corresponding to the levels of the classes 1/2, 3/4, 5/6. This formation of the themes has nothing to do with psychological reflection but attempts to provide a progression of themes at each stage in the school and to meet teachers' wishes to have themes dealt with at later as well as earlier stages of the school. This way of listing themes proved successful among teachers. However other problems turned up in biology teaching. At the moment the teachers prefer to treat animals as individual creatures without referring to the essential processes as genetics, nutrition, growth, protection. The dependence between man and nature, a very important theme, is neglected. At the moment we have reacted in the following way:

- in the introductory courses concerning the new curriculum we always refer to these aims and we develop teaching units together;

- we refer to literature which could assist the teachers in achieving such aims.

In retrospect, we can say that Thesis 5 was achieved successfully and that there is evidence, for example from school inspections, that blackboard-biology has disappeared.

The basic report of 1976 recommended a list of resources such as magnifying glasses, tweezers, needles, cages, breeding-cages, binoculars and microscopes as a kind of minimum equipment. We have now reduced this list and do not now include resources such as microscopes and binoculars, because they limit the direct contact between child and nature. There are still enough phenomena which could be observed directly with our own senses. This point of view is considered in Theses 1 and 5.

Thesis 6: The spiral curriculum provokes a continuous amalgamation of basic insights, working and thinking patterns.

In the basic report of 1976 the spiral curriculum was determined as follows: "Precisely determined teaching units will be treated during the course of the 6th primary class in a continuous increasing   complexity of the subject matter". The thesis was consequently developed and successfully introduced into the curriculum of 1982. An example, taken from the theme-circle "plants - creatures - living space" shows what is expected by the teacher. He chooses a theme from the listed suggestions (for example: living space "village-town": public gardens of Lucerne). He prepares a presentation of the chosen theme based on the following four knowledge and five process aims of this theme unit.

KNOWLEDGE AIMS:

1. The child has to be guaranteed a thorough insight into the diversity of life. Through the examination of various individual phenomena he should notice the variety of forms and species.

2. The child has an insight into different vital processes.

3. The child realises that plants, creatures and human beings live or exist together in mutual participation.

4. The child realises himself that he is part of nature, but that man on the other hand can modify nature and have an influence on the balance of nature.

PROCESS AIMS:

1. The child can observe plants, creatures and living spaces, collect, order and present observations by means of language or pictures.

2. The child can collect additional information from books and other media.

3. The child can make simple experiments with plants and formulate and test his expectations.

4. The child can compare different more or less similar beings (practises thinking patterns).

5. The child can take care of plants and animals developing his sense of responsibility (behaviour).

The spiral method consists of phenomenal and processual aims of different themes which reappear successively. From there, we expect a continuous development throughout the primary school which guarantees the teachers freedom in choosing themes. But the practical application of this thesis includes some difficulties. Our teachers are not accustomed to subordinating their themes to general aims. We only notice very slow progress, especially as far as the process aims are concerned. Therefore the teachers have been asked to put down theme and aims in their class-books (see Thesis 3). This helps to check whether or not the thesis is put into practice. The question about practical contribution of the curriculum towards environmental protection has been raised on several occasions between 1977 and 1982.

The commission in charge has a clear policy for environmental protection as far as the curriculum is concerned. But the children should not be overwhelmed by highly complex relationships. It is quite sufficient to offer the children intensive experiences with nature which should help to establish a positive attitude towards environmental protection.

Our solution seems to be simple, but the important things must be simple in order to put into practice; anything more might be counter-productive.

1.6.3 PROBLEMS ENCOUNTERED IN CURRICULUM IMPLEMENTATION

Our aim is to introduce the curriculum step by step until 1988. At the moment we face within that process the following problems:

i.   For the work with this curriculum the teacher has to adapt pupil-centred working patterns which force many teachers to change their general attitude towards teaching. Such changes cannot be achieved by the curriculum only but need additional teachers' courses and group work. Therefore the introduction of the curriculum requires time. As there is a lack of available models, progress is only made slowly. This explains why it took so much time to implement this curriculum.

ii. The parents are also involved in the new curriculum. They have to accept a new attitude towards the school. They must support the change from phenomenal to process methods, and they must understand why children have to make experiments instead of writing dictation at home. Parents in Switzerland can have much influence on schools via school commissions, political parties and the press. Therefore it is crucial to create in the public an understanding of such a reform. This is a priority for our commission. At the moment the political parties and the press fully support the change although this was not always the case. The second public consultation in 1979 especially produced a number of conflicts.

iii. Apart from the teachers involved, teachers' training colleges and school authorities must be included in the learning process within the coming years.

1.7 FORMULATING A SCHOOL POLICY FOR SCIENCE -
SUPPORT FOR TEACHERS IN SCOTLAND

by

Sinclair MacLeod, Scotland

1.7.1 SUMMARY

1.7.1.1 Recent surveys by HM Inspectorate in the United Kingdom, and other
references, indicate the importance of the need for schools to formulate
a policy for science.

1.7.1.2 In Scotland science is often included along with history and
geography as part of "Environmental Studies". Recent evidence (1980)
demonstrated that science is frequently neglected.

1.7.1.3 Since 1980 a number of developments are briefly described -
overall, by 1984, a more positive approach to science in many schools can
be detected. A national course for lecturers, advisers and promoted teachers
was held in July 1982.

1.7.1.4 A major initiative by the Scottish Education Department has been
the establishment of an action-research project to run from October 1981
till March 1985. The PRIMARY SCIENCE DEVELOPMENT PROJECT (PSDP), with
funds of £55,000 was asked to produce (i) support materials for teachers
and (ii) materials to assist schools to formulate policies for science.
The PSDP team was not asked to provide more curricular resources for pupils
and teachers to use; it was considered that sufficient of these were
available or in course of preparation.

1.7.1.5 An outline of the three phases of the PDSP strategy for development
is given. A key feature of the project has been the extent of consultation
with teachers, head teachers, advisers, lecturers etc. Work with infants
has identified good practice; the natural links between science and health
education have been investigated; the scope for introducing practical
activities, involving science concepts and skills, into the mathematics
programme explored; and the common features that schools encounter as
they formulate policy statements have been identified.

1.7.1.6 A series of eight booklets are being produced by PSDP along with
other support materials for teachers. (Drafts of these will be available
at the Research Workshop in Edinburgh.) A second national course for key
personnel in education authorities, colleges of education and schools will
be held in March 1985. This will constitute another part of the national
strategy to improve primary school science. The PSDP materials will be a
main feature of the course; copies of the booklets will then be sent to

D

every primary school, other materials, (case-studies, video, tape/slides) will be distributed to education authorities and colleges of education. It is expected that the use of PSDP materials after 1985 will be monitored.

1.7.2 GENERAL INTRODUCTION

Recently published surveys by Her Majesty's Inspectorate in different parts of the United Kingdom give indications of the state of science teaching in the primary school and emphasise the need for schools to formulate a policy for science.

1.7.2.1 Department of Education and Science 1978 - Primary education in England

"Few primary schools ... had effective programmes for the teaching of science."

"Although some science was attempted in the majority of classes, the work was developed seriously in only just over one class in ten."

"Yet the progress of science teaching in primary schools has been disappointing; the ideas and materials produced by curriculum development projects have had little impact in the majority of schools."

1.7.2.2 Scottish Education Department 1980 - "Learning and Teaching in Primary 4 and Primary 7"

"Science fared badly, with 60% of all teachers (P7) giving it little, if any, place in their curriculum."

"As a matter of priority, something has to be done for them (teachers) in science, but first it will be necessary to assess what schools can reasonably be expected to achieve."

1.7.2.3 Northern Ireland 1981 - Primary education

"It is considered to be absolutely essential that principals and teachers prepare guidelines of frameworks which will ensure progression and variety of experience as pupils proceed up the school."

Other publications have reinforced these surveys -

1.7.2.4 Lancashire looks at ... Science in the Primary School, Vol; 1, No. 2, 1981

"A school policy for science is not a syllabus ... It should make it clear to members of staff what is required from them and their children, offering many ideas yet leaving them free to use those most likely to be appropriate for their own children in their own particular school environment. It should however include some agreed structure so that children get a balanced science curriculum with logical progression."

1.7.2.5 *Department of Education and Science* - "Science in the primary
                                                      schools. A discussion
                                                      paper", 1983

"The benefits of a well-constructed scheme of work can hardly be over-
emphasised."

1.7.2.6 *Strathclyde Region Department of Education* - Science in the primary
                                                            curriculum 1982

"... schools should proceed with some caution while working gradually but
positively towards the establishment of a sound school policy for science."

1.7.2.7 *Scottish Committee on Environmental Studies* - Towards a policy for
                                                            science in Scottish
                                                            primary schools, 1980

"The school policy for science requires to be formulated, written down
and made available to all members of staff."

    "To be successful the policy should be the product of discussions
between the head teacher, assistant head teacher(s) and teachers."

1.7.3 THE SCOTTISH DIMENSION

It has always been acknowledged that nature study and science have a part
to play in the primary school curriculum as indicated by a memorandum from
HM Inspectors of Schools "Nature study and the teaching of science", 1908.

1.7.3.1 In 1965 HMSO published a policy statement on primary education in
Scotland "Primary Education in Scotland". This publication was to provide
an up-to-date appraisal of the best practices in primary schools in Scotland
and the principles on which primary education should be based. In this
publication science was included along with history and geography within
"environmental studies". Today many schools cover the scientific experiences
of children through environmental studies which is now thought of as including
history, geography, science and health education.

1.7.3.2 Since 1965 there have been a series of developments in the field of
science. Perhaps two of the most significant were Nuffield Junior Science
(1964-66) sponsored by Schools Council and Nuffield Foundation and the
Science 5/13 Project (1967-74) sponsored by Schools Council, Nuffield
Foundation and the Scottish Education Department. In 1971, a small team
in Scotland produced an audio-visual package based on Science 5/13. This
included an audio-taped interview with a class teacher, three video tapes
of her working with her class, an 8 mm film, and five tape slide
presentations.

1.7.3.3 The most recent report by HM Inspectors "Learning and Teaching in
Primary 4 and Primary 7" was published in 1980 and was based on surveys
of work being done in Primary 4 (8-9 year olds) and Primary 7 (11-12 year
olds) carried out by HM Inspectors of Schools in 152 primary schools in
1978.

"More thought needs to be given to relating the work of one stage to that of previous and succeeding stages; and teachers should be able to plan their own class activities against a whole school policy for environmental studies. Good work by the pupils was usually associated with good planning by their teacher and by the school as a whole."

The following tables from the surveys shed some light on the situation that existed in 1978 and indicate that there were many deficiencies in the scientific experiences of children in these classes.

Table 1: Over-emphasis and neglect of aspects of the curriculum in the survey classes

	Over-emphasised in classes		Neglected in classes	
	% at P4	% at P7	% at P4	% at P7
Arithmetic/Maths	14	22	9	1
Number/Computation	26	16	-	-
Practical Maths	5	-	17	19
Written English	1	3	16	18
Spelling	5	6	-	-
Spoken English (including drama)	2	1	26	29
Language Usage and Reading/Comprehension	38	41	5	4
Literature	-	2	9	10
Environmental studies generally	1	1	21	17
History	1	2	10	12
Geography	1	1	13	13
Science	-	-	30	36
Art	2	6	24	28
Craft	-	-	61	54
Music	1	2	14	17
Physical Education	-	-	5	8

This table illustrates the extent to which science was neglected in classes at both stages. In no class was science over-emphasised but in 30% of P4 classes (8-9 year olds) and in 36% of P7 classes (11-12 year olds) science was neglected.

"The evidence at both stages suggested that very little science was taught at all."

"The extent to which science is neglected, especially at the P7 stage, is of very real concern, and its contribution to the primary school curriculum will have to be examined."

Table 2: Programme of work: environmental studies

	% of P4 classes			% of P7 classes		
	Hist.	Geog.	Sc.	Hist.	Geog.	Sc.
The programme is based on available textbooks	9	5	2	11	5	3
The programme of environmental studies is strictly controlled by a school syllabus	7	9	4	7	7	3
A school syllabus exists but teachers do not necessarily adhere to it	7	7	5	9	11	5
The school programme allows the teacher to choose some of her own work	11	11	5	10	10	5
The teacher is free to organise work within a very broad framework	18	19	10	17	18	11
There is no school programme but the teacher organises her own in her class	26	26	32	32	34	28
There is no school programme and little attempt to organise a class programme	20	22	34	13	13	34

So far as this table is concerned the significance is in the last two entries. These may be looked at separately or combined to show where there was no school programme at all. Comparisons with other two components of environmental studies can also be readily made.

1.7.3.4 *Developments in Scotland since 1980*

Since the surveys and the publication of the report "Learning and Teaching in Primary 4 and Primary 7" a range of developments have been taking place in Scotland including the following:

1.7.3.4.1 Commencing in 1978 and continuing till 1983 about 260 schools have been involved in the Schools Council's Learning Through Science Project. The Scottish Education Department agreed to help fund this project between 1978 and 1983, similar support having been given to its predecessor the Science 5/13 Project. The Committee on Primary Education (COPE) allocated the funds and one of its sub-committees - Scottish Committee on Environmental Studies (SCES) - was asked to oversee the work and establish a Steering Committee. The project team, based in London, produced a discussion document on the formulation of a policy for science in primary and middle schools and a series of sets of work cards for children. Scotland has been involved in the trials of every set of Learning Through Science cards.

1.7.3.4.2 With the assistance of Jordanhill College of Education, over 100 schools in the west of Scotland have been involved in a four-year programme of science activities covering Primary 4 to Primary 7 stages.

1.7.3.4.3 Since session 1980-81 Aberdeen College of Education has been offering two distance learning courses: (1) "Learning Through Living Things" and (2) "Primary Environmental Studies: Biology". An average of 45 primary school teachers in the north of Scotland annually make use of each of these postal in-service courses.

1.7.3.4.4 A research project funded by the then Scottish Economic Planning Department has been carried out in a small number of schools, mostly in Glasgow. Engineering apprentices of several major local companies assisted Primary 6 and Primary 7 class teachers in their work with pupils using published science materials such as the "Craigie Science Kit" and "Learning Through Science".

1.7.3.4.5 Two pilot programmes for the BBC series "Science Workshop" were produced and tested in two primary schools in Lanark. A number of teachers from Lanark and Glasgow had the opportunity to preview the series and discuss its use. More than a third of primary schools in Scotland now make use of this series and in at least one area in-service training has been provided to promote good use of the series and its materials.

1.7.3.4.6 Schools from two regions have been involved with the British Association for the Advancement of Science; from this has developed the Awards for Young Investigators Scheme.

1.7.3.4.7 A national course was held for 70 participants in July 1982. A course report has been made available to regional authorities and colleges of education (copies will be available at the Research Workshop). A further national course is to be held in 1985 in order to assess progress in the intervening period and allow the teacher support materials produced by the Primary Science Development Project to be introduced at a national level.

1.7.3.4.8 After the publication of Learning and Teaching in Primary 4 and Primary 7 in 1980, the Scottish Education Department set up the Primary Science Development Project to run from October 1981 till March 1985, based at Moray House College of Education, Edinburgh.

1.7.4 THE PRIMARY SCIENCE DEVELOPMENT PROJECT (PSDP)

1.7.4.1 *The project team*

Director   Mr Sinclair MacLeod

Assistant   Miss M I Weir - October 1981 till November 1982
Directors
            Mr G Mills   - from January 1983

            Miss W Philip - from April 1983

1.7.4.2 The project proposal was -

"The aim of the project is to develop educationally acceptable science experiences in the curriculum of all Scottish primary schools. The team must make teachers more aware of the nature and aims of science in the primary school and how it relates to other aspects of pupils' education. Sufficient curricular resources in this field already exist or are in preparation, yet many schools do not make use of these. The major help which schools require is positive encouragement and guidance in the exploration and exploitation of these materials. In order to provide teachers with adequate guidance the team will evaluate the educational objectives which the use of the resources, already available, might be expected to achieve."

"Other factors in the failure of many schools to include science are the lack of a school policy, problems in the management of practical activities and the hesitancy of many primary teachers to become involved in science. The team will by direct discussion with schools' staffs (urban and rural; large and small) seek to establish the forms of support which the staffs think they require to overcome these factors."

"Following this appraisal the team will produce a package of resources which they will use with further groups of schools in order to assess the potential of this package in the development of science as an integral part of the curriculum. The intention is that this package in its final form will be available for use by schools through their promoted staffs, advisers, colleges etc."

"To achieve these aims it is envisaged that a three-year programme will be required. The team will liaise with education authorities and colleges of education and also be aware of current developments in the primary curriculum. The intention is to establish or utilise existing groups of head teachers, assistant head teachers and advisers, possibly in association with colleges of education staff.

A specific task which some of these groups could undertake would be an examination of how (1) science and health studies and (2) science and mathematics can reinforce each other."

1.7.4.3 An advisory committee, representing local authorities, schools, colleges of education and Her Majesty's Inspectorate was set up. These representatives were drawn from different parts of Scotland. The committee identified five main areas for investigation. These were:

A.   the scientific experiences of children in the early stages of primary education (5-8 years);

B.   interrelationships of science and health education for children between the ages of 8-12 years;

C.   interrelationships of science and mathematics for children between the ages of 8-12 years;

D.   the development of school policy documents;

E.   the particular needs of small schools in the formulation and implementation of a science policy.

1.7.5 STRATEGIES FOR DEVELOPMENT

PHASE 1: November 1981 - June 1982

1.7.5.1 Links were established with all education authorities, through
letters and, where feasible, meetings between project director and
representatives of the regions. Liaison persons were nominated by every
region in Scotland.

The project team produced questionnaires and interviewed 172 teachers
and head teachers to try to identify the "needs" of the schools ie what
they (the staffs of the schools) felt they required, in addition to
resources, in order to teach science in the primary school.

The two major issues highlighted by the responses to the questionnaires
were that teachers felt they needed help in the form of school guidelines
covering a programme for science and classroom organisation and also they
wanted adequate resources to be readily available.

Sub-groups of members of the committee were appointed to link with
schools in their local areas to examine -

a.   good practices in the early stages of primary education
     (age 5-8 years);

b.   interrelations between scientific experiences and health
     education for children in upper stages of primary school
     (age 8-12 years);

c.   interrelationships between scientific experiences and mathematics
     for children in upper stages of primary school (age 8-12 years);

d.   groups of schools in six areas were asked to work towards
     producing a policy for science within their own school.

PHASE 2: June 1982 - July 1983

1.7.5.2 *Early stages*

Members of the Advisory Committee working with infant teachers in 14 schools
carefully recorded all the work which related to science activities for the
whole school year. This included photographs, slides, tapes and videos as
well as written accounts. From this material the project team were able to
identify a number of case histories which exemplify good practices in the
early stages of the primary school.

1.7.5.3 *Science and health*

Three groups of schools in different parts of Scotland were set up, with
each group looking for relationships between scientific experiences and
health education. The teachers involved experienced little difficulty in
relating the two aspects of the curriculum and indeed felt that the
children's interest and performance improved in both areas. The teachers
also commented on the range of opportunities for language work that arose
from the combined study. Their detailed recording of the work covered
included useful examples of cross-referencing between resources for health
and science.

c. Development elsewhere.

d. What science in the primary school is.

e. The need for a school policy for science.

Booklet 2: A School Policy for Science - A Rationale

a. Why a policy for science is necessary.

b. What a policy for science should cover.

c. Some common features in approaches to formulating a policy.

d. Time scale for formulating and implementing a policy.

Booklet 3: Formulating a School Policy - A Strategy

a. Reviewing what is already being done in science in the school.

b. Deciding on an approach - either science core approach or thematic approach.

c. Implementing a science programme using these approaches.

Booklet 4: Science in the Primary School - Activities in the Early Years

a. Environments for science experiences.

b. The role of the teacher.

c. Centres of interest/theme approach.

d. On-going activities.

e. Collections.

f. Play.

g. Recording.

h. Assessment.

Booklet 5: Science in the Primary School - Links with Other Areas of Curriculum

a. Links with other areas of the curriculum.

b. Science/maths links.

c. Science/health links.

Booklet 6: Science in the Primary School - Class Organisation

a. Ways of organising a class.

b. The role of the teacher.

1.7.5.4 *Science and mathematics*

Two groups were set up in different parts of Scotland to try to introduce into the schools' programme for mathematics more practical work through related scientific experiences.

One group working with 10-12 year olds found that it was better for a school to establish a science programme on its own and that it was not possible to produce a complete science programme linked closely with their maths programme.

The other group working with 8-10 year olds found that links between science and maths, particularly in the topic "time" were easy to establish. Not only were good scientific experiences recorded but the teachers commented on how this more practical approach had benefited the teaching and understanding of mathematics. This group is producing an audio-visual package showing how the introduction of science activities enriched the schools' programmes for mathematics.

1.7.5.5 *Policy formulating groups*

The following procedure was adopted in all of the six areas:

i.   a member of the project team met with the local adviser and the head teachers of the schools to explain the purpose of the exercise. Head teachers chose resources to be used;

ii. each head teacher reviewed (a) what was being done in his school (b) what resources were currently in school;

iii. the head teacber (or member of project team) spoke to staff of school to illustrate the importance of scientific experiences for primary children and to highlight the need for a school policy in science;

iv. some teachers in school were given the resources previously chosen by head teachers, and guidelines on how to start using these resources;

v.   these teachers used the resources with their classes for about a term (three months);

vi. staff discussed experiences of these teachers - other teachers tried resources;

vii. promoted staff drew up draft policy statements.

PHASE 3: June 1983 on-going

1.7.5.6 Based on the results of Phase 2 the project team started writing small booklets covering different aspects as follows:

Booklet 1: Science in the Primary School - An Introduction

a.   Why include science in the curriculum?

b.   Developments in Scotland since 1980 HMI report.

Booklet 7: Science in the Primary School - Assessment, Evaluation and
Record Keeping

What form of assessment is appropriate in science?

Booklet 8: Science in the Primary School - Resources

a. Organisation of resources for science - a strategy.

b. Pupil materials.

c. Kits.

d. Books for pupils and teachers.

e. School broadcasts.

f. Microcomputer programme.

g. Documents for teachers.

Case histories

A number of case histories from schools are to be included in the package.
For example, how a school formulated its policy, science/health links.

These drafts were sent to members of the Advisory Committee, the
40 schools involved in the policy producing exercise and the Scottish
Education Department for comments. The comments were used to amend the
booklets which were then redrafted and sent out to a further 50 schools
for comment.

Once these last comments are received, the booklets will be further
modified. After a national course to be held in Moray House College of
Education, Edinburgh in April 1985, the booklets will be sent to every
school in Scotland. Some video and tape slide material will be sent to
education authorities. The dissemination will be accomplished with the
assistance of a small group drawn from different parts of Scotland as
part of the follow-up to the national course.

One important aspect that must be accepted by all parties is that the
formulation and implementation of a policy for science is a long-term
process. A minimum period of three years is envisaged as the time required.

1.7.6 FUTURE RESEARCH

1.7.6.1 As we see more science being developed in the primary school, the
whole question of the transition between primary and secondary becomes
important. How best can this transition be achieved?

1.7.6.2 The whole question of assessment in this area, at present being
covered by the Assessment of Performance Unit set up by the Department of
Education and Science, is a possible area for future research.

1.7.6.3 Does technology have a place in the primary school?

1.7.6.4 How can teachers in remote areas best be supported?

1.8 POSSIBLE USES OF COMPUTERS:
THE UNITED KINGDOM EXAMPLE

by

Alistair J Fyfe, Scotland

1.8.1 SUMMARY

1.8.1.1 *Introduction*

This section will introduce readers of the paper to the way in which microelectronics and computing has been introduced to schools in the United Kingdom. Mention is made of two specific projects in Scotland and the Department of Trade and Industry scheme which allow primary schools to purchase a microcomputer at 50% of the normal cost.

1.8.1.2 *Uses of microcomputers in the classroom*

This is the major part of the paper and describes the ways in which teachers are using microcomputers in primary schools. The applications covered are:

> simulation;
>
> calculation;
>
> information storage and retrieval;
>
> control;
>
> drill and practice;
>
> teaching the computer;
>
> problem solving;
>
> adventure games;
>
> electronic blackboard;
>
> extension to the curriculum.

1.8.1.3 *Conclusions*

The paper concludes by highlighting a number of areas of concern and by looking to the immediate future. The final conclusion is that Scotland has considerable experience of the use of computers in primary school classrooms to support and extend the existing curriculum.

1.8.2 INTRODUCTION

This paper describes the wide variety of ways in which primary teachers make use of computers in their classrooms. In addition, there is a short introductory section which outlines the relevant historical aspects of the introduction of computers to primary schools in the United Kingdom. The concluding section attempts to highlight some of the areas of concern which have arisen and some likely areas of development in the immediate future. It is not appropriate in this paper to present a detailed description of the education system in the United Kingdom; this information can be obtained from other sources but a few general facts may provide useful background for readers of this paper.

The first point is that education in Scotland is organised differently from education in the rest of the United Kingdom and, although the differences are perhaps more noticeable in secondary education, there are significant differences in primary education also. For example, children remain in primary schools in Scotland until the age of 12 whereas in the rest of the United Kingdom they normally transfer to secondary schools at age 11. To promote the introduction of microelectronics and computing into schools, central government established the Scottish Microelectronics Development Programme (SMDP) in Scotland and the Microelectronics in Education Programme (MEP) in the rest of the United Kingdom. These two organisations have different remits and roles which reflect the differences between the education systems. For such reasons, this paper is, in fact, a description of the uses of computers in primary schools in Scotland.

In general terms, the administration of education is undertaken by local government (there are 12 regional and island councils in Scotland) with some guidance given by central government. Such guidance will often relate to curricular matters and be based on advice from the Consultative Committee on the Curriculum (CCC) through its Committee on Primary Education (COPE). At present there are more than 25,000 primary schools in the United Kingdom (about 2,500 in Scotland) and on average there are 10 teachers in each school. Class size varies but does not exceed the contractual maximum of 33.

The first steps in the introduction of computers to Scottish primary schools were taken in the late 1970s with the establishment of some research and development projects. For example, a two-and-a-half year research project funded by the Scottish Education Department (SED) and by the Scottish Microelectronics Development Programme (SMDP) was established in Dundee College of Education. The chief aims of the project were to investigate the organisational and managerial constraints on microcomputer use in the primary school classroom and to develop software suitable for primary school children. The project team worked with schools in central Fife and Tayside regions and produced a report in 1982 (1). Also in 1979, the Committee on Primary Education (COPE) established a project through its Committee on Environmental Studies in the Primary School. This was based in the Curriculum Development Centre in Moray House College of Education and a number of primary schools in the Lothain region. The aim

_____

(1) Microcomputers in Primary Education, Dundee College of Education, 1982.

of this project was to produce software for use in primary schools on the theme of moving to a new community. The report on this project has recently been published by SMDP (1). These are only two of a number of projects which were established about this time and enabled primary teachers to develop their interest in the use of microcomputers in primary schools.

The introduction of computers to primary schools was encouraged by the Department of Trade and Industry (DTI) which established a scheme in September 1982 which would allow each primary school in the United Kingdom to buy a microcomputer system at 50% of the normal cost. DTI identified three different computer systems which they would support and, through the local education authorities, provided 50% of the cost of an agreed hardware specification. The package supplied also included a "Primer Pack" of computer software and other background material for teachers. This has led to a rapid increase in the number of microcomputers in primary schools.

1.8.3 USES OF MICROCOMPUTERS IN THE CLASSROOM

The uses made of computers reflect the curriculum of the primary school. As mentioned above, guidelines on curricular matters are issued by central and local government and may be based on recommendations from COPE. Advisory documents which are relevant to the introduction of computers include Primary Education in the Eighties (2).

There are many ways in which people have attempted to classify the uses of microcomputers in schools. None is entirely satisfactory. One reason for this is that programs which are developed for one purpose may be used by other teachers for an entirely different purpose which was not envisaged by the original program author. For example, a package which was written to introduce secondary school pupils studying computing to the ideas of word processing has proved to be just as useful in primary schools to provide motivation for certain children, particularly those with handwriting difficulties. It is inevitable, therefore, that in any classification some applications will be missed or particular programs may fit in more than one category. The breakdown used in this paper is based on that first published by W T Beveridge (3). In this case, the categories have been slightly modified and the examples given have been chosen to reflect applications of the use of computers in the primary school.

1.8.3.1 *Simulation*

Simulation is a powerful teaching technique which has been in use for many years before the introduction of computers into schools. However, the computer has made the technique available to a wider range of teachers who perhaps felt that the burden of managing the simulation was too great or

---

(1) The New Community, SMDP and Moray House College of Education, 1984.

(2) Primary Education in the Eighties, COPE.

(3) The New Era, Journal of Educational Fellowship, Volume 65, No. 2, 1984.

who now feel that the flexibility of the computer makes some simulations much more realistic. There are many good illustrations of which the following is only one.

In 1545 the English fleet set sail from Portsmouth to meet the French navy. King Henry VIII watched from the shore as his flagship, Mary Rose, led the fleet into battle. Unfortunately, Mary Rose foundered due to mishandling and sank with the loss of 400 men. In the early 1970s a group of enthusiasts located the wreck and a project was established to attempt to raise the remains of the Mary Rose and preserve them in a museum on land. The raising of the wreck was successfully completed in 1982. At about the same time an enterprising publisher produced a computer simulation of the raising of the Mary Rose.

It is an excellent example of the simulation type of program because it involves work at the computer and work away from the computer with additional support resources being provided with the teachers pack. There are, in fact, three stages within the program with the pupils first acting as navigators, then as divers and finally as archaeologists. This has proved to be an extremely popular program with schools, particularly in recent times because of the interest in the Mary Rose. It remains to be seen if the interest is sustained by using the program in a general way in connection with marine archaeology.

Like many other simulations, MARY ROSE involves a considerable amount of off-computer activity. This particular program generates much fascinating discussion between children as they discuss the decisions which have to be taken.

Simulation is a powerful technique which can be used when there is a need to give children experience of a situation which would be extremely difficult or impossible to set up in real life. This may be because an historical event has to be simulated or the situation in question is too dangerous, too time consuming or too difficult to set up. The introduction of the computer to support the simulation is an important development since it makes it easier for the teacher to pursue situations and, for example, to ask questions which begin "What if ...". The underlying model can be examined methodically using different sets of data and the changes in results studied. One of the great attractions of the computer simulation is that it may well allow a whole variety of outcomes to be considered while other approaches would force deductions to be made from very limited data.

1.8.3.2 *Calculation*

Computers were originally designed to assist mathematicians with complicated calculations. Modern machines are, of course, capable of much more but still retain their number-crunching power and this may be utilised on occasion in a primary school classroom. For example, the HISTOGRAM program can easily be used by children to analyse the results of some local survey which they have undertaken. The program will draw bar charts from a set of numeric data. The user can choose the interval width and whether horizontal or vertical bars are to be used.

It would also be possible to include within this section some applications in which the computer is being used to monitor external equipment. Some primary schools are experimenting with the use of their school computer to capture data from, for example, an electronic thermometer which allows them to accumulate data over either a long or a short period. The advantage of the computer is that it can accept values either at very long or very short intervals and then display the information graphically on the screen. Difficulties with manipulating data can be avoided allowing the prime concern to be the interpretation of results.

As with all uses of the computer, this one should be adopted with care. The computer should never be used to replace practical tasks which children can actually undertake. It should be used to extend the range of activities by allowing children to experiment or perform calculations which would be beyond their scope without the machine to assist.

The use of the computer in the classroom, like the introduction of calculators, will change the needs of mathematical learning. More emphasis will need to be given to the understanding of such things as place value. The computer will not merely complement the existing curriculum but will lead to its modification.

1.8.3.3 *Information storage and retrieval*

This covers a wide range of uses of computers in commercial applications where, for example, government, banks, supermarkets and airlines, use large computers to store huge amounts of information which can be accessed and updated quickly and regularly. In the primary school, it will be important to introduce children to the techniques which are used for storing and retrieving information from computers. Already teachers are taking up this task with enthusiasm. There are two main ways in which educational information retrieval systems such as FACTFILE or QUEST can be employed.

1.8.3.3.1 Teachers may use a previously constructed data base of information on a particular topic. A common example of this is information which has been selected from census data. This has already been done in various parts of the country and is available for use in schools from a number of sources. It may even be that the teacher is simply making use of local information which has been collected previously by the school. When the program is used in this way the children concentrate on the methods which may be used to access the information in the data base. The children, therefore, become familiar with the construction of logical expressions which enable them to make selective accesses of the data held in the computer.

With advances in technology, it is becoming increasingly possible that schools will be able to use their microcomputers to retrieve information from large commercial or educational data bases. In the last year there has been a significant increase in the number of schools using PRESTEL (a national viewdata system run by British Telecom). It is only a matter of time until they gain access to other data bases and encourage other schools to explore the possibilities of telecommunications.

1.8.3.3.2 An alternative way of using a data base package is as a resource
in a classroom project which involves the collection and analysis of
information. In this case, it is likely that the main thrust is not directly
related to the use of the computer program but to the way in which the
information is to be collected and organised. Children, therefore, are
given skills in the classification, collection and inputing of information
to a computer data base as well as its subsequent analysis.

One of the most important lessons to be learned from the use of
information retrieval packages concerns the type of classification used.
It is possible that essentially the same information may be organised in
slightly different ways for different purposes. For example, considering
information about pond animals, it would be possible to provide information
about a number of animals to programs such as ANIMAL (see Section 6 below),
FACTFILE or POND ANIMALS. With each program the information provided is
essentially the same but it will be organised in different ways. It is one
of the most important messages of the use of such packages that different
classification systems are possible and so the use of different systems
must be considered.

There is a need, which is already being met by certain packages
(eg FACTFILE and PICFILE), for children to be able to make mathematical
interpretations of data as well as logical selection. This leads children
into an awareness of some of the fundamentals of present day computing and
they will need to be conscious of the distinction between numeric and non-
numeric data. It also emphasises the fact that some children need the help
of graphical representation to enable them to make the appropriate
deductions. This is an interesting point worth noting because it is one
place in which the fact that equipment and software for primary schools
needs to be more sophisticated than that for older children.

1.8.3.4 *Control*

Another major commercial application of computers is beginning to find its
way into primary school classrooms for, even very young children can be
taught to control devices by using a computer. For example, Edinburgh
University and SMDP are investigating how infant children (5-7 years) can
be introduced to Turtle graphics using a BBC microcomputer controlling a
floor robot. This enables them to form certain geometric concepts as well
as allowing them to develop very simple programs for controlling the
device. Such programming concepts can be picked up again later in the
school (see Section 7 on problem solving).

As schools gradually acquire more equipment, they will increasingly
turn their attention to additional peripherals which can be used with their
micro. This will open up other possibilities for the use of computers to
control equipment. For example, with a suitable interface it is possible
to connect a school microcomputer to a Lego Technik model. The computer
can then be used to control motors allowing the children to move models
forward and back or turn left and right. This will be a valuable introduction
to the way in which computers are being widely used in the manufacturing
industry.

1.8.3.5 *Drill and practice*

There are probably more programs of this type than of all the other types put together. They are of variable quality and this, together with the fact that the use for drill and practice has been somewhat overplayed in the past, has meant that there has been a backlash against the use of school computers for drill and practice work. However, there are some advantages in this particular application. A computer may present problems in a much more attractive way, thus providing motivation for the children; it can be programmed to be patient and sympathetic to the child who is having difficulty; it may maintain a record of pupils achievement for subsequent examination by the teacher. The important question that any teacher should ask before using a program of this type (or of any other type) is

> "Does this program allow something to be done which cannot be done by other methods?"

If the teacher always keeps this in mind then drill and practice programs are a useful addition to a teacher's range of options and can usefully complement and supplement other materials.

1.8.3.6 *Teaching the computer*

It has often been said that if one wishes to know a particular subject, one should try teaching it. For school pupils the computer can help by playing the role of the student. The best example of this is the program ANIMAL in which the computer is expected to teach the computer how to differentiate between different animals. Most versions of this program begin with the computer knowing only two animals which can be distinguished by a single question with a yes or no answer. If the pupil thinks of an animal which the computer does not "know" then the computer will ask the child to define the animal by asking questions such as the following (input from the child is underlined).

Is it a blackbird? <u>No</u>.

I give up!

Please tell me your animal. <u>Dog</u>.

Please type in a question that would

> distinguish a dog
> from a blackbird.

<u>Does it fly</u>

For a dog the answer would be? <u>No</u>.

The "knowledge" of the computer is thereby extended and this process can be continued. At the end of the session, all of this information may be stored on tape or disc for use on subsequent occasions and so quite a comprehensive set of animals and questions can be accumulated.

The exercise provides excellent practice in the use of hierarchical structures and can be applied to many different topics. The program itself has been adapted and now exists in a variety of forms some of which allow the teacher to define the subject to be classified beforehand (eg SEEK). The idea can then be applied to a variety of situations such as animals, leaves or occupations.

1.8.3.7 *Problem solving*

In recent times, teachers in both primary and secondary schools have become increasingly conscious of the need to ensure that children are given practice in problem solving. Particularly in secondary schools the emphasis has been, perhaps, too much on the routine application of techniques and too little on problem solving. The result has been that children have difficulty in forming strategies for solving problems. Teachers are now looking for ways in which they can provide practice in problem solving and the computer can help at a variety of levels.

First there are some computerised versions of some well-known mathematical puzzles. An example of one such would be FARMER in which a dog, a chicken and a sack of grain have to be transferred to the opposite side of a river by a farmer who owns a boat only large enough for himself and one other passenger. The problem is to organise the transfer in such a way that the chicken is not left alone with the grain and the dog is not left alone with the chicken. Such problems are interesting but don't demand the use of the computer and once the solution is known, there is no further point in using the program.

At a slightly higher level are programs such as PAPER ROUND and WATCHPERSON. In these cases, the computer allows the pupil to have several attempts at finding a best solution. The context of the problem can then be slightly changed or made slightly more difficult so that the pupil can apply a similar strategy to solving the new problem. In this way, children can be introduced to the idea of searching for a strategy which they can then confirm by applying it to other problems. As with drill and practice, the computer is a patient tutor allowing the children to have as many attempts as necessary to form their strategy. Children should be encouraged to try different approaches and to examine why some work and some do not. They should be encouraged to keep trying if a chosen strategy does not work and should not be made to feel insecure if they do not get the correct answer first time.

The field of problem solving is perhaps the one in which the computer may have the greatest role to play in education. Careful use of Turtle graphics programs leading on to programming in languages such as LOGO should provide wide scope for the practice of problem solving. LOGO enables a structured approach to be used and children should be encouraged to develop the use of procedures at every opportunity. Successful completion of a program is not an end in itself and the method used to solve the problem is just as important as getting a program which runs.

1.8.3.8 *Adventure games*

There is little doubt that using the computer in the classroom is a
powerful motivation for children. There are many illustrations of
situations in which children will readily undertake tasks using a computer
while similar manual tasks are difficult to sustain. Consider, for
example, the Sinclair Spectrum version of THE HOBBIT. The book by Tolkien
is popular among teachers of upper primary children (10-12 years) and the
computer package consists of an adventure game and a copy of the book. The
computer program opens by displaying an attractive graphic of a country
landscape together with a brief description of the location. The pupils
have to describe the actions which they wish to take in a kind of natural
language, the limitations of which are described in the program
documentation. The computer keeps a score which increases as the pupils
get closer towards the goal of recovering the treasure. Familiarity with
the text undoubtedly helps the children progress through the adventure
game and they have been known to read the book several times in order to
be fully conversant with all the details of the story. By using the
computer program the children are motivated to read the book more carefully
than they would otherwise.

1.8.3.9 *Electronic blackboard*

There are still situations in which the teacher may wish to illustrate a
point to a group of children or even to the whole class. If this involves
reference to diagrams then the computer may be used instead of the
blackboard.

There are many good examples of this application to be found in
mathematics and science. For example, the program DIFFER illustrates
graphically the various methods which may be used to subtract numbers.
Another example would be the program LOCKS which demonstrates how canal
locks operate. Both of these programs are quite specific to elements which
may or may not form part of a curriculum in a particular school. There are
other more powerful programs which are "content free" and which may be used
in this way. One is the HISTOGRAM program mentioned in Section 2. Also
in this category is TELEDIT. One use is to allow teachers to construct
a series of screens which may be either text or block graphics to illustrate
teaching points. These can then be called up by the teacher in a
predetermined order. Again the teacher must provide the material to be
displayed and so the program can be used in a variety of situations. The
resolution of the graphics is not great but the quality of the text display
is good and a range of colours is available for highlighting purposes.

1.8.3.10 *Extension of the curriculum*

It could be argued that this category is redundant because the examples
given could be incorporated into earlier sections. However, it is
important to emphasise the fact that the computer will not only complement
the existing curriculum but will extend and modify it as well.

For example, primary schools are introducing pupils to word processing.
This is being done for two reasons. First, children whose handwriting is
not good are sometimes discouraged from writing stories simply because the
final product looks untidy or messy. Using the classroom computer as a

word processor, the final product of all children is much the same in terms of quality. Children with poor handwriting can produce a final product which is just as attractive as those whose handwriting is good. They are thereby stimulated to write imaginative stories knowing that they will be as attractively presented as those written by other children.

At the same time, children are being introduced to the skill of word processing. It is important that all children develop an awareness of how the computer can assist everyday tasks and this is just one way in which this can be achieved. In this way, the use of the word processor extends the curriculum.

Also, it is a well-known fact that children in the United Kingdom find the sound and graphics facilities of modern home and school computers quite addictive at times. These facilities allow the teacher to present children with material which is more attractive than would otherwise be possible. Sound and colour can combine to maintain the concentration of the child on the problem under discussion. Animation can be used to demonstrate situations which would be difficult to illustrate in any other way.

Many of the games programs for these micros use very sophisticated sound and graphics routines and so the children are very familiar with the machine's capabilities. There are two implications of this for teachers and educational software developers. The first is that these machines provide a unique opportunity to attract and maintain the attention of young learners. The second is that these young learners will be very critical of the kind of software which they are asked to use in schools and will compare it with the games software which they run at home.

1.8.4 THE SCOTTISH EXPERIENCE

The introduction of microcomputers to primary schools in the United Kingdom is proceeding rapidly. With six months of the DTI scheme still to run, over 80% of primary schools have already had applications accepted. It is too early to base any conclusions on the findings of research but some early impressions of success and failure will be of interest. A number of areas of concern for schools have already emerged and these are

1. hardware;
2. software;
3. teacher training;
4. support services;
5. effect on the curriculum.

1.8.4.1 *Hardware*

Initially there is great concern in schools about hardware. There are usually two main problems - where will the money come from and which machine should be bought. In fact, money has come from a variety of sources, for example:

- central government through the DTI scheme;
- local authorities;
- profits from fund-raising events.

In the case of primary schools, the choice of machine is usually
restricted to those supported by DTI even when additional machines are
being purchased. The choice may well be further limited by advice from
the local authority attempting to standardise on one particular model.
Greater difficulty for schools arises when there is no guidance from the
local authority. In such circumstances the choice, particularly of the
first machine, is very difficult.

It is impossible to be sure of the influence of certain factors on
the selection of equipment. It can hardly be coincidence that the numbers
of APPLE and Commodore microcomputers purchased by secondary schools
declined rapidly after the introduction of the Micros in Schools scheme
which supported other computer systems. Certainly, in primary schools,
the choice has tended to be almost exclusively between the BBC, RML and
Spectrum because of the support available from central government.

However, commercial and technical factors will be important as well
and it may be that many schools would have bought BBC and RML micros in
any case because of their high specification. Cost is an important factor
and, in some cases, an overriding one. It is difficult to believe that
BBC and particularly RML would have sold so well to primary schools had
DTI support not been available. Already it is becoming apparent that
problems related to hardware purchase are changing. The selection of
machine is easier and the difficult choice is between additional machines
and extra peripherals such as printers and disc drives. Generally, greater
concern is now being expressed about software and teacher training.

1.8.4.2 *Software*

If microcomputers are to be used successfully in schools then it is essential
that there is a good supply of high quality software which will meet the
requirements of the school curriculum. In the last two years in the United
Kingdom there has been a proliferation of software from small independent
companies, medium-sized firms and large publishing houses, all with programs
aimed at the primary school market.

A significant alternative method of developing software which will be
readily accepted by teachers is to have them closely involved in the
development process. In Scotland, for example, there is a Software
Development Project working at present to produce a number of new pieces
of software. In this project, the teachers have the major role; they have
to produce ideas and program specifications for the programmers. Once
programs have been written, the teachers are responsible for testing them
in schools and writing appropriate documentation. In this way it is hoped
that the software produced will meet the needs of the classroom teacher and
so greatly assist the development of the use of microcomputers in primary
school.

1.8.4.3 *Teacher training*

Pre-service training needs to reflect the changes being brought about by
the introduction of microcomputers to schools. Courses for primary teachers
are being radically altered for other reasons and this has given the
opportunity to ensure that all new teachers have received a minimum level
of training. However, this will have little influence on the expertise
among teachers generally. The demands for training from serving teachers
have been very considerable.

There are different types of expertise which are required. All teachers need to be familiar with the equipment provided and to have a basic knowledge of how to make use of the computer in the classroom. At a higher level, additional training is often required in the use of some of the more sophisticated software packages such as word processing systems or data base packages. Finally, there are demands for training teachers to a high level of technical competence so that they can assist and support other teachers. In the United Kingdom the demand for training from teachers has been very considerable and greater than the usual training agencies can cope with. The implications of this are being examined. Colleges and local authorities are concentrating on ensuring that there are trained teachers in each school which possesses a microcomputer. Other organisations such as the Open University and the BBC are making important contributions.

1.8.4.4 *Support services*

With the introduction of such a sophisticated piece of technology as a microcomputer to a primary school, it is inevitable that teachers will encounter problems and need assistance. They will have questions about equipment - how it operates; what additional equipment is available; how much it costs; from whom it can be obtained. They will be concerned about purchasing software and trying to ensure that they do not waste money on software of poor quality. They will have questions about classroom management and organisation since the computer may place strains on the classroom organisation or teaching style which is currently used. There will also be the question of maintenance of equipment; how should faulty equipment be repaired? In Scotland, there are many ways in which schools may obtain answers to such questions. COPE gives advice on curriculum matters, SMDP is involved in software development and distribution and the local authorities have advisers, working groups and software review groups which can help with a wide variety of problems.

1.8.4.5 *Effect on the curriculum*

Last, but not least, there is discussion about the school curriculum. It has already been stated that the introduction of microcomputers will lead to changes to and extensions of the curriculum. Existing priorities will change and the place of computer awareness in the primary school will need to be carefully examined. The important role to be played by computers must be recognised so that its influence may be taken account of whenever curriculum issues are discussed.

1.8.5 THE FUTURE

The previous section outlined the main areas of concern and, in each case, attempting to meet the identified needs is going to require additional resources. This demand for additional resources comes at a time when school rolls are falling and budgets are being cut. However, it is clear that attempts are being made to meet this demand at this difficult time.

As an illustration, one can refer to the situation regarding the acquisition of hardware for secondary schools about three years ago. At the time some schools were still struggling to find money to buy their first micro. They are still struggling to find money for micros but now it is to add to their pool of five or ten or even 20 micros. In a survey conducted in September and October 1983 it was found that in 25% of the secondary schools in the sample there were more than 10 microcomputers. More recent figures from one particular authority in Scotland indicate that the average number of micros in their primary schools is now three.

The conclusion is that although it is not easy to predict how immediate problems will be solved, solutions will be found. It will not be possible to meet all of the demands which have been identified above but local authorities and teachers are keen to go as far along the road as possible. Indeed, the highest priority must be to ensure that the present level of interest and commitment to the innovation is sustained.

The rapid pace at which the technology develops makes it difficult to make plans for much more than a year or two ahead. The education system is learning to adapt to this new situation in order that it may take advantage of the possibilities offered by the introduction of computers to schools.

Conclusion

The Scottish experience is that the computer has a fundamental role to play as a delivery system for learning. Computers are being used to support and extend the curriculum. The most important issue is not related to the number of machines in schools or to the range of computing topics being taught. Instead, it is related to the type of software which can be used to support a developing curriculum. This and other issues are discussed in the report of the New Community Project.

1.9 POSSIBLE USE OF COMPUTERS IN PRIMARY EDUCATION - THE EXAMPLE OF FRANCE

by

by Frédéric Robert

1.9.1 SUMMARY

Research into the use of computers in primary schools is still not very
advanced in France. The earliest studies, which had the most influence
despite some reservations which still exist, were based on the LOGO systems
and language (and it was LOGO, incidentally, that was chosen as the medium
for the current schemes for initiating schoolchildren in computer science).
The present climate of effervescence is reflected in the great efforts being
devoted to the design of software and various types of hardware as well as
systems suitable for schoolchildren. On the other hand, research (and the
evaluation thereof) into computer-aided education, in the traditional sense
of the word, is virtually non-existence in France at this level. The world
of innovation is not very interested in this aspect or is even fairly hostile
towards it on theoretical grounds: innovation enjoys no priority in the
official objectives of the introduction of computer science into primary
schools, precisely because of the lack of advanced research in this field.
The expectations of practising teachers contrast fairly sharply with these
conceptions, and substantial divergences are therefore likely. The advent
of telematics and the possible connection of micro-computers to these networks should open up prospects for communication between users, diversify
the products available, and allow children to learn to use documentary
services and consult databases designed for them.

1.9.2 INTRODUCTION

In the early 1970s there was virtually no interest in the use of computers
in primary schools in France, although a large-scale experiment was gradually
being set up in secondary schools. It was only in 1975, when the existence
of LOGO and the work of the team associated with S.Papert became known, that
the first studies, then the first trials began, at the Institut National de
la Recherche Pédagogique (INRP - National Institute for Educational Research)
and at various 'instituts de recherche sur l'enseignement des mathématiques'
(IREM - Research institutes for the teaching of mathematics). These
studies and projects are still fairly confidential. The image of computer
science in the education world was, then, still mainly negative (dehumanis-
ing technology, supervision, bureaucracy, etc), even among the most open-
minded members of educational movements who are usually the first to show an
interest in new facilities. Things changed fairly quickly however, with the
appearance of micro-computers and the resultant shift in attitudes. The
report on "Education and the computerisation of society" ("L'éducation et
l'informatisation de la société") prepared under the direction of

J.C.Simon at the request of the President of France and published in 1980,
contains a chapter on primary education. Reference is made in the report to
the need to introduce computer science into schools at primary level,
despite the lack of assessment of the use of computers as educational aids
at this level: the report argued that such introduction was justified by
the technical and social aspects of computer science. However, it clearly
stated that it did not seem advisable to envisage the widespread introduction of data-processing facilities into schools, mainly because of their
cost (primary schools are equipped by local authorities, whose financial
resources vary widely) but also because of the problem of teacher training,
which would necessarily take many years if undertaken on a general scale,
given the large number of teachers and the capacity of the training system.
The report therefore recommended that existing experiments should be
encouraged and extended in the hope that evaluation thereof would lead to
appropriate educational applications. It also set out precise recommendations for the initial and in-service training of primary teachers.

Three years later, even though the pace of research and experiments
had increased only slightly and some decision-makers were proving extremely
cautious about the advisability of introducing computer science into primary
schools, a series of political and ministerial decisions suddenly changed
the situation by shifting it to a different level. The speed-up in provision
of equipment (100,000 micro-computers in five years) at all levels of
education constituted a major innovation in France: for the first time in
the history of primary education, the state was to contribute to the
equipping of schools at this level. The process has already started - first
in 12, then in 16 "départements" designated priority areas. The Schools
Directorate (at the ministry) has been made responsible for organising the
training of teachers in the regions concerned and has published a memorandum
setting out recommendations on educational approaches and the implementation
of arrangements for initiating primary schoolchildren in computer science
and technology. The objectives of this memorandum were fairly substantially
based on the Simon report (mentioned above). We will come back to this
later. In fact, the whole context has changed: not only are the facilities
becoming available but public opinion has been galvanised by the advent of
micro-computers. This is resulting in somewhat light-headed prophetic talk
at all levels, with the media as usualy surpassing the propagandist zeal of
the neophytes. What is new is that teachers, who had shown little willing-
ness to allow themselves to be caught up in the "audio-visual" wave,
suddenly seem to want to jump on to the bandwagon - as much out of
curiosity, interest and hope of reforming an education system which no
longer satisfies its participants as out of any wish to be "with it" or a
fear of not being so.

Against this background, what has been the role of research, what has
been its influence and what scope has it offered for determining potential-
ities and objectives?

1.9.3 RESEARCH AND EXPERIMENTS BASED ON LOGO

When the work by S.Papert's team at the MIT first became known in France,
it aroused the interest and attention of a number of groups which can be
described as follows:

- academic computer scientists involved in the development of languages more advanced than those usually used - for example, the teams working on developments of LISP (from which LOGO came);

- the above-mentioned people may be sub-divided into those who are interested in learning problems for theoretical reasons mainly connected with research into artificial intelligence, and those who adopt an attitude of educational militancy in favour of a different conception of teaching and learning, a conception which they share with:

- educationalists involved in research into systems and methods which enable the usual conditions of education to be changed and encourage initiative and independence in pupils during their learning period;

- specialists in the teaching of scientific disciplines, particularly in the'instituts de recherche sur l'enseignement des mathématiques' (institutes of research into the teaching of mathematics), who find that the ideas developed in connection with LOGO converge with their own work.

There was thus a trend which, in spite of itself or through the will of certain people, soon found itself in a controversial situation with regard to computer-aided education of the type termed conventional because it in no way alters traditional educational relationships. This controversy is a revival - on the theme of computer science and education - of the equally traditional controversy which has been going on among educationalists about learning methods, so-called active methods, the independence and responsibility of pupils, etc. It usually results in attention being focused on the use of facilities instead of on the aim of an overall strategy concerning the organisation of the relations and work of the various participants in education.

The first experiments began in 1977-78, and until 1980-82 there were very few terminals: five "GENERAL TORTUE" (LSI11) appliances in five universities, and one LOGO version on a large computer with a terminal controlling a floor turtle at the INRP (National Institute of Educational Research). The French versions of the language came from Quebec (Franco-Quebec co-operation). Some of these experiments took place in primary schools. Since the material conditions of these experiments left a lot to be desired (one terminal per site), some teams chose to operate in environments more akin to a laboratory than to the normal educational situation: tuition on an individual basis or in small groups outside the classroom, supervised by one or two of the experimenters. During this first trial phase, the children's usual teachers were mostly excluded from these activities, doing no more than providing support when the activities took place in the actual classroom and when they themselves had been given some basic training. The reasons given for this were the inadequacy of the hardware available, the teachers' lack of training and their fear of using a fairly complex system. A less charitable explanation is that the experimenters did not have a proper educational policy for the situation and were anxious to get their hands at last on a tool they had been waiting for for such a long time. The other side of the coin is obvious: all too often the experimenters were too involved in their role as "supervisors" to be able to record the various measures and results systematically. Their observations were therefore confined to general statements in the form of chronological reports and overall impressions that were more anecdotal than analytical.

However, some teams did equip themselves for observing and collecting data more systematically, either by operating in supervisor/observer tandems or by using the micro-computer itself to record everything the children did on the keyboard, the time taken and the results obtained. In fact, these first experiments were of a highly exploratory kind. They all related to the manipulation of mechanical floor turtles or symbolic screen turtles and therefore, whether by accident or design, were all concerned with the universe described by concepts of "turtle geometry". That was the common basis of all this research work, whose objectives varied according to whether the teams concentrated on:

-   observing and studying the children's assimilation of the language (LOGO), their initiation in computer science through the construction of procedures, the manipulation of variables, the use of editors, keyboards, etc;

-   describing and analysing operations relating to the control of "turtles" and the mastering of space and the concepts necessary for constructing and calculating the paths, figures and designs of turtle geometry (which are the ones with the greatest relevance to thought and learning Processes);

-   setting up educational systems around the data-processing system in order to show the phenomena of communication between the different participants, the relations between individuals and groups, etc.

There was a range of situations extending from highly controlled experimentation with children working individually on set tasks, where all their operations with the machine were recorded, to complete "trial and error", where the children had to suggest projects, "discover" operating modes for themselves, including vocabulary, without any tools (language function) being given to them unless they asked for them or explicitly suggested them! In fact, since there is no detailed chronological description of the conversations between children and adults, it is always difficult to tell exactly what happened in such cases, who asked or suggested what, and precisely what suggestions and information were supplied during such exchanges. Curiously, the same designs or fairly similar products were found to recur in different experiments and places, which raises questions about the spontaneity of the children's suggestions.

On the other hand, clear differences were to be observed in the structure of the procedures written by the children. Those who were taught by experimenters with a concern for language, methods and reasoning produced more structured procedures (use of a larger number of parameters, "REPEAT",loop procedures, etc) than the others, who often lined up long series of patiently repeated instructions. Of course, these tools were supplied by the experimenters who often explicitly asked the children to use them to construct this or that figure.

These first experiments in primary schools were carried out mainly with children aged between 9 and 11-12. The experiment conducted with the greatest degree of control took place with children aged between 8 and 9 years. The experiments lasted for varying periods, ranging from several sessions to a complete academic year, at an average rate of one session per week, ie about 30 sessions inthe case of the longest experiments.

Despite the often unsatisfactory conditions of these experiments and the vagueness of some of the reports (offset by the lyricism that characterises many LOGO enthusiasts), the results are nevertheless interesting:

- Firstly, a general remark which applies to all situations: the children showed great interest in the activities offered and were able to concentrate for sessions lasting up to an hour or even longer, whereas their normal powers of concentration are supposed to be much more limited. As will be seen later, it is likely that the enthusiasm and dedication of the experimenters and the novelty of the occasion greatly influenced the pupils' motivation;

- The same may be said of the assessments of the communications between children, the exchanges and the collaboration within and between groups. They were not always confirmed subsequently: they obviously varied according to the teaching situations set up. In addition, in order to judge their relevance, it would be necessary to have a description of the organisation of normal relations in the classes concerned, but this has never been described with any accuracy;

- The analyses of the children's behaviour patterns and methods of reasoning when dealing with the relationships and concepts of turtle geometry give a fairly good idea of their validity, especially when the experimenters laid emphasis on this aspect. By the end of the session, the children had tackled, manipulated and often mastered the following:

  . rotation quantities and angle measurements, relations of supplementarity and concordance, closure and apex in the calculation of regular polygons (the closed path theorem);

  . addition and subtraction of numerical values of movement, sometimes including manipulation of negative numbers;

  . symmetrical relations within figures;

  . analysis of regular repeated paths and their breakdown into basic elements (periods) with the aid of the instruction "REPEAT";

  . the parameters of procedures (functions with n arguments), notions of variables and their possible co-variations (reducing or enlarging a figure, halves, quarters, etc).

The fact that the children used a proper experimental approach, with hypotheses, testing and verification, rejection or acceptance of a theory, was closely linked to the guidance they received from the adults. They immediately tried to find a solution to the problem, starting with some invariables serving as a basis for calculations, rather than carrying out a series of tests in order to infer other rules from them. Without guidance, the children re-used whatever empirical procedures proved to work, without really trying to analyse the task or to reduce the amount of writing.

The youngest children (aged 8-9), placed in the situation of guided individual work (reproducing paths with dotted lines starting from various positions), had much more difficulty in manipulating spatial relations (orientation of the symbol to L/R, rotation quantities and measurement of movements). Learning and progress were to be observed only in those who showed an analytical attitude from the outset. The others got no further than a mass of more or less random commands, which confirms by default the importance of interactions with other children and with adults.

Extension and development of research

From 1980 onwards, the teams working on LOGO became grouped together in a 'Recherche co-opérative sur programme' (RCP - Co-operative research group on programming), supported firstly by the INRP (National Institute for Educational Research) and by the Information Technology Agency of the Ministry of Industry, then by the CNRS (National Centre for Scientific Research).

In order to remedy the lack of LOGO equipment in France, and propose other applications, some teams have embarked on the development of software and hardware:

-   implanting of LOGO language models on a micro-computer;

-   construction of prototypes of mechnical floor turtles which can be controlled from a micro;

-   studies of programmable keyboards or simplified input systems: punched-card reader for small children.

Here is a description of one of these as an example of a project which has proved successful with decision-makers:

The INRP team, being interested in the ways in which young children might use turtles (from the age of five, in other words at the end of nursery school and the beginning of primary school), decided to construct a simplified control system which would be independent and easy to use. It took up the idea of a "slot-machine" tried out by the MIT team, and developed a small micro governing a prototype mechanical turtle with input controls in the form of punched cards (eight holes) in a reader-storage unit. This system is a small scale version of LOGO, since it does not just enable the moving unit to be directly controlled by the same commands (forward, reverse, turn right, left, etc) with pre-determined amounts of movement, but also allows the system to be modified for the following purposes:

-   to make the system receptive, the input instructions being memorised but carried out, in sequence, only when the signal is received (EXECUTE);

- to correct errors, remove instructions, delete sequences, etc;

- to transfer a memorised sequence to one of the free addresses with which "blank" cards (so-called procedure cards) correspond.

In this way the children were able to build up procedures a posteriori as with ordinary LOGO and to join them together, if necessary, in order to produce new ones. The card system was chosen both to overcome the lack of a micro-computer (at that time) and to provide a practical manipulation medium for children who were not yet able to master the reading and writing of orderly sequences.

This system was tested with children aged between five and seven. The aim was not only to watch them tackling the spatial operations necessary for controlling the moving unit, but also to see whether they were capable of anticipating and organising a number of instructions in order to draw a path or construct a line. Although, as would normally be expected, many of the children had great difficulty in mastering the spatial relations of directional and rotational operations, particularly when the turtle was in a direction different from their own or when it was necessary to foresee a series of movements, some (albeit uneven) progress was observed in the manipulation of the directly controlled turtle as well as an increasing ability to "pre-programme" a series of instructions (up to a dozen) in order to complete a design (simple figures, capital letters, etc) through compilation of the list of successive commands (the series of necessary cards being lined up on a medium). Children aged between six and seven were initiated in the analysis of a simple repetitive figure (eg staircase, cross, radiating figures, borders, etc) where only the periodic sequence is programmed and is then repeated as often as necessary. About a third of the children managed to manipulate these operations successfully; they were, incidentally, the children who had the least difficulty with spatial relationships. In the course of the experiment, all the children were initiated in the notions of code (of the cards), organisation of a series of instructions, memorisation and execution of a series of memorised series etc, ie various operations typical of data-processing systems.

In 1982, the Ministries of Education and of Industry (Information Technology Agency) decided to have a hundred of these systems manufactured commercially in order to increase the scope for experimentation. The systems were intended for training centres, documentation centres and, above all, teacher training colleges. Since then, the system has become available commercially, the floor turtle being controllable either by a micro-computer or by the card system. Since the beginning of the 1980s, then, there has been the problem of extending the LOGO area of experimentation. The French translation of the language is beginning to become available on various machines, not usually those available in educational establishments. It is necessary to wait for new versions to be installed on the hardware chosen by the ministry. Nevertheless, the number of users, if not experimenters, is growing steadily. At present, various experiments in the use of LOGO are being carried out with children aged between five and eleven, either in the schools themselves or in children's clubs, day hospitals, re-education centres etc. Their results cannot yet be outlined, as there are no reports on them. While the LOGO research teams continue their work, the teacher training colleges and training centres for special education are joining in and carrying out a number of experiments in collaboration with the INRP or the Schools Directorate. The work now in progress may be summarised on the basis of the main trends:

- Some are carrying out work on turtle geometry, concentrating on learning problems from the epistemological and mathematical point of view rather than that of computer science.

- Others are more interested in the problem of introducing children to a technological and data-processing culture and are therefore looking at LOGO primarily as a simpler way of achieving this.

- Yet others are trying to extend the field of application to subjects other than graphics and geometry, eg manipulations of language (syntactic and semantic), music, other robots and models (lifts, cranes, etc).

- Lastly, some are concerned with ways of integrating and using such systems in the education system itself. This is a considerable and as yet unresolved problem liable to hamper the widespread introduction of this system into schools. Assuming that several terminals will be available in each educational establishment (an optimistic hypothesis at the moment), at least two approaches are possible: one terminal could be allocated to one class, which would manage its use and integrate it into normal activities, which is feasible only if individualisation of work or a system of more or less independent small groups is already the established method of functioning. Otherwise, it is necessary to group all the terminals together in one place and assemble the pupils for sequences at regular intervals, which entails the risk of cutting this activity off from other activities and interfering with the interaction between individual or small-group work and the subsequent general exchanges. One training college has tried to investigate a different solution by including parents in the organising team.

What is relatively new in some current experiments is a desire to assess LOGO's contribution by means of techniques other than a simple record of observations, which has been the main procedure up to now. Although it has been possible to describe and analyse methods of reasoning, stages of learning, etc, this has always been done on the basis of specific individual cases or statements relating to "a certain number". However, there is very little information on a quantitative evaluation of the results of the work of all the children and on their ability to solve or deal with this or that problem after 10, 20 or 30 sessions. Some people propose to produce evaluation techniques suited to the types of activities offered and the concepts they support; other think that it is possible to carry out measurements with more general techniques, such as those used in non-verbal tests (particularly spatial tests). However relevant the techniques used may be, it seems only right to begin to look into the problem of evaluation more rigorously than has so far been the case in this field. In this way, it would be possible to compare something else than the claims of the various lobbies. In particular, it seems that even if all the children are still as interested in the LOGO system, the speed and quality of their learning generally correspond fairly closely to those of their normal academic performance. In the light of such observations, it is difficult to continue to claim that LOGO and computer science will provide means of combating failure and reducing inequalities, if one keeps within the same framework and does not use other forms of action. Moreover, it has also been observed that in the case of children with difficulties, their initial enthusiasm wanes quickly if the errors and obstacles accumulate: intolerance of failure is considerable in many, and patience limited in the face of the system's constraints. In such cases, putting too much confidence in spontaneity is likely to lead to serious upsets.

A somewhat impertinent remark may be made to conclude this section: one of the reasons why LOGO is arousing so much interest among those concerned with the introduction of computer science into primary schools is that they see it as a suitable means of developing thought processes, construed, for example, as operations necessary for implementing the experimental method. They believe that it teaches children to analyse difficulties and deal with only one problem at a time. From this point of view, experimenters do not seem to be greatly influenced by the excellence of the system they are offering the children: when they describe the objectives of their research, most of those I mentioned above are included higgledy-piggledy, and it should therefore be expected that a variety of problems will be dealt with simultaneously, such as those concerning initiation in computer science, the development of logical thinking, and the assimilation of operations necessary for geometry, communication and socialisation. However, perhaps that is just one of the ruses employed by researchers to try to interest as many people as possible in their work so as to get financial support for it! That is a constant concern of everyone. Nevertheless, some people are beginning to encounter a problem: if the aim envisaged is to initiate children in the operations and concepts necessary for analysing a task and organising the instructions which must be given to a machine in order for it to carry the task out, the world of turtle geometry is perhaps a minefield: the younger the children are, the more difficulty they have in mastering spatial and geometric relations. Not that the aim should be abandoned, as it is highly significant and concerns fundamental learning processes, but it is perhaps wrong to mix the two things from the outset. That is why so many attempts are now being made to vary the systems and subjects offered.

1.9.4 THE PROBLEM OF COMPUTER-AIDED EDUCATION

Computer-aided education has a poor reputation in France among teachers involved in research, innovation or reform projects who refer more readily to the learning theories derived from Piaget than to those of the behaviourists, whether or not followers of Skinner, who are supposed to be the originators of the conceptions applied to computer-aided education. In fact, the term "computer-aided education" has become a very general expression, which accommodates not only all software of the "dialogue" type, questions and answers, drills and exercises, but also software for the simulation or more or less guided manipulation of data.

The guidelines issued by the Schools Directorate on the introduction of computer science and technology in primary schools set out the following objectives:

-    social and human initiation in the socio-cultural phenomenon of the development of data-processing;

E

- introduction to technology; What is a computer? How does it work? How can it be used in work processes (eg robots, automatons) etc;

- introduction to logistics: What is a programme? How is a task for a machine analysed and organised, concepts of algorithms, etc);

Inorder to achieve the last two aims, the use of LOGO systems is recommended. Moreover, it is clearly stated that the general approach is not that of computer-aided education, ie a learning process aimed at specific contents. Its use is envisaged only for helping children with learning difficulties or in areas where the characteristics of computers are relevant (eg coaching in reading).

In teacher training colleges, most of the staff are afraid, probably quite rightly, of computer-aided education being used inconsiderately for the automation and "dialoguing" of traditional exercises. It is quite apparent that a large number of rank-and-file teachers expect the computer to be an instrument enabling sequences, exercises and drills in arithmetic, mathematics, spelling, grammar, etc to be offered ad lib. It would be dangerous to allow the gap between the conceptions of some and the aspirations of others to widen, otherwise there would be no limit to what could be passed off as computer-aided education. The reason why little material is being published at present is simply that there is not yet a market for it, owing to a lack of hardware; but things are likely to develop rapidly.

On the one hand, even in primary schools, computer-aided education should not be reduced to mere "drills and practice"; but even at that level, of course, problems are posed by the choice of vocabulary and wordings, by division and progression of the content, by the role of duration and tempo etc. At present, however, despite the fact that there are teams and individuals involved in producing computer-aided education software, no research in France has gone beyond the stage of planning and using products designed for primary schools to the stage of systematically evaluating their use in a particular place with a given population.

The only evaluation involving quantitative data (even though the numbers covered were small) was carried out in a private school (Ecole Bossuet in Paris) by means of a series of arithmetic and problem-solving drills derived from the products by the Suppes team at Stanford. This system (DIDAO) works with a server feeding eight terminals. It records the pupils' results and guides their progress from one drill to another. The evaluation covered a year's use with children aged between 9 and 11/12. The school in question used fairly open teaching arrangements, with open-plan classrooms and individualised work. However, the results were not conclusive, and even the children's response was lukewarm. The odd thing was that the system set up was at variance with the school's normal organisational principles. There was no liaison between the computer-aided education workshop's functioning and the work of the ordinary class teachers, who were not concerned with what was going on and did not even watch the children tackling the exercises.

There was therefore a rift - clearly felt by the children - between classroom work and computer work, with virtually no link between the two, and that, together with problems of ill-adjusted tempo and progression, was probably the reason for the failure that occurred.

There is another software package that is notable for the amount of exercises it contains, the number of sessions it offers and the guidance of pupils' progress it permits, namely a package for coaching in reading (ELMO), designed and produced by a team of INRP researchers and teachers belonging to the 'Association française pour la lecture' (AFL - French Association for Reading), who are campaigning for a reading method conceived of as the processing of graphic information received mainly through visual perception. The programme, aimed at improving reading ability beyond the initial learning stage (other programmes are being developed for the initial stage), uses the specific capacities of the computer as a technical instrument for monitoring the parameters of item presentation duration, hence speed, and variations in spatial positioning, division, appearance and deletion, as well as answering times and success rates. The pupils' results are recorded and enable subsequent exercises to be modulated; assessment tests are carried out at regular intervals.

The package has been in regular use in several primary schools for more than a year. The children involved are generally self-sufficient in using the machines, which are either in the classrooms or, more often, in the school's main library. The system is generally distributed to circles which share its authors' ideas. A large-scale experiment, involving not only primary schools but also all levels of education, youth training centres, libraries etc, was proposed two years ago in order to evaluate the performances of various samples of the population as well as the effects of this type of coaching, which is fairly controversial. A decision has still not been taken, partly for financial and technial (choice of media) reasons and partly because reading is at present one of the major problems of education and arguments are rife between the supporters of conflicting approaches. Even on a smaller scale, for example in primary schools, assessment of this type of instrument is indispensable in order to weigh up views put forward by the various sides, or simply to improve methods and products.

Owing to a lack of space, I will leave aside other studies in progress, particularly as they are only just beginning and it is therefore impossible to talk about any results, even in general terms. The position of computer-aided education in France seems unique. Some people talk about an intoler--ble backwardness; this could be taken advantage of to ensure that France does not repeat mistakes made elsewhere, but the opposite is also quite possible. Arguments about learning theories are tending to shift towards the use of instruments as though it was a question of strategies on which the development of everything else depended, whereas it is almost invariably the "everything else" that is immutable and causing the best suggestions (as well as the less good ones!) to get bogged down.

1.9.5 TELEMATICS

Considerable effort is being devoted to telematics in France. There are several experiments that concern education, and at least two of them have involved primary schools since 1982-83. One is the TELETEL project in the Versailles area; the other is the TELEMEDIATHEQUE project in the Bordeaux area. The systems used are the TELETEL ones, and the terminals are of the MINITEL/VIDEOTEX type. In the Versailles area, five schools have been given access to the network. In Bordeaux, it was planned that all primary schools in the Gironde département (approximately 200) will be linked to the network.

Both these systems offer documentary services, games, some computer-aided education software, and an electronic service allowing correspondence between users. However, the documentation which can be accessed on the Versailles network is not specifically aimed at schoolchildren, whereas the Télémediathèque system was primarily designed as a documentary service for children, with the aim of improving the running of a resource centre (that of the 'Centre Régional ou Départemental de Documentation Pédagogique' - the Regional or Departmental Centre for Educational Documentation) which was being used to only 10% of its capacity, by giving its potential users direct access. A base of 2,200 documents was chosen, which can be accessed from about 4,000 descriptors. Access is not by a series of logical choices as is normally the case, but by a series of approximations based on key words which are freely inputted and associated. The system provides a list of documents available on the subject concerned, and the children can ask for them to be sent (by minibus). It has been so successful that the documentary network is now working at full capacity and the number of works ordered by the children has increased considerably. It is assumed that they do not read everything completely, but interest has been maintained and this is a clear sign that it is being used properly.

The other service which has become increasingly important in the two experiments is an electronic system of communication between users. Children in different schools send messages to one another, and in this way a new type of academic correspondence is becoming established. This function is destined to develop considerably. It is of direct value to teachers belonging to Freinet-type educational movements who are investigating the setting up of such networks between their schools.

1.9.6 PROSPECTS AND PROBLEMS

Leaving aside the earliest research based on LOGO, the advent of computer science in primary schools has been a practical issue for only a short time. The emergence of a political will to foster the general introduction and use of such facilities at all levels of education, together with the concomitant shift in public opinion, has resulted in research and thinking on the merits of this or that strategy being caught on the hop. This may be the cause - or the effect (?) - of the inadequacy of research in this field. The state of emergency and turmoil which characterises the current situation means that people are far more involved in the design of hardware, software and systems suitable for use at this level than in assessing them. In addition, the groups which act as "pioneers" in schools, whether they comprise researchers, teacher-trainers or school teachers, are traditionally supporters of methods and tools which encourage activity and independence in children during their learning process - hence the marked lack of interest in computer-aided education, at least in the most conventional sense of the term. The lack of more advanced research in this field is liable to result in an increase in the discrepancy between, on the one hand, experiments which, however interesting, are difficult to put into practice outside their context and, on the other, the daily use of reassuring traditional techniques.

1.10 BROADCASTING AND PRIMARY SCIENCE:
A SUPPORT FOR THE TEACHER

by

Jacqueline Johnstone, Edinburgh

1.10.1 INTRODUCTION

The BBC has supported the development of science in primary schools since
1959 when Junior Science was introduced and was used by more than 70% of
the radio audience. Schools television first became involved with
Exploring Your World in 1965 and Science All Around in 1969. In its 12 year
run, Science All Around underwent a major rethink after six years, and
individual programmes were being modified right up to its last year of
transmission.

Recent reports from the Inspectorate of both the Department of
Education and Science (DES) and the Scottish Education Department (SED)
have issued clear statements about the importance of science for primary
schools and have stressed the need for head teachers to develop this
area of the school curriculum.

However throughout the many projects to encourage primary science one
aspect has always posed a problem - how do you gain the confidence of those
teachers who, for many and very understandable reasons, are afraid of
getting started?

At about the time of these reports, the School Television Department
was planning a replacement for Science All Around and rather than develop
the series for the existing audience of teachers who were confident of
working with science, the opportunity was taken to develop a new series to
help those teachers who were being encouraged to get involved for the
first time.

The result was "Science Workshop" - a series of weekly science
programmes which began in autumn 1981.

1.10.2 SCIENCE WORKSHOP

The series attempted to provide programmes that would help all teachers to
involve children in the age range 9-12 in the practical experience of
science - the focus was on learning skills.

During 1981-82 there were 12 topics in the series. Each topic was
chosen to provide the practical activities which would develop certain
identified skills. For example the first topic of fruits and vegetables
was about observing and recording. Each topic was supported by two

20 minute programmes. The first programme contained core work and was
largely prescriptive. It aimed to take both the teachers and pupils through
the preliminary stages leading to a single practical classroom activity. As
well as introducing the topic and the skill, the programme also provided
an in-service training element for teachers. Where possible, it was filmed
with one of the presenters, David Hargreaves, himself an ex-teacher, talking
with children to illustrate for teachers the sort of situation they might
find themselves in and how they might control and use it to develop the
children's ideas.

Since the first programme of each topic always led to a particular
classroom activity, it was felt that the teachers would require a
permanent record of what was expected of them. The broadcast by its very
nature can only provide an ephemeral experience. Video recording does
offer greater opportunities for more flexible use, but armed with the
knowledge that only a small percentage of United Kingdom primary schools
had recording facilities the extra support came from a pupil book
(published by Longmans) entitled Science Workshop and a set of teacher's
notes published by the BBC.

Particular care was taken over the choice of practical activities.
Not only had they to provide the opportunity to practise skills, but they
had also to involve the teacher in the minimum of preparation and use only
material easily available in every classroom - or in extreme cases from the
local secondary school. Field tests were held in schools all over the
United Kingdom to find out what was practical and possible. A good example
of this was the choice of the runner bean and marrow which were used in the
pilot and were not found to be growing in Scotland. At the request of the
Scottish teachers these were taken out of the final programme.

Another important point was that the work suggested in the first term
(autumn) did not involve the children moving from their seats - an
important consideration for any teacher who is not quite sure what is
going to happen!

The book gave full details of the necessary practical work and
identified the "core" objectives of each topic. In addition the summer
term's teacher's notes placed an emphasis on helping teachers assess for
themselves how the work was progressing in their own classrooms.

The second programme in each topic was of a magazine type aimed to
broaden the children's knowledge and provide opportunities for discussion.
It was not expected that all teachers would follow up the second programme
but rather that they would look on it as providing for themselves and
their pupils an opportunity for enrichment and enjoyment. There were
nonetheless built-in incentives and ideas for further practical work if
teachers wished to go beyond the core.

Topics for 1981-82:

Autumn: fruit and vegetables, materials, fabrics, stability, highlights.

Spring: stretch, weigh and bounce, dissolving tracks, cleaning, animals
of the soil.

Summer: seeds and plants, floating.

Additional topics for 1982-83:

Autumn: bread, paper, analysing colours, joins, hearing.

Spring: sliding, fish, basic patterns, water, stiff shapes.

Summer: twigs and wood, levers.

Although a two year series Science Workshop did not aim to achieve a great deal of scientific progression in any one topic - it set out to use the topics to get the pupils involved in the processes and skills used in science. For example, what is meant by

Observing and recording like a scientist?

When is a test fair?

How can things be sorted out?

How can material and objects be classified?

Each topic was a starting point for short units of practical work - all aimed at encouraging investigation and discussion.

1.10.3 IN-SERVICE TRAINING IN SCOTLAND

Since Scottish teachers had contributed greatly in the piloting of the new series, it was suggested to the producer by HM Inspectorate that some form of useful in-service training might be set up by HMIs, advisers and BBC education officers.

Primary advisers in Lanark and Glasgow selected 11 and 8 schools respectively in each of the divisions. These schools were given between one-and-a-half to two hours in-service training directly linked to the series. At each session the HMI gave a short introduction to the series and the BBC education officer presented the first programme. Teachers were taken through the core follow-up work and introduced to some of the possible extension work which was detailed in the pupil books. Teachers were asked to keep a personal diary of their experiences under certain headings to aid them with later discussions. Each school was visited at least twice by the primary adviser, HMI or BBC education officer. Teachers were also encouraged to write comments direct to the programme producer.

Those schools which had been given a small amount of in-service training directly linked to the series used the programmes in a most effective way. Teachers involved easily moved on to a large amount of practical follow-up, grew greatly in confidence and understood the relevance of the back-up materials. One of the most useful points to emerge from schools not having any introductory in-service was that they found the BBC teacher's notes off-putting and preferred the pupil book. Although this was initially disappointing it has been possible to reflect on comments and to rewrite the teacher's notes for use with the repeat of the first 12 topics in session 1983-84 - more detailed programme content, more direct links to the pupil book, and more specific help with follow-up were a few of the teacher's needs.

In March 1981 after the first two terms of Science Workshop the producer visited a range of Glasgow and Lanark schools to discuss the series with staff and pupils. In addition follow-up meetings were held for those who had received in-service training.

All of these were of great value to the production team - as were teacher's diaries, samples of pupil materials and children's letters.

1.10.4 UNITED KINGDOM REACTION

Since 1981 the response to the series throughout the United Kingdom has been very encouraging. BBC education officers who visit schools to monitor the progress of new series have found the programmes not only to be effective but to achieve what they set out to do - teachers in the target audience are getting enough confidence from the series to do good basic practical science in the classroom and are realising that a skill based series offers them a way towards understanding of what science at this age is all about.

SECTION 2: NATIONAL REPORTS

2.1 THE TEACHING OF SCIENCE IN
IN BELGIAN PRIMARY SCHOOLS

by

Prof. Romain Decambray, Torhout

For some years our Institute Saint-Joseph in Torhout has been pursuing
an original approach to training future primary school teachers how to teach
natural science. On the basis of this approach it has devised a method which
is systematically used during teaching practice. This report outlines the
approach and its implications as regards teaching methods, curriculum and
syllabuses. It concludes with an impression of the results achieved by
this method with primary school children.

2.1.1 CONCEPT OF THE FUNCTION OF NATURAL SCIENCE EDUCATION IN PRIMARY SCHOOL

Teaching is one of the means of providing education. The purpose of
education is to make young people independent. This implies that they must
be capable of taking responsibility for the decisions which need to be taken
in a very wide variety of situations. To this end, they must UNDERSTAND.

The only way to understand is to arrange knowledge, after thinking
about it, in a logical order. Knowledge is made up of observations anchored
in the memory. Furthermore, rational understanding can serve as knowledge.
Since the knowledge used must be accurate if it is to elicit a thorough
understanding, the best form of observation is total observation, that is,
the observation of reality. This kind of observation makes it possible to
use the senses and anchor a complete, undistorted picture of reality in
the memory.

All other methods are incomplete. A photo or slide usually provides
only a two-dimensional image. One simply "looks at" it: the other senses -
hearing, touch etc - are not used. Artificial means are nevertheless
useful for the purpose of abstraction.

If pupils are to receive a good education, they must therefore be
taught careful observation. They must also be taught to think clearly.
Since thinking requires language, the ability to define is also an
essential part of education.

Science has its own thought process - scientific method - comprising
the following stages: observation, description of the problem, formulation
of a hypothesis, experimentation and conclusion. This method tallies
exactly with the process of understanding.

Scientific method	State of the process
1. Observation	1. Observe → know
2. Description of the problem	2. Know → think
3. Formulation of hypothesis	3. Know → think
4. Experimentation	4. Observe → know → think
5. Conclusion	5. Know → think → understand

The teaching of science should therefore be geared to learning to observe, think and, if possible, apply scientific method.

2.1.2 IMPLICATIONS OF THIS APPROACH AS REGARDS CURRICULUM, SYLLABUSES AND TEACHING METHODS

2.1.2.1 *Implications as regards teaching methods*

Since it is important for the pupils to learn to observe, the observation of reality constitutes the starting point for each lesson wherever possible. This is what we call the principle of impression of reality. As the pupils are young, the teaching is confined to external features visible with the naked eye. Internal structure and microscopic and sub-microscopic features will be studied later, in secondary school. It is the pupils who must observe, think and understand. In other words, it is they who must be active during the lessons. The teacher's function is to co-ordinate, organise and guide. Moreover, the activity must not be confined to one pupil or a few pupils: they must all be involved and take part in the activities. This is the second important teaching principle: the principle of active involvement.

2.1.2.2 *Implications as regards curriculum*

The curriculum takes account of the pupils' level of development. In the first four years the teaching of natural science is not included as a separate discipline but is incorporated in what are called "life lessons". It is only in the last two years that provision is made for an hour's "nature study". Accordingly, it is logical that during the early years of primary school attention should be focused on language and concept. Language, which is the basis for thought, must be learnt and developed. In the first and second year the structure and parts of plants, animals and environmental objects of all kind are observed and given names.

From the third and fourth year onwards the focus is not only on concepts but also on the relationships between structure and function, environment and the lives of plants and animals. The pupils learn to see relationships and are encouraged to think. In scientific terms, the relationships they find correspond to the hypothesis. As from the fifth year they can begin to apply scientific method and carry out experiments. Needless to say, the experiments are no more than simple tests and the pupils are not given the terminology corresponding to the various stages of scientific method. The teacher supervises the lesson, follows the scientific method of thought but leaves it to the pupils to formulate the observations, hypotheses and conclusions themselves.

2.1.2.3 *Implications as regards syllabuses*

Since the starting point is always reality, the only subjects dealt with are those for which sufficient material can be found in the immediate surroundings of the school, and hence of the child. It is therefore likely that a school near the coast will choose different topics from a school near a wood or in a town.

Accordingly, the curriculum must be fairly flexible. In this approach it is not, in the final analysis, the topic which is important but the formal training provided by scientific thought. Dealing with topics from the children's immediate surroundings will give them a greater involvement and interest in what is being taught. The tests are carried out with simple materials so that the children realise that they can continue with their experiments on their own at home.

2.1.3 IMPRESSIONS OF THE RESULTS OF THE METHOD

We have learnt from experience that primary school children enjoy natural science lessons: they find them fascinating, take them seriously and have a keen interest in reality and in experiments. This interest obviously has a beneficial effect on their behaviour at school and even prompts them to raise some small problems themselves for critical study.

As to whether they will be able to achieve a higher level of thought more quickly by this means, a much more detailed survey would be needed to answer the question.

2.2 RESEARCH AND DEVELOPMENT IN SCIENCE IN FRENCH SCHOOLS

by

the Experimental Science Team of the
French National Institute for
Educational Research, Paris

There are two papers summing up research work done in this field at the French National Institute for Education Research (INRP) or in co-operation with it:

- The ASTER Bulletin published by the Experimental Science Team of INRP. It sums up a research project on "Pupils' learning processes in experimental science education at primary, lower and upper secondary level (Procédures d'apprentissage des élèves en sciences expérimentales, à l'école primaire, au collège et au Lycée)".

  In this research the team has decided to focus on energy concepts and ecosystems. INRP will publish an intermediary report early in 1985.

- An internal working paper reporting on a series of working sessions concerning a pilot experiment conducted by the School Education Directorate of the Ministry of Education in co-operation with the Experimental Science Team of INRP. This experiment concerns formative evaluation of science education at primary schools, mainly in biology, and in-service education and training of teachers ("l'évaluation formative des activités d'éveil scientifique, à dominante biologique, et formation continue").

The final document summing up the results will be available in the course of 1985.

Anyone interested in this work are kindly invited to make themselves known to INRP, 29 rue d'Ulm, F-75230 PARIS Cedex 05.

2.3 PRIMARY SCIENCE EDUCATION IN THE
FEDERAL REPUBLIC OF GERMANY

by

Prof. Karl Frey and Dr. Roland Lauterbach,
Kiel

2.3.1 THE INSTITUTIONAL FRAMEWORK

The Constitution of the Federal Republic of Germany decrees a period of
schooling as compulsory for all. The authority for the school system lies
with the 10 Länder (states) and West Berlin. Authoritative control
includes regulations on the curriculum, time schedules, professional
requirements, teachers, school buildings and equipment as well as hiring
recruitments of teachers. Costs are commonly covered by the states, the
local community and in some cases by the federal government.

Children must be enrolled in school at the age of six and must continue
their schooling for nine years. The primary level is comprehensive ending
with the fourth year. Thus, primary education generally lasts four years.
The children are 6-10 years old. To pass from one grade to another they
need to accomplish certain requirements, mostly marks based on tests given
during the school year and on the personal judgement of their individual
teacher. German compulsory schooling does not use course credits or central
achievement tests.

2.3.2 THE PLACE OF SCIENCE EDUCATION IN THE OVERALL CURRICULUM

The curriculum consists of the usual school subjects (mother tongue,
mathematics, physical education,etc). These are taught by one to three
teachers. A five or six day school week is divided up into 20 or 25 class
periods built into the daily time frame between 8 am and 1 pm. Students
go home for lunch except in the few all-day schools. Thus, the daily
routine does not correspond to patterns of an "integrated day" or a "school
community life". On the other hand, a teacher is not strictly required to
hold her/his two to four subjects per day in the same order and during the
same time periods. Generally speaking the curriculum is organised as a
flexible series of lessons each devoted to one subject.

Among the subjects one is called "Sachunterricht", which could be
translated as "teaching about things" or "teaching about real objects".
These are phenomena of everyday life such as nutrition, climate, helping
neighbours, social institutions, windmills, bicycle, our ancestors or the
rainbow after a spring shower. Principally, the range of topics is not
delimited except for those instances of a topic which are already
incorporated within the domain of other subject areas.

The "Sachunterricht" was introduced to enlarge, update and redirect the concept of environment. It was to encompass all objects, phenomena and events which children encounter today, including those of technology, television programmes and travel experiences. Moreover, the pupils were to be acquainted with the complex and highly structured physical and social world of an industrialised society, reflecting its technical, scientific, economic, judicial and political dimensions. Emphasis was placed on science and technology as moving forces for industrial progress, adding the view of man-made factuality in two forms:

1.   The explained and   2.   the constructed world.

These two ideas joined with a second line of educational change, ie the notion of "Wissenschaftsorientierung" (science orientation).

The place in the curriculum to implement these ideas was the earlier mentioned "Sachunterricht". It was not a separate subject science per se and it was not meant to be a set of individual disciplines like chemistry or physics. During its short history of 10-15 years this subject has established itself.

2.3.3 THE TIME SCHEDULE

The "Sachunterricht" starts in grade 1 and continues through to grade 4. It is taught throughout the entire school year, since the weekly timetable does not vary during the whole year (from autumn to autumn). "Sachunterricht" averages 3-4 lessons with 45 minutes each per week.

2.3.4 CHARACTERISTICS OF THE SCIENCE CURRICULUM

About half of the topics covered in the natural sciences in primary education are like those one finds in primary schools of all industrialised countries, for example properties of matter (eg states of aggregation, dissolution), electric circuits, light sources, heat, nutrition, basic ecosystems etc. The topics, mainly, are not to be presented by the teacher in lectures, demonstration experiments, blackboard writing or audio-visual media. It is intended that students have opportunities to make direct observations, to build simple experimental devices, to collect and classify objects or phenomena from their surroundings. Generally students can fill out their own work sheets or work books. Thus, it is safe to say that in this respect primary science education in the Federal Republic of Germany intends to cover a broad range of student activities. And this is more or less accomplished in comparison with science education of the secondary schools. Note that neither primary science nor the whole subject "Sachunterricht" has a decisive role in the selection process for the different paths in secondary schooling.

2.3.5 CODIFICATION AND DYNAMICS OF THE CURRICULUM

Over the last 30 years, the following general characteristics of stability and change are noted:

1.   Science education has roots in nature study which was restricted to the childs' immediate neighbourhood. It now represents a relatively clear and delimited part of the large subject "Sachunterricht", where distinct positions of biology, physics

and, to a lesster extent, chemistry can be identified. Experimental work and learning of notions replaced the more intuitive and narrative mode of dealing with nature and the constructed environment. More recently, science education has tried to regain a lost dimension by reinstating a more child-centred approach.

2. Instead of radical changes effected by administrative measures the complexity of the system allows only for a slow evolutionary change.

3. No need was felt to introduce achievement tests or other evaluation in order to guarantee equal standards of learning outcomes. The clusters of programmatic curricula together with the mode of supervision and financing made such assessment unnecessary. That is true for most of the secondary level as well.

2.3.6 TEACHER EDUCATION

Teacher education undergoes three phases. The first phase lasts three or four years and is located either at universities or teacher colleges. It corresponds to a Bachelor degree plus a one or two year Master's degree. The course of study consists of two to four special subjects and educational sciences. Next comes the second phase which lasts one-and-a-half years with approximately 15 class periods of theory per week and between 6 and 15 hours of supervised teaching. Upon passing the exam after the two phases one can get a teaching position. The third phase is a one to ten day in-service education per year, generally on a voluntary basis.

In spite of the comparatively high standard of teacher education in the Federal Republic of Germany there are some difficulties concerning the teaching of "Sachunterricht" and especially its nature, science and technology contents. The legislative and executive autonomy of the Länder in matters of culture and education and the relative independence of universities and teacher colleges in setting up their teacher training courses are responsible for a wide variety of study programmes leading to the teachers' first certificate for primary education. After their three or four years of academic study future teachers may have had neither courses in "Sachunterricht" nor the sciences, or even in primary education. More often, only one of these requirements is lacking.

To be able to cope with these difficulties more effectively, a group of teacher educators from universities, teacher colleges and institutions of second phase (many of whom are also engaged in the third phase) joined in a working group organised by the Institute of Science Education (IPN) and endorsed by the "Arbeitskreis Grundschule", an organisation of some 8,000 primary school teachers, university teachers and parents. This group worked out suggestions on how to qualify teachers for "Sachunterricht" during the first and second phase of training. After consultation with administrative officials and a symposium held in 1982 the suggestions were disseminated as a proposal for possible measures to be taken (Lauterbach, Marquardt 1982, Lauterbach, Marquardt, Bolscho 1983).

2.3.7 CURRICULUM DEVELOPMENT

Curriculum development understood in its traditional sense means the construction of learning and teaching material in a certain systematic way. The overall moving and conserving forces as well as the instances of codification have been characterised in the last sections. Now it might be useful for an international comparison to look at four specific points of interest.

2.3.7.1 *School books*

The editors and groups of authors for the large publishing companies which share a large part of the market have the heaviest impact on curriculum. They almost constantly improve and adjust their curricular systems. The quality of the common school books and worksheets has improved considerably during the last 10 years using a rather broad variety of sources, among them half a dozen journals dealing partly with science education as well as assorted grey materials (such as pamphlets, correspondence, newsletters and the like).

Presently more than 50 different books, worksheet collections and curricula are published for "Sachunterricht" due to the different syllabi in the 10 Länder and West Berlin, the various approaches teachers prefer, and the dozen or so publishing companies engaged in this subject. Insofar, none of these publications represents a typical approach or dominates the market, though some are more favoured by teachers and teacher educators or have a greater regional influence than others.

2.3.7.2 *Journals, grey material, action groups, publications*

Another large impact is due to the journals, which schools or school teachers normally subscribe to. The journals outline regularly or even exclusively prototypique teaching units which can be implemented by the teachers since the syllabi of the states permit them a lot of flexibility. The authors of these units are professors in teacher education or active teachers and/or former teacher students. The latter are required at the end of their academic and practical studies to write a paper each between 50 and 200 pages in length.

Every year several hundred of these people choose a curriculum topic in which a specific approach is dealt with such as verbalisation of body experience, comparing the image of wild animals in fairy tales and in ethnological descriptions, about the origin of the universe, approaching natural phenomena by rational argumentation and deliberation, consequences of the theory of symbolic interactions for teaching physics and chemistry, curriculum sequence based on Galperin and Brunner etc.

One ought not leave the topic of curricular dissemination through journals, grey material, and action groups without mentioning the "Arbeitskreis Grundschule" again. This organisation comes up every year with a series of teaching suggestions and conceptual considerations. Furthermore, the curricular institutes of the Länder, IPN as institute with a national function, the in-service training institutes and many other groups or institutions are also enriching the curricular field.

2.3.7.3 *Projects*

As a third characteristic of curricular development in the Federal Republic
of Germany one might mention the usual projects. Some were sponsored by
Volkswagen Foundation as part of the two programmes "Curriculum der
Institutionalisierten Elementarerziehung" - CIEL (Bennwitz, Weinert 1973,
Garlichs, Knab, Weinert 1983) and "Curriculum Naturwissenschaft" - CUNA
(CUNA-Autorengruppe 1981), others are results of initiatives at universities,
research and development institutes and teacher training institutions
often backed financially and logistically by publishing companies.

Several of these projects lie on the international mainstream.
Spreckelsen's programme, for instance, is conceived as a spiral curriculum
organised around the concepts of particle, interaction and conservation
(Frey, Schreiner 1977, Spreckelsen 1977). The Arbeitsgruppe für
Unterrichtsforschung (one of the CIEL-projects) started with an adaptation
of "Science - A Process Approach", but redefined the approach to integrate
processes, concepts and attitudes. The group then identified topics of
immediate interest to children, substituted the artificial material by
common ones from the children's environment, and generated situations that
permit children and teachers to bring in their own experiences and ideas
(Arbeitsgruppe für Unterrichtsforschung 1971, Haller et al 1983).

Besides the projects just described which correspond to the international
mainstream there are other projects that differ significantly. Special
attention will be given to two of them.

The first one has been developed on the background of Hiller's
"Konstruktive Didaktik" (Constructive Didactics) within the CIEL-programme
(Hiller 1973). Giel, Hiller, Krämer and Nestle (1974, 1975) together with
a group of teachers created a new approach to "Sachunterricht". The
curriculum's name is "Stücke zu einem mehrperspektivischen Unterricht" -
MPU (roughly "Pieces for Multiperspective Instruction"). It relies on the
implications drawn from the theories of constructivism and symbolic
interactionism.

The second "project" is probably inaptly called a project as by now it
has developed a private school system of its own. It has its roots in
R Steiner's philosophy of nature and education. Sharing Goethe's
encompassing view of nature which embeds all phenomena in a religious whole
(in a "Naturreligion") R Steiner at the beginning of the century drew up
examples for a holistic comprehension of nature. The distribution of
Steiner's "Waldorf-Schulen" and the involvement of dozens of scientifically
educated people with Waldorf education led to a differentiation of Steiner's
original ideas. Many of Steiner's writings have been organised into an
instructionally feasible programme influencing primary science education
experience (Lindenberg 1975, v. Mackensen 1976, 1979).

2.3.7.4 *National and international comparisons*

Given this enriched and energetic state of curriculum production, one can
make certain historical and international comparisons. The following might
be typical. Several years ago certain themes were much more evident than
today, among them biological aspects of sex education, introducing

disciplinary concepts into primary level, optimising learning processes relative to time needed for achievement, ie using programmed instructions or techniques of concept formation.

We discern an increase in work which tries to identify and further develop students' pre-scientific understanding of the physical world, their locally-based experiences and their contact with nature. It is not, what one is calling social orientation of primary science. There has been some of that, too. Rather this work comes closer to the notion of "endogenous education" in the same sense as represented by the recent UNESCO programmes. Endogenous primary science education places great importance on the curricula process especially as it concerns the genesis of the learning situation. Not only the topic, the theme or the given scientific principle provide educational substance but also the way the students and teachers are building up their learning process in concrete situations. Thus student relevance goes far beyond Ralf Taylor's rationale, because interaction and, furthermore, curricular legitimation is added. Endogenous science education has a sense of pragmatism akin to Dewey's or Pierce's ideas: the emphasis is not theory but practical process.

Looking at recent international tendencies several areas did not receive the same emphasis in the Federal Republic of Germany. For instance there are practically no projects using computers in primary education. Few efforts exist for special education and education for gifted children. An integration of science and mathematics has not been attempted for primary education. Piaget is much less used as a reference point for curriculum development than in the Ango-Saxon world. The reason is obvious. Constructs such as equilibrium, accommodation, and adaptation or his theories on the development of knowledge through a transformation of action into logical systems are either too specific or too general to play a structuring function throughout a curriculum. Yet, very limited, carefully specific implications have been drawn for teaching topics of classical mechanics (Kubli 1981). Also the clinical interview has been developed further as a tool to view pupils pre-instructional state vis-à-vis a phenomenon of the physical world and elaborating it through instruction (Frey et al 1982).

2.3.8 RESEARCH

It might be helpful to divide research very pragmatically into the following categories:

A.   developmental work with accompanying research activities;

B.   research with practical implications or technological research;

C.   analytical research.

2.3.8.1 *Developmental work with accompanying research activities*

The curriculum projects mentioned earlier were flanked by research activities. Unlike the North American project funding policy of the last 15 years (quantitative) evaluations of such project were not required. Nevertheless, a variety of specific concerns were dealt with.

    With Spreckelsen's programme "Science in Primary Schools" the influence
of different factors on students' achievement was investigated, such as
homogeneity of the learning group concerning age, previous achievement,
intelligence, class size, sex, mathematics teaching and teachers' experience
in science (Wiebel, Spreckelsen 1977/1,2). Except for slight effects of
previous achievement and teacher experience no marked effects could be
identified. In addition, the teachers' reception of the programme was
evaluated. Besides the usual interest in the specific understanding of
programme objectives and contents, the evaluation study tried to identify
the degrees of freedom teachers perceived when following the detailed
outline of prescribed steps in the curriculum (Wiebel/Spreckelsen 1977/3).

    The Arbeitsgruppe für Unterrichtsforschung evaluated their pilot
adaptation of "Science - A Process Approach" by investigating its influence
on intelligence development and by assessing achievement with activity-
based competency measures following the mastery learning concept of Gagne,
Carroll and Bloom (Arbeitsgruppe für Unterrichtsforschung 1971). Thereafter,
while developing their curriculum "Children and their natural environment"
they emphasised student interaction and self-regulating group work.
Accordingly, changes of teachers' classroom behaviour and role perception
as well as modes of interaction between teachers and curriculum material
were focused on. This more elaborated format of a curriculum reception
study assumed and accepted that in the confrontation with a curricular
prototype teachers will change their previous behaviour somewhat while at
the same time changing the intentions of the prototype. Piaget's paradigm
of accommodation and assimilation was used to describe teacher and
curriculum interaction. Four influencing variables on the teacher behaviour
were proposed: reflexiveness role understanding, planning behaviour and
level of pretentiousness (Haller, et al 1983).

    In a follow-up implementation study of three of the CIEL projects,
one of which was the just described science curriculum, the project history
was reconstructed and the curriculum effects assessed. Additionally, it
was investigated, how written curriculum materials are transformed into
action by teachers. Three phases were identified: (1) copying attempts,
(2) flexible adaptation to own aims, and (3) reflection of own interaction
behaviour and attempts of modification (Mühlhausen 1983).

    More specific questions were researched in close association to those
curriculum developments which were in the responsibility of university
professors or at least supervised by them. These research activities
usually were tied to masters or doctoral theses. H Schütze (1970), for
instance, identified criteria to determine concept and process orientation
in science curriculum materials. W Nestle (1972) investigated the concept
of time and time measurement. W Kuschmann (1973) looked at aspects of
developing a science curriculum for primary schools in the Federal Republic
of Germany. R Lauterbach (1974) devised a scheme for analysing primary
science materials. J Bloch (1978) identified the steps needed to implement
an individualised science programme. K J Trottmann (1978) developed and
evaluated curriculum units on "potential" and "energy" for grades one and two.

    Another type of scientific activity has been brought to developmental
work in primary science: that is a focused or multiperspective awareness
of what is going on in a project. This was demonstrated first by the state-
wide project of developing and implementing the school curriculum for the
state of Hessen together with teachers within the framework of teacher
in-service education (Haller, Wolf 1973).

Other developmental projects proceeded similarly. Such activity yields a narrative description of specific steps, contexts, problems and break-throughs. Often, quotations and photographs are added. The acceptance and use of this new type of scientific record keeping is attributable in part to several factors: (1) the popularised knowledge about the restrictiveness in quantitative modelling, (2) the application of action research along the lines of Brunswick and Lewin (eg Hameyer, Haft 1977), and (3) the substitution of Dilthey's "Geisteswissenschaft" (committed to hermeneutics) by the political intentions of the scientists (Herrmann 1978).

2.3.8.2 *Research with practical implications or technological research*

The German Council of Education (Deutscher Bildungsrat 1970) put down a programmatic outline for primary science education in its "Structural Plan for the German Education System" ("Strukturplan für das Deutsche Bildungswesen") triggering a number of developmental activities. The most renowned of them was the already referred to CIEL project. Other programmatic designs had only a modest influence on research in primary science education (Ziechmann 1982).

A stronger impetus came from the research projects described in the previous chapter and it can also be expected from the discovery learning approach which argues with psychological theory and research (Klewitz, Mitzkat 1977, Soostmeyer 1977, Einsiedler 1979), from a system theoretic algorithm, in which students decompose a given system in order to reconstruct it after a phase of subjectivation to a system with a new quality (Walgenbach 1979) or from theories of games dealing with interaction systems (Schwedes 1982, v. Aufschnaiter et al 1980). The broad revitalisation of the project method is promising.

Up to date, the major effects on developmental as well as technical research as far as breadth is concerned were due to the fundamental revision of the state syllabi between 1969 and 1975. With the introduction of "Sachunterricht" into primary education science was established at this level with explicit concerns for its objectives, contents, structure and sequence. The conceptual frameworks differed widely. The first move was that some states extracted and transposed contents from the secondary science level to the primary (eg North Rhine-Westphalia or Rhineland-Palatinate). Then suggestions of curriculum development groups were picked up and modified in accordance with the assumed acceptability by primary school teachers (eg Bavaria and Spreckelsen or Baden-Württemberg and Giel, Hiller, Krämer, Nestle). Later on, syllabus commissions worked out approaches of their own (eg Hessen, Lower Saxony or Bremen). The practical implications of the syllabi were threefold: curriculum development tried to meet these demands; this was especially the case with developments tied to publishing companies. Teacher education complied with it by having students prepare and evaluate curriculum units or parts thereof during their studies or for their final papers. Teacher in-service education offered courses and aided groups of teachers in developing and evaluating new materials for primary science teaching. These products were then made available in special publications of the teacher training institutions, published in journals, or they were distributed as "grey materials".

One can already cite a few studies which survey students' interests
and preferences in science education (Todt et al 1974, Frey, Bayrhuber,
Lehrke, Lind 1982). The newer affective tests differ from the
internationally known attitude, interests and cognitive preference tests.
They involve more instructional material and provide enlightening
information before soliciting student reactions - in contrast to former
questionnaire formats.

The second research area deals with concept formation. Some of the
most sophisticated investigations have been conducted by W Jung and
associates. They studied notions children have of concepts from mechanics,
eg force, impulse, energy, inertia (Jung, Wiesner, Engelhardt 1981),
electricity (Maichle 1979, Stork, Wiesner 1981) and optics (Jung 1981).
To get at the notions of the students, questionnaires, association tests,
and small tasks to study physics understanding were given to them.
Additionally, interviews were conducted. Unlike Piaget, these researchers
confronted the children with views and interpretations held by the
interviewer and interpreted their problem solving process using the
psychological network theory of concept formation. Thus, Jung and
associates have been able to give teachers a relatively clear picture of
the meaning children attach to some concepts and processes in physics.
While most of the studies concentrated on grades 7 to 10, some studies
were also made in grades 4 to 5 with the intention of developing a sequence
in mechanics for this level.

Similar investigations were conducted for the energy concept
(Duit 1983). They supplemented Piaget-like studies on the energy concept
with children aged 6 to 16 (Jenelten-Allkofer, Duit 1980). Of special
interest may be a study of the Piaget-type on the concepts of density and
buoyancy in which the interview is arranged as a learning situation
(Klewitz, Mitzkat 1982).

In regard to the international mainstream one finds studies of concepts
in physics. But there are also some studies concerning chemistry, eg
investigation to students' notions in chemistry (Haupt 1981, Pfundt 1982).

This research may characterise many of the already described attempts
to improve primary science education in the Federal Republic of Germany.
The approach comments basic principles of the educational relationship in
the original sense of the "Geisteswissenschaftliche Pädagogik" from the end
of the 19th century. It is a basic premise that education is an interaction
between two individuals - teacher and student - with the purpose of promoting
the self-development of the student and not of maintaining the status of
the adult teacher. It implies the necessity of legitimation of educational
measures in which theory and scientific rationality only have a function
in relation to other concerns such as interactions, expressing needs for
activity and finding agreements for common activities. From the perspective
of the teacher or curriculum constructor there is more than theoretical
conceptions to defining the child-centration of a curriculuml It seems to
be typical of the German research scene that these well-known and often
taunted principles of education are being (a) conceptualised in strong and
systematic ways and (b) translated into new methods of teaching.

2.3.8.3 *Analytical research*

It goes without saying that from any methodological viewpoint one pure frame of reference for analytical or explanatory research is not possible. Thus analytical research is understood as research which yields knowledge about primary science education and which does not lead to direct applications or use per se.

We have to acknowledge the absence of national assessment studies of primary science education. There is no tradition, often no need felt to carry out national assessment studies. The lack of assessment may be associated with the character of the federalistic organisation. It also may be attributed to a process of curricula development that is proactive instead of one that is retroactive, ie comes about through achievement tests and other monitoring systems. The proactive nature of curricula development was mentioned earlier.

Primary science topics have been used in new applied psychological experiments. Demonstration experiments using the balance beam have studied problem solving strategies (Spada 1978). Ratios in mathematics and in physics have been used to test Piagetian hypothesis of the prerequisites for complete logical structures to handle mathematically any ratios (Häussler 1981). Using principles of light defraction and refraction in geometrical optics, an experimental situation is designed such that pupils of different ages each try to predict a solution path in regard to how light travels. The solution paths are interpreted by Rost's theory of knowledge acquisition (Häussler, Miecke-Ehrens, Rost 1982). The researchers created a potential teaching tool though at present it is only useable as a laboratory kit. Bear in mind that the main purpose of this methodologically outstanding experiment is to test the theory of knowledge acquisition.

Comparing science education with mathematics far fewer analytical research findings are available. It might be that open boundaries to the social sciences in the common subject "Sachunterricht" render empirical research more difficult. It might be also true that the less firm and stable curricular structure of primary science education does not afford the proper conditions for analytical educational research. Frame factors are changing very rapidly and replications seem hardly possible.

2.3.8.4 *Comparisons*

Relative to the other two types of research in science education, the number of investigations accompanying practical measures is much greater. The emphasis in this area reflects the self-image of most university scholars. They are engaged in efforts to improve primary science education or at least they try to translate some ideas or findings from physics, chemistry and biology or the educational sciences into practice. No major changes in their intentions or procedures are expected in the near future. However, it is very likely that the methodological standards and the complexity of the theoretical background from the educational sciences will increase rapidly. This increase is probable now that the majority of scholars working in the field of primary science education have several years experience in their professional positions and are by now well acquainted with at least one educational research field. That does not mean that primary science education will undergo automatic improvement. It does mean that at least one potential factor will have been strengthened.

150

2.3.9 BIBLIOGRAPHY

Arbeitsgruppe für Unterrichtsforschung: Weg in die Naturwissenschaft. Ein
    verfahrensorientiertes Curriculum im 1. Schuljahr. Stuttgart:
    Klett Verlag 1971.

Aufschnaiter, St. v., et al: Spielorientierung im naturwissenschaftlichen
    Unterricht. In: Naturwissenschaften im Unterricht, Physik/Chemie,
    28 (1980) 12, S. 405.

Bennwitz, H/Weinert, F E (Hrsg): CIEL - Ein Förderungsprogramm zur
    Elementarerziehung und seine wissenschaftlichen Voraussetzungen.
    Göttingen: Vandenhoeck & Ruprecht 1973.

Bloch, J A: To a Model for the Adaptation of Curriculum Materials and its
    Use in the Work with "Individualised Science" in West Germany.
    IPN-Arbeitsberichte 30, Kiel: IPN 1978.

CUNA-Autorengruppe: Unterrichtsbeispiele zu Natur und Technik in der
    Sekundarstufe I. Köln: Aulis Verlag 1981.

Deutscher Bildungsrat: Empfehlungen der Bildungskommission. Struktur-
    plan für das Bildungswesen. Bonn: Bundesdruckerei 1970.

Duit, R: Energy conceptions held by students and consequences for science
    teaching. In: Helm, H/Nova, K (Ed): Proceedings of an International
    Seminar on "Misconceptions in Science and Mathematics". Ithaca:
    Cornell University 1983.

Einsiedler, W: Entdeckungslernen im Grundschulunterricht. In: Einsiedler, W
    (Hrsg): Konzeptionen des Grundschulunterrichts. Bad Heilbrunn/Obb:
    Klinkhardt 1979.

Frey, K/Schreiner, H-R: Der physikalisch-chemische Lehrgang von
    Spreckelsen aus curriculumtheoretischer Sicht: Analyse mit Hilfe
    eines curricularen Referenzrahmens. OE 3 Didaktik der Physik,
    Arbeitsbericht 5. Kassel: Gesamthochschule 1977, S. 5 - 19.

Frey, K/Bayrhuber, H/Lehrke, M/Lind, G: Surveying and Considering Pupil
    Interests in Curriculum Development: New Questionnaire Techniques
    and Findings. In: Wanchoo, V N: World Views on Science Education.
    New Delhi/Bombay/Calcutta: Oxford & IBH Publishing Co.

Frey, K/Pfundt, H/Lehrke, M/Bayrhuber, H/Jenelten-Allkofer, C:
    Utilisation des Methodes et Connaissances Psychologiques pour le
    Developpement des Curricula des Sciences Naturelles au Niveau
    des Ecoles Primaires. Les conférences au Centre Universitaire
    Protestant. Genève: Faculté de Psychologie et des Sciences de
    l'Education 1982.

Garlichs, A/Knab, D/Weinert, F E (Hrsg): CIEL II - Fallstudie zu einem
    Förderungsprogramm der Stiftung Volkswagenwerk zur Elementar-
    erziehung. Göttingen: Vandenhoeck & Ruprecht 1983.

Giel, K/Hiller, G G/ Krämer, H: Stücke zu einem mehrperspektivischen
Unterricht. Aufsätze zur Konzeption 1 und 2. Stuttgart: Klett 1974
und 1975

Haller, I/Wolf, H: Curriculum konkret. Neuorganisation der Lehrerfortbildung
als Teilstück schulnaher Curriculumentwicklung, 1, 73.
Frankfurt/M: Union-Druckerei 1973.

Haller, H-D u.a.: Entwicklung eines naturwissenschaftlich orientierten
Curriculum: Kinder und ihre natürliche Umwelt. In: Garlichs, A/
Knab, D/Weinert, F E (Hrsg): CIEL II - Fallstudie zu einem
Förderungsprogramm der Stiftung Volkswagenwerk zur Elementarerziehung.
Göttingen: Vandenhoeck & Ruprecht 1983.

Hameyer, U/Haft, H: Handlungsorientierte Schulforschungsprojekte in der
Praxis. Voraussetzungen, Realisierungsprobleme und Entwicklungstendenzen.
In: Hameyer/Haft (Hrsg): Handlungsorientierte Schulforschungsprojekte.
Weinheim und Basel: Beltz 1977.

Haupt, P: Welche Vorstellungen entwickeln Schüler von Phänomenen der
Verbrennung und inwieweit werden Kenntnisse aus dem Chemieunterricht
zur Deutung herangezogen? Härtel, H (Hrsg): Zur Didaktik der Chemie
und Physik. Alsbach/Bergstrasse: Leuchtturm-Verlag 1981.

Häussler, P: Denken und Lernen Jugendlicher beim Erkennen funktionaler
Beziehungen. Bern/Stuttgart/Wien: Verlag Hans Huber 1981.

Häussler, P/Mielke-Ehrens, L/Rost, J: Kognitive Umstrukturierung
physikalischen Wissens - Ergebnisse eines Lernexperimentes im
Bereich der geometrischen Optik. (Cognitive Restructuring of Physics
Knowledge - Results of a Teaching Experiment in the Field of
Geometrical Optics). IPN-Arbeitsberichte 49, Kiel: IPN 1982.

Herrmann, U: Pädagogik und geschichtliches Denken. In: Thiersch, H/
Ruprecht, H/Herrmann, U: Die Entwicklung der Erziehungswissenschaft.
München: Juventa 1978.

Hilfrich, H G/Switalla, B: Natur sprachlich begreifen. München: Verlag
Urban & Schwarzenberg 1977.

Hiller, G G: Konstruktive Didaktik. Düsseldorf: Pädagogischer Verlag
Schwann 1973.

Jenelten-Allkofer, C/Duit, R: Entwicklung des Energiebegriffs bei 5- bis
16-Jährigen. In: Naturwissenschaften im Unterricht Physik/Chemie,
28, 1980, 408 - 413.

Jung, W: Conceptual frameworks in elementary optics. In: Jung, W/
Pfundt, H/Rhöneck, C v. (Ed): Problems concerning students'
representations of physics and chemistry knowledge. Ludwigsburg:
Pädagogische Hochschule 1981, 441 - 448.

Jung, W/Wiesner, H/Engelhardt, P: Vorstellungen von Schülern über Begriffe
der Newtonschen Mechanik. Bad Salzdetfurth: Didaktischer Dienst 1981.

Klewitz, E/Mitzkat, H (Hrsg): Wir und unser Körper/Wir entdecken Farben. Stuttgart: Klett 1977.

Klewitz, E/Mitzkat, H: Grenzen und Möglichkeiten didaktischer Einflussnahme auf die Entwicklung naturwissenschaftlicher Begriffe. In: Lauterbach, R/Marquardt, B (Hrsg): Sachunterricht zwischen Alltag und Wissenschaft. Frankfurt/M: Arbeitskreis Grundschule e.V. 1982.

Kubli, F: Piaget und Naturwissenschaftsdidaktik. Köln: Aulis Verlag 1981.

Kuschmann, W: Aspekte einer Curriculumentwicklung für naturwissenschaftlich-technischen Anfangsunterricht. Diss. Technische Universität. Berlin 1973.

Lauterbach, R: Analyse naturwissenschaftlicher Curricula für die Primarstufe in der BRD. Probleme der Konsistenz zwischen Zielen, Inhalten und Unterrichtsplan. Magisterarbeit (MA): Universität Göttingen 1974.

Lauterbach, R/Marquardt, B (Hrsg): Sachunterricht zwischen Alltag und Wissenschaft. Frankfurt/M: Arbeitskreis Grundschule e.V. 1982.

Lauterbach, R/Marquardt, B/Bolscho, D (Hrsg): Lehrerbildung Sachunterricht. Frankfurt/M: Arbeitskreis Grundschule e.V. 1983.

Lindenberg, C: Waldorfschulen ... Reinbek: Rowohlt-Verlag 1975.

Löscher, W (Hrsg): Sand und Wasser. München: Don Bosco Verlag 1979.

Mackensen, M v.: Die Chemieepochen der 7. und 8.Klasse. Clausthal-Zellerfeld: Bönecke-Druck 1976.

Mackensen, M v.: Klang, Helligkeit und Wärme und weitere Gebiete eines Physikunterrichts der 6. bis 8.Klasse. Clausthal-Zellerfeld: Bönecke-Druck 1979.

Maichle, M: Schemata als Organisationsprinzipien beim Erwerb physikalischer Inhalte aus dem Bereich der Elektrizitätslehre. Naturwissenschaften im Unterricht Physik/Chemie 27, 1979, 33 - 39.

Mühlhausen, U: Unterrichtsreform durch curriculare Materialien? Erfahrungen mit der Erprobung eines Sachunterrichtsprogramms. In: Garlichs, A/Knab, D/Weinert, F E: CIEL II, Fallstudie zu einem Förderungsprogramm der Stiftung Volkswagenwerk zur Elementarerziehung. Göttingen: Vandenhoeck & Ruprecht 1983.

Nestle, W: Didaktik der Zeit und Zeitmessung. Empirische Konstruktion eines Teilcurriculums zur Revision des Lehrplans im Sachunterricht der Grundschule. Diss. Universität Tübingen 1972.

Schütze, H: Kriterien zur Unterscheidung von begriffs- und prozessorientierten Curricula, dargestellt am Vergleich von "Science - A Process Approach" und "Science Curriculum Improvement Study". Magisterarbeit Universität Göttingen 1970.

Schwedes, H: Schülerorientierte Unterrichtskonzepte im Physikunterricht.
   In: Fischler, H (Hrsg): Lehren und Lernen im Physikunterricht.
   Köln: Aulis Verlag 1982.

Soostmeyer, M: Das entdeckende und forschende Lernen als Ansatzpunkt einer
   Didaktik der Denkerziehung im naturwissenschaftlich-technischen
   Sachunterricht der Grundschule. Fachperspektive Physik. Versuch
   einer Grundlegung. Diss. Universität Essen 1977.

Spada, H: Understanding Proportionality: A Comparison of Different Models
   of Cognitive Development. In: International Journal of Behavioural
   Development 1978, 1, 4.

Spreckelsen, K (Hrsg): Der Lehrgang "Naturwissenschaftlicher Unterricht
   in der Grundschule" in der fachdidaktischen Diskussion. OE 3 Didaktik
   der Physik, Arbeitsbericht 5. Kassel: Gesamthochschule 1977.

Stork, E/Wiesner, H: Elektrizitätslehre in der Primarstufe. Über einen
   Versuch zur Integration von fachdidaktischer Forschung und
   schulpraktischer Ausbildung. In: Härtel, H: Zur Didaktik der Physik
   und Chemie. Alsbach/Bergstrasse: Leuchtturm-Verlag 1981.

Todt, E/Arbinger, R/Seitz, H/Wildgrube, W: Untersuchungen über die
   Motivation zur Beschäftigung mit naturwissenschaftlichen Problemen
   (Sekundarstufe I). Universität Giessen 1974.

Trottmann, K J: Potential und Energie. Planung, Entwicklung und Erprobung
   eines strukturorientierten Curriculums des Faches Physik und Chemie
   im Sachunterricht der ersten beiden Grundschuljahre. Diss.
   Pädagogische Hochschule Rheinland 1978.

Walgenbach, W: Ansätze zu einer Didaktik ästhetisch-wissenschaftlicher
   Praxis. Weinheim und Basel: Beltz Verlag 1979.

Wiebel, K H/Spreckelsen, K: Evaluationsergebnisse des Lehrgangs
   "Naturwissenschaftlicher Unterricht in der Grundschule - physikalisch-
   chemischer Lernbereich", Teile 1, 2, 3. Kassel: Gesamthochschule
   Kassel 1977.

Ziechmann, J: Das Fliegen - Ein Projekt im offenen Sachunterricht. In:
   Lauterbach, R/Marquardt, B (Hrsg): Sachunterricht zwischen Alltag
   und Wissenschaft. Frankfurt/M: Arbeitskreis Grundschule e.V. 1982.

2.4 PRIMARY SCIENCE EDUCATION IN ITALY:
PRESENT SITUATION AND DEVELOPMENT PROSPECTS

by

Nunzio Rizzoli, Parma

2.4.1 INTRODUCTION

In order to provide adequate information about science education in Italian
primary schools and development prospects, it is necessary to describe the
Italian school system and the reforms of the last 15 years. In particular,
educational innovation and institutional reforms in pre-school, primary and
lower secondary (scuola media) education and their impact on curriculum
development have to be considered. Proposals for reforming initial and
in-service education of teachers are also relevant.

Since 1955 free compulsory education of eight years has been
institutionalised, but it became operational only in 1962 after the creation
of the unified middle school (scuola media, a sort of comprehensive lower
secondary education for the age group 11-14). Now it ranges from 6 to 14.
Following an increasing demand, state pre-school institutions were set up
in 1968 to supplement the many private institutions. At present the question
of extending compulsory education is under discussion; there are proposals
to start school at five (third year of pre-school education) and to prolong
schooling to the age of 15 or even 16. One might claim that in practice
basic education in Italy covers the age range from 3 to 14. The aim is
comprehensive general education for this age range combined with
corresponding teacher mobility. All teachers should have an academic
qualification (university level), based on solid educational as well as
subject matter studies.

Over the last 10 years declining birth-rates and, consequently, a
decreasing school population have made it possible to organise the public
school system in a more efficient way. It is hoped to come to better
solutions with regard to the selection of teachers and their in-service
education and training (INSET).

2.4.2 BASIC SCHOOLING AND SCIENCE EDUCATION

It is necessary to examine the syllabuses of pre-school, primary and lower
secondary (ie middle school, scuola media) education to get an idea of the
role and quality of science education in Italy.

2.4.2.1 *Pre-school education*

The "Suggestions for educational activities in state pre-school
institutions" (1969) stress "the importance of science education in
contemporary society, highly influenced by scientific and technological

research". They suggest making "the best possible use of the children's curiosity about natural phenomena and everyday scientific problems in order to encourage them, through play and games, to start observing natural processes. This would obviously not presuppose any logical co-ordination. The aim would be to develop their ability of identifying not only the most striking features of things and situations, but also the more hidden ones, always with a view to comparing and distinguishing things. A specific aim would be to make the children distinguish between instinctive fear and real danger and to make them understand that certain dangers have to be avoided in any case, whereas others may be faced with a certain amount of caution".

Teachers are advised to build upon the knowledge and ideas of kindergarten children and to initiate them gradually into science; science education should be a continuous process from kindergarten up to 14 years, ie the end of compulsory schooling. The above-mentioned "Suggestions" recommend activities such as handling, cutting, kneading, playing with water, floating things, balance games, gardening, breeding, daily health care. It is felt that this might help the children to observe and reflect things and exercise a certain self-control.

2.4.2.2 Primary education

There is a uniform national primary school syllabus dating back to 1955 and still in force, but it is more or less out of date, in particular with regard to science education. "It now appears quite obsolete and absolutely inadequate for children living in a society highly influenced by science and dominated by an increasing amount of science programmes in the mass media" (F Emiliani, 1983).

Primary science education in Italy followed the trend of the state school system which could be observed over the last 10 years, namely to group science together with history, geography, aspects of economics, and civic education under the heading of "social studies". Early this century science education came under "various information"; under the terms of the 1955 syllabus it is limited to the natural and social environment. The prevailing stress on culture favoured a subjective concept of science. Science teaching enjoyed less prestige than history and literature teaching. According to Mauro Laeng (1982), the role of science education is restricted to one of forming not only descriptive but also explanatory concepts. The reason is that mathematics are seen as a basic language, whereas science is only seen from the point of view of teaching contents.

The 1955 syllabus contains a few paragraphs about science education, not specifying any contents in detail, only setting the general framework for the teaching of the natural sciences. For the first two years it is recommended to let the children explore their environment but not to overburden them with information. The text speaks of "direct observation of the environment in relation to space and time" and suggests excursions into the neighbourhood to observe animals and plants and to collect come of them.

During the following three years of primary education (8-10 age group) the children "should proceed along the same guidelines extending their observation to minerals; they should also learn some elements of meteorology, physical geography and earth science. Excursions are recommended as well as

keeping a terrarium, an aquarium or small mammals in the classroom"
(L Borghi-De Stefano, 1983). Science is dealt together with geography in
the same paragraph with a view to exploring the environment which is
introduced in a way focusing on man. In particular, a "more and more
analytical way of observation" is recommended. The children should observe
"vegetables, animals, minerals found in their local environment and then
proceed to comparing them with those found in other countries". After
referring to hygienics (including also "the fundamental functions of the
human body"), the syllabus concludes by stressing the "spritual and
aesthetic importance" of environmental studies and calls for "the maximum
respect 'to nature" ... (F Emiliani 1983).

Many primary school teachers have never had adequate science education
themselves; they therefore limit themselves to simply passing on knowledge
in science education. Science education is thus not taken very seriously
in most Italian schools.

2.4.3 EVALUATION

As from 1970, a number of studies tried to evaluate the state of science
education in Italy:

2.4.3.1 The first IEA study (started in 1970 and published in 1977)
involved 166 teachers all over Italy. The results were presented at the
so-called COASSI meeting in 1982. The study showed that teachers still
prefer "learning by listening" to "learning by doing" and tend to simply
describe things. The study, carried out by a team of research workers at
the University of Pavia, "reveals that topics of chemistry and physics are
only introduced by less than 50% of the teachers. Moreover, pupils are
usually not taking an active part in experiments but take almost all
information from the teacher or the textbook. In fact only 14% of the
teachers organise practical activities in the classroom. Germination of
seeds is the most frequent activity (7% of the teachers)".
(L Borghi-De Stefano,1983).

2.4.3.2 The Regional Institute for Learning Psychology and Education (IRPA)
of the Region of Emilia-Romagna carried out a study on the number, type and
use of equipment and teaching aids available for science and technology
education. The enquiry involved 135 teachers in pre-school, primary and
lower secondary education in Bologna and Ravenna; 49 of them were primary
school teachers working in 16 classes. The list of equipment (grouped
according to various topics of science) gives a rather poor picture.

2.4.3.3 A more in-depth analysis of the situation was made in 1982 at the
so-called COASSI meeting. The title was: "The value attached to science
education in the education of primary school teachers; ideas and proposals".
A step further was made at the joint Italian-American (USA) meeting on
primary science education held at Villa Falconieri, Frascati, in
November 1983. The report is in preparation. A meeting on natural
environment and science education at primary school organised in Venice
in January 1983 by the Municipal Museum of Natural History in co-operation
with the IRRSAE of the Region of Veneto may also be of interest in this
context.

The situation is better in all-day primary schools the number of which has been increasing; here science education assumes a new educational dimension (see the recent report of the Ministry's Schools Inspector on the general situation of primary school education and the evaluation of developments 1978-83). "The situation is best where the teacher does not limit himself/herself to passing on information but tries to solve problems, to explore things, to gather information and to carry out experiments together with the pupils; in short when he/she aims at doing science with them" (F Emiliani 1983).

It is clear from these sources of information that most primary school teachers are not prepared for a more advanced approach to science education. At university level, several research teams engaged in research about teaching methods have - over the last 10 years - tested various teaching units and curricular innovations. In most cases this was restricted to a single subject, however, eg to physics and chemistry, but earth science, integrated science and environmental studies (ecology) were also covered. A list of the most advanced research teams is available. They are involved in teacher education and INSET and are running classroom pilot experiments all over Italy. Some of them presented their findings at international meetings or in international journals.

Financial and organisational support given by local authorities (regions, provinces, municipalities etc) also helped to stimulate numerous experiments and innovations in primary science education, mainly in the field of environmental studies. Initiatives of this kind were not always linked to merely cultural, social or historic aspects but involved knowledge about the management of natural resources and nature conservation. Environmental education also developed after distribution of the Italian Government's report on UNESCO's Environmental Education Conference (Tbilissi, USSR, 1977). CIREA noted profound changes in the approach to environmental education; teachers passed from violent ecologic commitment to integrated field studies of nature at work, of the specific human responsibility and means of controlling the quality of the environment.

2.4.4 LOWER SECONDARY EDUCATION (SCUOLA MEDIA)

Based on reform legislation (Act No. 348 of 16 June 1977) a ministerial decree of 9 February 1979 laid down the new syllabus, timetable and examination requirements for compulsory lower secondary education (scuola media) strengthening the interdisciplinary approach to science education in subjects such as mathematics, chemistry, physics, and natural sciences (see the introduction to the decree and the paragraphs devoted to education in science and technology). The new syllabus (fairly advanced from a European point of view) calls for

-   a reform of science education also at upper secondary level (still not approved by parliament);

-   new university curricula for future mathematics, physics, chemistry and natural science teachers.

What matters is that the new syllabus stresses an integrated approach based on problem-solving by pupils: <u>doing science rather than teaching science</u>. Scientific working methods are to be taught: field work and laboratory experiments should help the pupils to learn by doing things, to identify problems and to try and solve them.

2.4.5 THE PROPOSED NEW PRIMARY SCHOOL SYLLABUS

The Ministry of Education set up a committee to make proposals for a new primary education syllabus. The committee completed its work in November 1983. It is hoped that the new syllabus will become operational as from 1985-86.

The committee's report, an interesting document full of new ideas, is at present under discussion. It attached great value to science education (see for instance the paragraphs devoted to mathematics and science education) and asks for better preparation of primary school teachers.

The introduction of the report defines the aims of science education as follows: to teach knowledge and abilities enabling pupils to understand the world and to act responsibly. What matters is the promotion of certain attitudes and techniques of enquiry.

The chapter on "Objectives, contents, and activities" describes the common core as follows: to acquire basic knowledge by means of activities related to everyday problems and to learn certain scientific working methods (learning by experimenting). The main topics to be dealt with are:

1. the living environment;

2. health;

3. earth as part of the universe;

4. management of natural resources;

5. materials.

At the end of primary schooling the children should be able to apply scientific methods in simple situations: observing, measuring, classifying, defining relations of space and time, collecting and interpreting data, identifying and distinguishing variables, communicating in oral and in written form. The committee's report gives a long and rather detailed list of activities suitable for the various stages of primary education.

The second chapter is entitled "teaching suggestions" and recommends

- adapting the teaching programme to the pupils' state of development;

- starting with local environment and its resources;

- organising laboratory work and excursions;

- to follow a spiral-shaped approach in introducing the main topics.

In the same way as the new lower secondary syllabus priority is given to

- methodological objectives;
- experimentation, operational activities, combination between doing things and thinking them over.

More or less the same objectives, criteria and perspectives for a new science education syllabus were put forward at a meeting in Florence in 1980 by a group of educational research workers (see summary conclusions by C Pontecorvo).

2.4.6 THE KEY PROBLEM: REFORM OF PRIMARY SCHOOL TEACHER EDUCATION

The law provides for academic (university) education of future primary school teachers. So far most of them only have gone through upper secondary education (Istituto Magistrale). Their training is quite inadequate. The science education, timetable and practical training (tirocinio guidato) they had are insufficient both in the cultural (ie general education) and the professional sense. They are not prepared for the proposed new primary education syllabus.

Over the last few years Italian universities have been experimenting with new types of degree courses for primary school teachers. The results were evaluated both at national and international level. Within the framework of the current university reform the new primary school teacher courses will have to be offered throughout the country for 1986. At the last COASSI meetings it was stressed that the faculties of science and the faculties of humanities (including education) would have to co-operate closely in the attempt to improve the science education of future primary school teachers.

The universities will also have a vital role to play in INSET, considering the fact that more than 200,000 primary school teahcers will require some form of retraining.

Over the last seven years the Centre for Environmental Education at University Level (CIREA) - rather unique in its way - carried out field as well as laboratory research about INSET both for primary and lower secondary school teachers (often taking them together). The idea was to develop teaching materials introducing ecological aspects into integrated science teaching. Special reference should be made to the local and regional natural environment, resource management and nature conservation. Experimental training courses are being organised with the help of the ministry, the European Communities and the Region of Emilia-Romagna both in the form of school-based INSET courses and residential courses. Study of the British field study centres (aims, contents, methods) has been helpful in this context. The results were laid down in reports and textbooks supporting the new approach to primary science education.

2.4.7 BACKGROUND MATERIAL (AVAILABLE ON REQUEST)

1. Primary school syllabus 1955, paragraphs on science education.

2. Results of the IEA research project (team at the University of Pavia) presented at the COASSI meeting in 1982.

F

3. List of equipment and teaching aids available for science education (IRPA research project, Emilia-Romagna).

4. Report of the Ministry's Inspectorate for Schools on developments 1978-83.

5. List of main research teams at Italian universities engaged in science education at school level.

6. New lower secondary (scuola media) syllabus, in particular the introduction and the chapters on mathematics and science.

7. List of members of the committee set up by the ministry to make proposals for a new primary education syllabus (1983).

8. Proposed new primary education syllabus 1983 (chapters on mathematics and science).

9. C Pontecorvo, summary conclusions of the Florence meeting 1980 on science education.

10. English translation of the science syllabus and timetable for primary school teacher training at the "Istituto Magistrale" which is out-of-date but still in force (kindly supplied by Prof. F Emiliani).

11. Report and leaflet on the Centre for Environmental Education at University Level (CIREA).

12. Bibliography (Italian literature).

2.5 PRIMARY SCIENCE EDUCATION IN IRELAND

Report submitted by the
Department of Education, Dublin

2.5.1 PLACE OF SCIENCE EDUCATION

Science in Irish primary schools is an essential part of the total social
and environmental education programme which is taught by all primary
teachers.

Social and environmental studies are primarily concerned with human
activity, with the child's physical surroundings and the natural phenomena
with which he is familiar. The child has a natural urge to explore and
investigate his own environment and it is perceived as good practice that
this curiosity should be directed and channelled so as to enable the child
to differentiate his experiences, to organise his knowledge and to form a
satisfactory concept of his environment.

A primary aim of the programme is to stimulate and foster in the
child an interest in the world around him and to answer in a natural way
many of the questions he may ask about things which confront him in
everyday life. For example: What makes a rainbow? What makes our door-
bell ring? Why had we to be vaccinated in school today?

The essential basis for much of the knowledge gained is the child's
own observation, and therefore, a wide range of opportunities is provided
for activity, exploration and discovery. This leads to a sharpening of
his powers of accurate perception, thinking and recording, and gradually
a firm basis is laid for intelligent action and independent enquiry. As
the child is the principal agent in his own education, the emphasis is on
learning, rather than on teaching.

2.5.2 HISTORY AND CONCEPT OF SCIENCE EDUCATION

Since the foundation of the national school system the practical home crafts
and rural sciences were encouraged but were ousted from the schools
programme of work occasionally by what was regarded as more pressing
priorities. Botany and nature study always received some attention but
other aspects of science suffered from lack of emphasis. However the
new primary school curriculum which was introduced in 1971 acknowledges
the basic principle of child-centredness and advocates the central role of
pupils as active agents in their own education. Consequently the discovery
and scientific method takes precedence over traditional didactic pedagogy.
Also strategies and methods of learning are more beneficial educationally
than is the attainment of knowledge per se.

Environmental studies is not thought of as simply a subject with its own body of factual information but as a way of learning through organised enquiry. It is defined as an approach, through activities, based on the child's physical and social environment, which leads to the progressive development of attitudes and skills required for the observation, recording, interpretation and communication of scientific data.

2.5.3 AIMS OF SCIENCE EDUCATION

The broad aim of science in the Irish primary school is to develop in the pupil an enquiring mind and a scientific approach to problem-solving which emphasises understanding and constructive thinking.

Science, as traditionally studied in secondary schools even when suitably simplified for younger children, has no place in the primary school.

In practice therefore the progress of any scientific investigation in Irish primary schools has the following five-stage sequence:

a. observation of objects of phenomena under investigation;

b. sorting or classifying into groups which share similar characteristics or properties;

c. hypothesis or prediction of what will happen under varying conditions;

d. experimentation or testing of hypothesis to prove or disprove the hypothesis;

e. explanation of outcome, involving discussion, communication and recording.

The skills of measurement, recording and communication are essential to the scientific method and these are developed and refined by and derive meaning and stimulus from their use. The important point is that science, at this level, is process-based rather than content-based. How the pupil investigates is more important than the object of the investigation. This is not to suggest that the matter or theme of the research is unimportant.

2.5.4 TIMETABLE

Science is included in the timetable in one of two ways:

a. it is given a specific period of time in the class during which a programme in elementary science is followed;

b. it can be drawn out of the existing curriculum when the opportunity presents itself.

2.5.5 PILOT SCHEME 1984-85

During the academic year 1984-85 a special pilot scheme in the teaching of science will be conducted in a number of primary schools.

The experience of the pilot scheme will lead to guidelines on issues such as:

a. timetabling: the amount of time that should be devoted to elementary science together with implications for other areas of the curriculum and, especially, for social and environmental studies;

b. an integrated approach to social and environmental studies which would include a definite elementary science section;

c. pre-service and in-service needs of teachers;

d. basic supply of scientific equipment required;

e. realistic expectations and outcomes from science;

f. strategies for extending science to the whole school and to all schools;

g. items of content: description of modules suitable for varied environments;

h. indications as to whether/how the programme recommended at present should be revised or amended.

2.5.6 USE OF COMPUTERS

Also during the academic year 1984-85 a pilot project on the role and function of microcomputers in primary schools will be conducted in a selected number of primary schools in Ireland. The aim of this project is to examine the feasibility of introducing microcomputers into all primary schools. As a result of this project guidelines on the role and function of the microcomputer across the primary school curriculum will be drawn up.

2.5.7 SCIENCE PROGRAMME FOR THE SEVENTH AND EIGHTH YEAR

The primary school cycle in Ireland lasts eight years. The science programme for the last two years in primary schools is as follows:

a. Animal life: birds, animals, fish. An investigation into how they live.

b. Plant life: parts of a flower, pollination, dispersal of fruits and seeds, germination. Trees and their uses. Plant growth, soils, fertilisers. Fungi, bacteria, weeds etc. Nature table, school garden, vegetable plot. Simple experiments.

c. Air. Breathing. Oxygen cycle. Expansion, burning, rusting, pressure etc.

d. Water. Different forms. Solution of solids. Purification and fluoridation.

e. Electricity. Fuses. Dangers etc.

f. Heat. Conduction. Convection. Radiation. Energy from different sources.

g. Sound and light. Telephone, radio, television etc.

h. Gravity and levers.

i. Simple experimental study of everyday objects, eg bicycle pump.

2.6 NORWEGIAN RESEARCH - A BRIEF SURVEY

by

Svein Sjøberg, Oslo

2.6.1 INTRODUCTION

Science plays no central role in the common national curriculum for
Norwegian schools at the primary level (grade 1-6, age approximately 7-13).
From grade 4 to 6 it is, however, taught, either as an integrated course
or as part of an even more extensive subject, encompassing also social
science, history etc.

Teachers at this level generally have a very weak background in
science. They are educated in teacher training colleges where science
subjects are either non-existent or chosen by a very small minority. In
addition, most students who enter these colleges have a very weak science
background from their upper secondary education.

Quite a few research studies have focused directly on the science
part of the curriculum in the primary years. The following points emerge
from the few studies that are known. Some projects looking at science
education in secondary schools also shed light on the situation in primary
schools.

2.6.2 RESEARCH EVIDENCE

With a very weak science background teachers rely heavily upon the use of
textbooks. (This is also part of the Norwegian teaching tradition.)
Research has shown that teachers with the weakest science background are
the ones who most strictly follow the textbooks page by page. Paradoxically,
the same teachers are the ones who state that they do not feel the need for
a stronger science background.

The central role of the textbook justifies a closer textbook analysis.
This has been done from different perspectives: in general, the level of
abstraction is unrealistically high, which has been revealed by analysis
of Piagetian level of demand. Even for 11-13 year olds, formal operational
thought is required to grasp the concepts that are introduced. High-level
generalisations are presented on areas where very few children have the
necessary concrete experience. Piagetian-type tasks show that only a small
minority of the pupils operate on the level required by the textbook.

The factual contents of the books have also been analysed from a
scientific point of view. Concepts are often treated in such a way that
it is obvious that the author does not have a firm grasp of the material
presented. One often notes survival of so-called "textbook errors", which
indicate that new generations of textbooks repeat the mistakes of the
former. In the hands of a teacher with a very weak science background
such books may be responsible for the forming of hostile attitudes to
science. When neither teacher nor child understand the textbook, the
teacher has to resort to an authoritarian and dogmatic style of teaching
"by the book" in order to hide her/his lack of grasp of the contents.
It is well documented that rather negative and persistent attitudes to
science are formed at this level of schooling. This tendency is reinforced
by explicitly negative statements in some of the newer books. For instance
is "chemical" equalled with "poisonous", and "technology" is presented as
nearly synonymous to degradation of quality of life, exploitation of
resources etc.

The situation is again paradoxical: textbooks at higher levels are
written by science experts with a non-critical and positive faith in
science as a benevolent source of unproblematic progress for mankind. In
these books, very few social and ethical issues are treated, at least not
critically. Textbooks at the primary level are, however, written by people
with a very weak background in science, but with the commonly held
negative attitudes to science and technology. "Science" in these books
is often "integrated" with social science, where the author feels more at
home.

These two extremes of textbooks both neglect a serious treatment of
pros and cons of science and technology in today's and tomorrow's society.
And the result from both these extremes is that many pupils, also the very
gifted, and especially the girls, turn their backs to science, and drop
it at the first point of choice.

The situation for the girls has been studied in some detail. The
reason is of course that very few girls opt for "hard science" and
technology at higher levels in their education. In fact, Norway and other
Scandinavian countries are near the bottom of the enrollment statistics
in these areas, in spite of a very strong women's liberation movement, and
in spite of more than half of all students now being female!

The reasons are thought to be manifold. Textbooks play an important
role. Girls are both quantitatively and qualitatively badly treated. Very
few girls are depicted in text, examples and illustrations, and when they
are, it is often in passive and traditional roles. More important is
probably the fact that science textbooks are written by men, who most
often use male experience in their choice of examples.

Even more important is probably the open hidden messages on what
science is all about, and how scientists are as people: the values inherent
in school science is next to antithetical to the values girls are socialized
to stand for: school science is oriented towards things and not people and
their needs, science is presented as cool, abstract, disinterested reasoning,
devoid of subjectivity, feelings, creativity. It is needless to say that
the image of school science is rather different from the picture emerging
from recent studies of the philosophical and sociological foundations of
science.

Attempts are now being made to give a richer and more reflected view on the positive and negative aspects of science and technology. This is being substantiated both in current curriculum reform and in the publishers' attempts to produce new textbooks. The girls are of particular concern in this work.

2.6.3 FUTURE DEVELOPMENT

A curriculum reform has recently commenced and is influenced along the lines just described. An ongoing study will probably also have some influence on these reforms: Norway took part in IEA's Second International Science Study together with some 35 other countries. The target populations are pupils of 10 - 14 - 18 years of age and also the science teachers at these levels as well as the schools. The Norwegian version of the study has included national items to elicit the pupils' interest and attitudes, the teachers' priorities, needs etc. It is expected that the results from this comprehensive, large-scale study will have an influence also on the development of science teacher education, the form and content of in-service education and on the new curricula.

Some new studies of children's learning are also promising. They follow the international tendency to move away from studies of logical form and put more emphasis on the contents of children's thinking. Children's preconceptions (or "alternative frameworks") are now being studied in different areas of science, and these empirical findings are interpreted in the light of a constructive epistemology and a constructive theory of instruction.

2.7 NEW METHODS FOR THE TRAINING OF
SCIENCE TEACHERS IN SPAIN

by

Elena Martin, Madrid

2.7.1 THE ORIGIN OF THE PROJECT

During the past years of research and experimentation the team (1) working
at the Institute for the Teaching of Science discovered something which is
actually quite well-known: neither elementary nor secondary schoolchildren
learn science properly, and they are unable to assimilate the knowledge
to explain daily phenomena. Research on the assimilation of physical
notions pointed out the difficulties children experience in understanding
certain concepts and in explaining phenomena which occur around them every
day and which are closely related to what they study at school. Subsequent
research on the understanding of certain mathematical research notions
demonstrated that abstract concepts taught to children are not acquired
in an abstract way but always appear in concrete representations which are
therefore not really mathematical.

Out studies, along with many others on the learning of science, clearly
pointed out the main shortcomings in teaching which cause pupils to
misunderstand scientific concepts. At no time, however, they offered
either an alternative to the school-work the children did or concrete
proposals on what should be done in the classroom to avoid these
misunderstandings.

Aware of the need to overcome these limitations we decided on the
idea of working on methods of science teaching which would be both new and
different but which could at the same time be applied to the normal school
curriculum. We studied the possibility of setting up a system of science
based on recreational science which would shun the pitfalls produced by
the traditional educational system. Our contact with UNESCO's Science
Education Section and the interest they showed in our project, constituted
a great stimulus to our work.

---

(1) Juan Delval, Director, and Amparo Moreno, Elena Martin, Carlos Palacios,
     Maria Jesus Posada, Aurora Iovar Alberto Navarro and Elvira Rocha.

2.7.2 DEVELOPMENT OF THE PROJECT

Thus a project supported by the Ministry of Education and UNESCO emerged
and gradually developed which we called "The Formation of a Scientific
Mind in Children", based on the well-known work of the French philosopher
Gaston Bachelard. Our project is so entitled because we believe that
one should not begin by teaching sciences but by helping the children form
attitudes towards nature which might be entitled "the scientific mind".
However, in order to accomplish this objective it was necessary to bear
in mind the children's interests and their approach to problems, both
factors being determined by their intellectual development. Our principal
idea is that <u>children should be taught science as applied to normal
situations and with ordinary materials before they learn the principles
of a scientific discipline.</u>

In order to teach in this way, we thought it necessary to develop
new kinds of materials designed for teachers' use. Perhaps it would now
be appropriate to explain how we arrived at this conclusion. From the very
beginning our main intention was to design materials for science teaching
which could be used in the classroom even though we believe it is up to
the student to construct his own ideas and the teacher does not really
teach but rather establish and control the conditions under which the
student learns. However, the teacher does play a vital role in the
organisation of the work to be done in the classroom. For this reason
we thought it necessary to develop materials which would enable the teacher
to carry out a different method of teaching.

Furthermore, as we were able to verify in many grades, a great number
of teachers is convinced that the education they are giving their pupils
is unsatisfactory and aware of the shortcomings of the current methods of
teaching, mentioned above. It is less obvious to them what they can do
to improve the traditional methods. For this reason, they need materials
which allow them to work creatively within the classroom, innovative
materials for science teaching. This is precisely the type of material
we decided to develop.

The goal of our project consists, therefore, in producing modules so
that teachers can explain various aspects of science. These modules are
sets of structured suggestions which enable the teachers to organise the
classroom work of their pupils.

Each module has a wide usage and the teacher can either follow it
literally or use it simply as a teaching aid. One of our objectives is
precisely that the teachers use these modules as stimuli to create others.

The materials are designed for the average teacher and for neither
the specialist science teacher nor the teacher with special scientific
knowledge. We have tried to go step by step, not by leaps and bounds, in
such a way that a person not specialised in the subject can learn to teach
it properly and that a person who knows the subject well can use the
material to introduce variations.

2.7.3 THE DEVELOPMENT OF TEACHING MATERIAL

We then attempted to create teaching materials which would fulfil the above-mentioned conditions but which would differ from those produced by other projects. Our goal was to gradually cover the different sciences and establish a connection among them. We used different systems for the development of our materials, but we always worked with psychologists and science teachers, due to the peculiar characteristics involved in the production of these materials. The reason we used psychologists stems from our conviction that it is necessary to pay a great amount of attention to the development of cognitive processes in children.

We therefore formed teams of psychologists and science teachers and studied the genesis of the scientific concepts in question by means of interviews with the children and revision of current publications on the subject. We subsequently produced an initial version of the material which we tried on small groups of pupils. Then courses were organised for teachers, instructing them in the usage of our materials in the classroom and with the information teachers provided us we amended the material. Due to its special characteristics our material is in a constant state of modification.

Coinciding with this work on the production of materials we analysed the shortcomings found in current science teaching and the characteristics which more suitable teaching methods should display. Part of the result of this work can be observed in our paper Science Teaching by Juan Delval produced as a part of this project.

Although our goal is to cover the different fields involved in science teaching and to produce materials for the greatest possible amount, we have concentrated on only a few fields, some of which we have developed further than others. We believed it preferable to carry out a deep study which would provide us with a work method rather than to try to cover all possible fields of science teaching. The main subjects studied are heat, light, colour and growth. In addition to these we have begun to work on material which could be used in studying water, the hydrostatics and the production of certain substances from others.

2.7.4 COURSES GIVEN TO TEACHERS AND DISSEMINATION OF MATERIAL

One of the possible causes of the failure of certain didactic innovations might be the lack of relation between the persons who develop the materials and the teachers of the subject in question who should contribute their specific experiences to the work in the classroom. For this reason, in conjunction with the experiments we have been carying out to develop our modules, we have also been offering a series of courses to teachers in order to introduce them to our new methods and to evaluate and circulate the material.

Furthermore, if we take into account that our material is neither a set of laboratory practices nor a recreational science but rather an integration of both in an understandable teaching system, it is easy for teachers to misinterpret it and to take it for something it is not (ie a set of laboratory experiences). Consequently the task of introducing our material through courses, seminars and articles is becoming increasingly important.

Different types of courses have been organised. We temporarily rely on the collaboration of a group of teachers belonging, for the most part, to centres related to the ICE who have revised and repeated the experiments suggested by the modules and introduced modifications which make it more applicable to real conditions in the science classes of our schools.

Courses have also been offered to teachers in several public schools located on the outskirts of Madrid. These teachers, after doing the experiments suggested by the module and after discussing with us the validity of the approach insofar as science teaching is concerned, have used the module in their classrooms. The data obtained from the evaluation of the material with teachers and students from different backgrounds proved of great utility in introducing new modifications which we hope will facilitate the practice of the proposed method.

We have also taught courses in the summer schools which have been open for years in the big Spanish cities and constitute one of the most important movements for bringing teachers up to date in their fields as they unite a great number of highly motivated members of the teaching profession. One group of these teachers is using our material during this school term and we meet periodically with them to evaluate the results.

2.7.5 EVALUATION OF THE MATERIAL

Although the evaluation of our work is at present in the initial stages and we have no results based on big groups of teachers, we can still draw some conclusions. The first impression is that this type of teaching is more attractive to pupils since they participate to a greater extent in the work. The system seems to be especially useful for students of average ability and restless children with small attention spans.

Problems arise, above all, due to the lack of the teachers' familiarity with experimental teaching and in many cases with the scientific concepts in question. We believe his lack of practice and initial insecurity can be overcome in most cases without difficulty. Some teachers claim that this method is difficult to use with big classes does not really present a serious obstacle since the pupils must work on their own during a good part of most of the activities. The availability of good-sized classrooms does seem to constitute an important factor so that the students can be grouped in different ways.

From our viewpoint the work done up to now has been extremely valuable for it has enabled us to make important gains in the search for better science education. We have worked with teachers and not just criticised present methods or discussed general solutions, but we have attempted to formulate concrete proposals on specific contents. Notwithstanding, we consider our work only a beginning for future research and study.

2.8 PRIMARY SCIENCE EDUCATION IN WALES

by

Neville Evans, Cardiff

It has always been recognised that the curriculum of primary schools for pupils from 3 to 11 years of age should include an introduction to features of the world of nature. In most schools for a long time this took the form of information about living matter, with some attention to scientific method, for instance, in studying the development of plants and small animals kept in school. On the whole, however, the emphasis was on second-hand knowledge, mostly conveyed in a predominantly verbal descriptive mode, and the context was biological.

By now there are clear signs of change, helpfully indicated by a more frequent reference in school schemes of work and on timetables to "science" than to "nature study", even for very young pupils. Not only is there the continuing acknowledgement of the need to give pupils knowledge of the world around them, but also a more discerning appreciation of the desirability of enabling pupils to appreciate, through first-hand investigation studies, how that knowledge is obtained and thereby to understand its status significance and limitations.

Over the past five years there has been a substantial increase in the use by schools of commercially produced schemes. In part, perhaps, this is a reflection of the desire of schools to give science a secure place in the curriculum, but also it is a tacit recognition that hitherto little structure existed in schemes of work. However, of more significance in the long term for science education has been the establishment and activity in all parts of Wales of voluntary curriculum development groups of teachers. The deliberations of these groups have resulted in the production of discussion documents for schools and of workcards, usually grouped to present a range of pupil experiments on a variety of themes. Assistance has been rendered to these groups by local education authorities and by teachers' centres, for instance, in the provision of printing facilities at the final stages of development. Specialist advice and training has also been arranged in various ways by staff of institutions of higher education.

An interesting and beneficial instance of curriculum development in primary science was sponsored financially by the Welsh Office over the period 1980-83. It involved teachers in the education authorities of Gwynedd, Clwyd and Powys, with administrative and professional support from the staff of the Faculty of Education at University College of Bangor, North Wales. In the exercise several schools within a small geographical area - the number of schools varied according to their sizes - worked together on agreed topics over a period of time. The common area of study facilitated discussion and corporate support. Each group of schools had its own co-ordinator who, in most cases, was a teacher of science at the local secondary school. This arrangement assured the primary teachers of specialist science support available at very short notice, a facility that is not usually easily arranged. The whole project had a director, a primary school head teacher on full-time secondment for part of the duration of the project, and a part-time deputy director, a primary school teacher. The director and deputy visited schools throughout the region, called meetings of the group co-ordinators and organised courses for teachers in the participating schools. Reports on the work of the groups were written and in one instance a video film of classroom practice was produced.

These various developments of the past five years are most encouraging. There remains the need to secure a better balance of course content to ensure that pupils study both living and non-living matter and that they are helped to appreciate the general applicability of scientific method. Among the challenges that school will have to meet continually in the future are:

a. avoiding an unthinking adoption of published schemes, ie there is more to the science education of pupils than simple completion of the exercises on workcards;

b. organising classes (all pupils doing the same science together or not) and timetables (designated science sessions or not) in such a way that whenever pupils do science and for whatever length of time and frequency they delve in some depth into a topic, thus retaining more than an uncertain memory of having been engaged, albeit contentedly, in doing something to something;

c. striving to secure a progression in pupils' understanding of specific science topics and of general scientific principles; there ought to be several discernible differences between the responses of 10 year olds and 4 year olds to the same investigation.

SECTION 3: APPENDICES

3.1 LIST OF ONGOING RESEARCH

compiled by the Secretariat of the
Council of Europe

This list is by far not exhaustive and gives only a few examples.

FINLAND

- J LAUREN
  Institute for Educational Research
  University of Jyväskylä

. An Evaluation Project on Learning Results in Science Education

- SECOND IEA SCIENCE STUDY (IEA/SISS)

. Aims and expected outcomes

  The aims of the study are:

  a. to assess the current state of science education across the world;

  b. to identify factors which explain differences in achievement and
      other outcomes of science education, with particular attention to
      the role of the science curriculum as an explanatory factor, and

  c. to examine changes in the descriptive picture of science education
      and in the patterns of explanatory relationships (in (a) and (b)
      above) since the early 1970s in the countries that also
      participated in the first study.

HUNGARY

- ORSZÁGOS PEDAGÓGIAI INTÉZET
  Gorkij Fasor 17-21
  H - 1071 BUDAPEST

. Project No. 121
  Co-ordinated science instruction in the primary school

  Head of project: Mr Jozsef BAN HALMI, Bessenyei György Teacher
  Training College, Sostoi u 31/b, H - 4401 NYIRGYHAZA

. Project No. 122
Elaboration of a methodologically new system of physics instruction
and of physics curriculum for the 6th, 7th and 8th grades of primary
school

Head of project: Mr Rezsö KARACSONY, Department of Physical Chemistry
and Radiology of the Science Faculty of ELTE, Muzeum Krt. 6-8,
H - 1088 BUDAPEST

. Project No. 123
Student activity in science education

Head of project: Mr György MARX, Department of Nuclear Physics of the
Science Faculty of ELTE, Puskin u. 5-7, H - 1088 BUDAPEST

. Project No. 124
Elaboration and experimental control of co-ordinated science teaching
programmes for the age group 10-14

Head of project: Mr Károly MOHOLT, Juhasz Gyula Teacher Training College,
Aprilis 4 u. 1, H - 6701 SZEGED

. Project No. 125
Establishing the basic notions of physics in the first four grades of
primary school

Head of project: Ms Györgyné PÁLFFY, Department of Physics, Janus
Pannonius University, Ifjusàg utja 6, H - 7644 PECS

. Project No. 131
The co-ordination of technical-scientific and social science subjects

Head of project: Mr Barna SZUCS, National Institute of Education,
Gorki fasor 17-21, H - 1071 BUDAPEST

. Project No. 132
Development of technical education

Head of project: Mr Ervin SZUCS, Group on Technics of the Science
Faculty of ELTE, Råkóczi n. 5, H - 1088 BUDAPEST

ITALY

– Prof. Paolo GUIDONI
Istituto di Fisica
Via Archirafi
I - 90123 PALERMO

. Research on the development of physical notions in the case of children

- Prof. Matilde VICENTINI MISSONI
  Prof. Clotilde PONTECORVO
  Gruppo Università Scuola
  Istituto di Fisica
  Università di Roma
  Piazzale Aldo Moro
  I - 00100 ROMA

. Research on science and primary school: new curricula

- UNITA DEL GNDF (Gruppo nazionale di didattica della fisica) of the
  University of GENOVA

  M DE PAZ
  M PILO
  G PUPPO

. Research on the following subjects:

  1. analysis of science teaching in Italian schools;

  2. development of methods and techniques for experimental physics
     teaching at various levels (from first grades to university);

  3. educational learning of experimental and theoretical science
     teaching related to the age of students;

  4. relationships between school and society;

  5. study of interdisciplinary subjects applied to school work.

- Centro Europeo dell'Educazione (CEDE)
  Villa Falconieri
  I - 00044 FRASCATI

  1. CEDE participates in the Second IEA Science Study on Educational
     Achievement Evaluation (IEA-SISS); the first data (including data
     about primary education) will be available in autumn 1984.

  2. CEDE is launching the IRIS Project (Iniziative e Ricerche per
     l'informatica nella Scuola) on basic computer education,
     including the primary education level; an experimental version
     is being tried out in a sample of schools.

  3. In October 1983 CEDE contributed to the organisation of a "Joint
     Italian-USA Seminar on Science Education at Primary Level". The
     proceedings will be published around summer 1984.

  4. CEDE collects information and documentation for the Italian Science
     Education Information Project.

Italian research groups engaged on science education at primary level

Prof. B BERTOLINI
Via G Tommasetti 3
I - 00161 ROMA

Prof. C PONTECORVO
Via Nomentana 399
I - 00141 ROMA

Prof. F Emiliani ZAULI
Via Puccini 1
I - 43100 PARMA

Prof. N Tomasini GRIMELLINI
Via Fleming 5
I - 40100 BOLOGNA

Prof. M VICENTINI
Istituto di Fisica
P. le A. Moro 2
I - 00185 ROMA

Prof. G FABBRI
Istituto di Chimica
Fisica
Via Campi 183
I - 41100 MODENA

Dott. N LANCIANO
Laboratorio di didattica
Nuovo Istituto di Fisica
P. le Aldo Moro 2
I - 00185 ROMA

Prof. A BARGELLINI
Istituto di Chimica
Organica
Via Risorgimento 35
I - 56100 PISA

Prof. G PEDEMONTE
Istituto di Petrografia
Palazzo delle Scienze
Corso Europa
I - 16132 GENOVA

Prof. P VIOLINO
Istituto di Fisica
P.za Torricelli 2
I - 56100 PISA

Prof. G BONERA
Via Franchi 3
I - 27100 PAVIA

Prof. M RIGUTTI
Via Moiarello 16
I - 80131 NAPOLI

Prof. F TONUCCI
Via U Aldovrandi 18
I - 00197 ROMA

Prof. P GUIDONI
Istituto di Fisica
P. le Aldo Moro 2
I - 00185 ROMA

Prof. O Andreani DENTICI
Istituto di Psicologia
Universita di Pavia
C.so Strada Nuova 65
I - 27100 PAVIA

Prof. P BOERO
Istituto di Matematica
Universita di Genova
V. le Benedetto XV 5
I - 16132 GENOVA

Prof. M DE PAZ
Istituto di Fisica
Universita di Genova
I - GENOVA

Prof. R SPERANDEO
Istituto di Fisica
Universita di Palermo
Via Archirafi 20
I - 99123 PALERMO

Prof. BOSMAN
Istituto di Fisica
P.za Torricelli 2
I - 56100 PISA

LUXEMBOURG

- Alex STORONI
Inspecteur de l'Enseignement primaire
121 rue Prinzenberg
L - 4650 NIEDERKORN

. Structural approach of science teaching
Level: primary education: 1st-6th school year in Luxembourg

NORWAY

- Dr. Svein SJØBERG
  IMTEC (International Movement Towards Educational Change)
  Dynekilgt. 10
  S - OSLO 5

  (in co-operation with the Centre for Science Education at Oslo
  University)

- . IEA/SISS: Norway is taking part in the Second International Science
  Study. The internationally defined target populations are 10, 14 and
  18 years, where large samples are tested for achievement, interests,
  attitudes and background variables. Norway is also carrying out a
  large survey among the science teachers for these student populations.
  Testing took place in early 1984.

- Ass. Prof. Svein SJØBERG
  Centre for Science Education
  Oslo University
  Box 1048
  Blindern
  S - OSLO 3

- . "Girls and physics"

  This action-oriented research is funded by the Ministry of Education.
  The aim is to identify factors that act against higher participation
  of girls in science and technology and to propose possible actions to
  increase the proportion of girls in such studies and occupations.
  The project group arranged the second GASAT (Girls and Science and
  Technology) Conference in September 1983. Reports are available in
  English.

SWEDEN

- Ass. Prof. Björn ANDERSSON
  Department of Educational Research
  University of Gothenburg
  Box 1010
  S - 431 26 MÖLNDAL

- . Pupils thinking and course requirements in science teaching (EKNA)

- Dr. Anita KOLLERBAUR
  Department of Information Processing and Computer Science
  University of Stockholm
  S - 106 91 STOCKHOLM

- . Research on interactive computer based educational systems

–   Assoc. Prof. Richard NOONAN
     Institute of International Education
     University of Stockholm
     S - 106 91 STOCKHOLM

.   Swedish science subjects in an international perspective: curriculum,
     teachers and pupils (SNILLE)

UNITED KINGDOM

–   National Foundation for Educational Research in England and Wales

     Dr. Wendy KEYS
     The Mere
     Upton Park
     Slough
     GB-Berks SLI 2DQ

CURRENT EDUCATIONAL RESEARCH PROJECTS supported by the DEPARTMENT OF
EDUCATION AND SCIENCE

–   Prof. D CHILD
     Centre for Studies in Science Education
     University of Leeds

.   The assessment of performance in science of pupils in schools in
     England, Wales and Northern Ireland

     Project No. B29

–   Prof. P J BLACK, Prof. P J KELLY
     Chelsea College
     University of London

.   The assessment of performance in science of pupils in schools in
     England, Wales and Northern Ireland

     Project No. B30

     (An extension of the existing project at both Chelsea and Leeds, which
     undertakes the monitoring of performance in science of pupils aged
     approximately 11 to 15.)

–   Dr. R H DRIVER
     University of Leeds

.   Childrens learning in science

     The aim of this project is to describe levels of understanding of
     secondary school pupils in a number of conceptual areas in science.
     The analysis will be based primarily on data from the APV science
     surveys at age 15.

3.2 LIST OF PARTICIPANTS

3.2.1 CHAIRMAN, RAPPORTEUR GENERAL AND LECTURERS

Mr George PATON (Chairman), Deputy Director, Scottish Council for Educational Technology, 74 Victoria Crescent Road, GB - GLASGOW G12 9JN

Mr Frank ADAMS (Rapporteur General), Principal Curriculum Officer, Scottish Curriculum Development Service, Moray House College of Education, Holyrood Road, GB - EDINBURGH EH8 8AQ

Prof. Björn ANDERSSON, Department of Educational Research, University of Göteborg, Box 1010, S - 43126 MÖLNDAL

M Armin BEELER, Seminarlehrer, Seminar Musegg, Museggstrasse 22, CH - 6004 LUZERN

Prof. Paul J BLACK, OBE, KSG, Centre for Science and Mathematics Education, Chelsea College, University of London, Bridges Place, GB - LONDON SW6 4HR

Mr Alistair FYFE, SMDP (Scottish Microelectronics Development Programme), Dowanhill, 74 Victoria Crescent Road, GB - GLASGOW G12 9JN

Prof. Dr. André GIORDAN, Professeur Ordinaire à l'Université de Genève, Directeur du Laboratoire de Didactique et Epistémologie des Sciences, FAPSE/UNI II, 24 rue Général Dufour, CH - 1211 GENEVE 4

Dr. Roland LAUTERBACH, Institute for Science Education (IPN), University of Kiel, IPN - Gebäude, Olshausenstrasse 40 - 60, D - 2300 KIEL

Mr Sinclair MACLEOD, Director of PSDP, Moray House College of Education, Holyrood Road, GB - EDINBURGH EH8 8AQ

M Frédéric ROBERT, INRP (Institut National de la Recherche Pédagogique), 91 rue Gabriel Péri, F - 92120 MONTROUGE

Ms Jacqueline JOHNSTON, Secretary and Senior Education Officer, School Broadcasting Council for Scotland, Broadcasting House, 5 Queen Street, GB - EDINBURGH EH2 1JF

3.2.2 REPRESENTATIVE OF CDCC'S PROJECT No. 8

Mr Peter HONETH, Director of Primary and Lower Secondary Education,
Ministry of Education, S - 10333 STOCKHOLM

3.2.3 DELEGATES

BELGIUM

Prof. Romain DECAMBRAI, Institut Saint-Joseph, 16 August Vermeylenlaan,
B - 8100 TORHOUT

Mlle Brigitte DENIS, Laboratoire de pédagogie expérimentale
(Prof. G DE LANDSHEERE), Chargée de recherches à l'Université de
Liège, Sart Tilman, B - 4000 LIEGE

M Pierre CHARLIER, Service de pédagogie générale et de méthodologie de
l'enseignement, Université de Liège, Sart Tilman, B - 4000 LIEGE

DENMARK

Prof. Tom Plough OLSEN, Associate Professor, Cand. Paed., Royal Danish
School of Educational Studies, Emdrupvej 101, DK - 2400 COPENHAGEN NV

FRANCE

M Frédéric ROBERT, INRP, 29-31 rue d'Ulm, F - 75230 PARIS CEDEX 05

FEDERAL REPUBLIC OF GERMANY

Dr. Werner SCHROM, Regierungsschulrat, Bayrisches Staatsministerium für
Unterricht und Kultus, Salvatorstrasse 2, D - 8000 MUENCHEN 1

IRELAND

Mr John C MACNAMARA, The Curriculum Unit (Primary), Department of Education,
Marlborough Street, IRL - DUBLIN 1

ITALY

Mr Nunzio RIZZOLI, Università degli studi di Parma, Centro Italiano di
Ricerca ed Educazione Ambientale, Via Copernico 3, I - 40300 PARMA

Mr Livio NUZZOLO, Centro Europeo dell' educazione, Villa Falconieri,
I - 00044 FRASCATI

NETHERLANDS

Drs. Ph C GROENEWEG, Project Manager SVO, PO Box 19050,
NL - 2500 CB THE HAGUE

Mr P PILGRAM (Director of the Dutch project "Science in primary education
(NOB)"), Stichting voor de Leerplanontwikkeling (National Institute
for Curriculum Development), PO Box 2041, NL - 7500 CA ENSCHEDE

184

NORWAY

Mr Svein SJØBERG, Centre for Science Education, Universitetet i Oslo,
    Institute of Physics, PO Box 1048, BLINDERN, N - OSLO 3

Mr Paul HOFSETH, the Council for Natural Science and Environmental Subjects
    (Rådet for Natur - og Miljøfag), Universitetet i Oslo, BLINDERN,
    N - OSLO 3

SPAIN

Mme Elena MARTIN, Universidad Autonoma de Madrid, Instituto de Ciencias de
    la Educacion, Ciudad Universitaria de Canto Blanco, E - MADRID 34

SWEDEN

Prof. Björn ANDERSSON, Department of Educational Research, University of
    Göteborg, Box 1010, S - 43126 MÖLNDAL

SWITZERLAND

Prof. Dr. André GIORDAN, Professeur Ordinaire à l'Université de Genève,
    Directeur du Laboratoire de Didactique et Epistémologie des Sciences,
    FAPSE/UNI II, 24 rue Général Dufour, CH - 1211 GENEVE 4

M Armin BEELER, Seminarlehrer, Seminar Musegg, Museggstrasse 22,
    CH - 6004 LUZERN

UNITED KINGDOM

SI Mr A J ROSE, 19 Talisman Square, GB - KENILWORTH, Warwickshire CV8 1JB

3.2.4   OBSERVERS

UNESCO

Ms S HAGGIS, Chief of Science Education Section, Division of Science,
    Technical and Vocational Education, UNESCO, place de Fontenoy, BP 307,
    F - 75700 PARIS

OECD

Excused

COMMISSION OF THE EUROPEAN COMMUNITIES

Excused

WORLD CONFEDERATION OF ORGANISATIONS OF THE TEACHING PROFESSION (WCOTP)

Mr Marc Alain BERBERAT, Deputy General, WCOTP/CMOPE, 5 avenue du Moulin,
    CH - 1110 MORGES

INTERNATIONAL FEDERATION OF TEACHERS' ASSOCIATION (IFTA)

M Jean DAUBARD, FIAI, 3 rue la Rochefoucauld, F - 75009 PARIS

WORLD FEDERATION OF TEACHERS' UNIONS (WFTU)

Mme Sylvia SAYLE, Field Officer, Educational Institute of Scotland,
46 Moray Place, GB - EDINBURGH EH3 6BH

EUROPEAN TRADE UNION COMMITTEE FOR EDUCATION (ETUCE)

Miss Aileen BECK, head teacher of Inverkeithing, Turris Law, Pitliver Road,
Charleston, DUNFERMLINE, GB - Fyfe KY11 1NP

CANADA

Mr Gary S POPOWICH, Assistant Director of Curriculum, Science and
Mathematics, Alberta Department of Education - CDN - EDMONTON

M Maurice MORAND, Directeur de Programmes, Direction Générale de
Développement Pédagogique, Hôtel du Gouvernement, Ministère de
l'Education à Québec, QUEBEC, CDN - Province de Québec

HUNGARIAN INSTITUTE OF EDUCATION

Ms Zsuzsa KERESZTY, Head of Department, Hungarian Institute of Education,
Gorkij Fasor 17/21, H - 1071 BUDAPEST VII

FEDERATION-LAENDER COMMITTEE FOR EDUCATIONAL PLANNING AND RESEARCH PROMOTION

Frau Dorothee ENGELHARD, Bund - Länder - Kommission für Bildungsplanung und
Forschungsförderung, Friedrich - Ebert Allee 39, D - 5300 BONN 1

3.2.5 UNITED KINGDOM PARTICIPANTS

SI Mr A J ROSE, 19 Talisman Square, GB - KENILWORTH, Warwickshire, CV8 1JB

Mr Roddy DUNCAN, Assistant Director of Education, Woodhill House, Ashgrove
Road West, GB - ABERDEEN AB9 2LU

HMI Dr. Neville EVANS, Inspectors' Sector, Welsh Office, Education
Department, Cathays Park, GB - CARDIFF CF1 3NQ

Dr. Malcolm R GREEN, Strathclyde Regional Council Headquarters,
20 India Street, GB - GLASGOW G2 4PE

Mr I W MILLIGAN, Principal Inspector of Science in Northern Ireland,
58 Vannview Heights, GB - BANBRIDGE, County Down BT32 4NT

Mr George MILLS, Head of Department of Primary Science, Jordanhill College
of Education, Southbrae Drive, GB - GLASGOW G13 1PP

Miss Wilma PHILIP, head teacher, Lasswade PS, 10 Pendreich Drive,
GB - MIDLOTHIAN EH19 2DX

Mr Dan TAYLOR, Adviser in Primary Education, Moray Divisional Education Offices, Academy Street, GB - ELGIN IV30 1LL

Mr William D F THOMSON, Physical Science Department, Aberdeen College of Education, Hilton Place, GB - ABERDEEN AB9 1FA

Mr Willie SHAW, Glenburn, Etive Drive, GB - AIRDRIE

Mr Kevin GAVIN, Adviser in Primary Education, Newton Centre, Greenstreet Lane, GB - AYR

Ms Jane STEWART, Sales Centre for Mathematical Education, University of Nottingham, University Park, GB - NOTTINGHAM NG7 2RD

Mr C SCHENK, Micro-electronics Programme, National Primary Project, St. James Hall, King Alfred's College, GB - WINCHESTER

HMI Mr John W BURDIN, Scottish Education Department, HM Inspectors of Schools' Office, Overgate House, 133 Marketgait, GB - DUNDEE DD1 1QT

HMI Mr J C RANKINE, Scottish Education Department, Room 206, Chesser House West, 502 Gorgie Road, GB - EDINBURGH EH11 3YQ

HMI Mr J Gerry L WRIGHT, Scottish Education Department, Room 214, Chesser House West, 502 Gorgie Road, GB - EDINBURGH EH11 3YQ

3.2.6 ORGANISERS

3.2.6.1 SCOTLAND

HMCI Mr Jim H THOMSON, Scottish Education Department, New St. Andrew's House, GB - EDINBURGH EH1 3S4

Mr John L POWELL, Assistant Director, the Scottish Council for Research in Education, 15 St. John Street, GB - EDINBURGH EH8 8JR

3.2.6.2 COUNCIL OF EUROPE

Dr. Michael VORBECK, Head of the Section for Educational Research and Documentation, Council of Europe, BP 431 R6, F - 67006 STRASBOURG CEDEX

Mlle Anna CAPELLO, Administrator in the School Education Division, Council of Europe, BP 431 R6, F - 67006 STRASBOURG CEDEX

Mme Danièle IMBERT, Secretary in the Section for Educational Research and Documentation, Council of Europe, BP 431 R6, F - 67006 STRASBOURG CEDEX

3.2.7 INTERPRETERS

Mr Anthony KERR, 52 Castlegate, GB - JEDBURGH

Mrs Jennifer MACKINTOSH, 10 Gledstanes Road, GB - LONDON W14 9HU

P.106

3.3 LIST OF SCHOOLS VISITED

1. Aberlady Primary School
   GB - Aberlady EH32 ORQ

   Head teacher: John Roy

2. Balbardie Primary School
   Torphichen Street,
   GB - Bathgate EH48 4HL

   Head teacher: Mrs Myra Macpherson

3. Inverkeithing Primary School
   Roods Road
   GB - Inverkeithing KY1 1NP

   Head teacher: Mrs Aileen Beck

4. Longniddry Primary School
   Kitchener Crescent
   GB - Longniddry EH32 OLR

   Head teacher: Mrs Anne McLanachan

5. Paradykes Primary School
   3 Mayburn Walk
   GB - Loanhead EH20 9HG

   Head teacher: Jack Smith

6. Springfield Primary School
   141 Springfield Road
   GB - Linlithgow EH49 75N

   Head teacher: Mrs Pamela Slater

7. Toronto Primary School
   Toronto Avenue
   Howden East
   GB - Livingston EH54 6BN

   Head teacher: William Kerr

CONTENTS

Introduction

SECTION 2: NATIONAL REPORTS

SECTION 3: APPENDICES